$\int$

COMPLEX CARBOHYDRATES IN FOODS

COMPLEX CARBOHYDRATES IN FOODS

The Report of the British Nutrition Foundation's Task Force

The British Nutrition Foundation

Published by Chapman and Hall
for the British Nutrition Foundation

UK	Chapman and Hall, 11 New Fetter Lane, London EC4P 4EE
USA	Van Nostrand Reinhold, 115 5th Avenue, New York NY10003
JAPAN	Chapman and Hall Japan, Thomson Publishing Japan, Hirakawacho Nemoto Building, 7F, 1-7-11 Hirakawa-cho, Chiyoda-ku, Tokyo 102
AUSTRALIA	Chapman and Hall Australia, Thomas Nelson Australia, 480 La Trobe Street, PO Box 4725, Melbourne 3000
INDIA	Chapman and Hall India, R. Seshadri, 32 Second Main Road, CIT East, Madras 600 035

First edition 1990

© 1990 The British Nutrition Foundation

Typeset in 10/12pt Helvetica by Mayhew Typesetting, Bristol
Printed in England by Clays Ltd., St. Ives PLC

ISBN 0 412 39180 5   0 442 312881 (USA)

British Library Cataloguing in Publication Data

Task force on complex carbohydrates
  Complex Carbohydrates in Foods
  1. Man. Diet. Role of Fibre
  I. Title
  613.28
  ISBN 0-412-39180-5

Library of Congress Cataloging-in-Publication Data
available

CONTENTS

BNF Task Force on Complex Carbohydrates in Foods

Chairman

Professor Dame Barbara Clayton
Honorary Research Professor in
Metabolism
University of Southampton
Southampton General Hospital

Members

Dr C.S. Berry
Head of Nutrition and Food
Safety Section
Flour Milling and Bakery
Research Association

Dr D.M. Conning
Director General
British Nutrition Foundation

Dr M.A. Eastwood
Gastrointestinal Unit
Western General Hospital
Edinburgh EH4 2XU

Dr S.J. Fairweather-Tait
AFRC Institute of Food Research
Norwich

Dr K.W. Heaton
Department of Medicine
Bristol Royal Infirmary

Dr M.J. Hill
PHLS Centre for Applied
Microbiology and Research
Porton Down
Salisbury

Dr J.O. Hunter
Gastroenterology Research Unit
Addenbrooke's Hospital
Cambridge

Dr A.R. Leeds
Department of Nutrition
Kings College
University of London

Dr G. Livesey
AFRC Institute of Food
Research
Norwich

Professor N.W. Read
Sub-Department of Human
Gastrointestinal Physiology and Nutrition
Royal Hallamshire Hospital
Sheffield

Professor D.A.T. Southgate
AFRC Institute of Food Research
Norwich

Observers

Dr D.H. Buss
Ministry of Agriculture, Fisheries and
Food

Dr A. Stone
Medical Research Council

Dr M. Wiseman
Department of Health

Secretariat

Dr Margaret Ashwell[*]
Science Director
British Nutrition Foundation
(Editor of the Task Force Report)

Miss Anne Halliday[†]
Nutrition Scientist
British Nutrition Foundation
(Secretary to the Task Force)

Dr R. Cottrell[‡]
Science Director
British Nutrition Foundation

Miss M. Sommerville[§]
Nutrition Scientist
British Nutrition Foundation

[*†] from January 1989
[‡] until December 1988
[§] until September 1988

TERMS OF REFERENCE

1. To review the nutritional attributes of complex carbohydrates (primarily in foods) in relation to current dietary advice to the population to increase the consumption of such foods. Complex carbohydrates for the purpose of the remit of the Task Force include all polysaccharides containing 20 or more monosaccharide residues. Reference to polysaccharides less than 20 monosaccharide units are made where appropriate.
2. To prepare a report and, should it see fit, draw conclusions and identify areas for future research.

ACKNOWLEDGEMENTS

The Task Force gratefully acknowledges the help received from Dr J.H. Cummings (MRC Dunn Nutrition Unit), Professor W.M. Edgar (University of Liverpool), Dr H. Englyst (MRC Dunn Nutrition Unit), Dr T. Grenby (Guy's Hospital), Dr S. Kingman (MRC Dunn Nutrition Unit), and Dr M. Lean (University of Glasgow).

FOREWORD

The British Nutrition Foundation organises independent 'Task Forces' to review, analyse, and report in depth upon specific areas of interest and importance in the field of human nutrition.

These expert committees consist of acknowledged specialists and operate completely independently of the Foundation.

The *Complex Carbohydrates in Foods* Task Force has reviewed and discussed much published information. This report summarises the deliberations and findings of the Task Force, and gives its conclusions and recommendations.

I am most grateful to the members of the Task Force who have contributed their time and expertise so generously. My sincere thanks also go to the Secretariat for their excellent support.

Professor Dame Barbara Clayton
Chairman of the Task Force

CHAPTER 1
INTRODUCTION

The value of 'fibre' in the diet was even recognised by the Greeks. Hippocrates, in the fourth century BC, commented 'To the human body it makes a great difference whether the bread be made of fine flour or coarse, whether of the wheat with the bran or the wheat without the bran'.

In the nineteenth century, Graham and Kellogg in the United States and Allinson in Britain tried to draw attention to the importance of 'fibre' in the diet, all with limited success.

Modern interest in carbohydrates and health began with Surgeon Captain Cleave's exposition of 'The Saccharine Disease'. Under this title, Cleave (1966) brought together a variety of conditions characteristic of the Western World which he thought were due to consumption of refined carbohydrates. This hypothesis was then developed by Burkitt and Trowell (1975) who suggested that it was the diets of Africans which protected them from most of the chronic non-infective diseases characteristic of Western culture. They suggested that many Western diseases were due to lack of 'fibre' in the diet rather than to the direct ill-effects of refined or 'fibre'-depleted foods. At about the same time, Painter (1975) presented his evidence that diverticular disease could be successfully treated with bran. A full account of the contribution made by the early 'pioneers' of the 'fibre' hypothesis has been given by Trowell (1985).

Their ideas stimulated much research, and in 1980, The Royal College of Physicians published a report on 'Medical Aspects of Dietary Fibre' (Royal College of Physicians, 1980). The RCP committee concluded that 'On present evidence, we think it highly probable, though not fully proved and possibly not susceptible of rigid proof, that increasing the proportion of "dietary fibre" in the diet in Western countries would be nutritionally desirable'. They highlighted two reasons why their conclusions and recommendations had to be tentative:

(i) the diversity of compounds which are loosely grouped together as dietary 'fibre'.
(ii) the imprecision of the epidemiological comparisons between populations consuming a high-'fibre' diet and those consuming a low-'fibre' diet.

The Report recommended that further research was required before any detailed dietary recommendations could be made to the general public.

In 1988, the British Nutrition Foundation decided to convene this independent Task Force, to see what progress had been made. Complex carbohydrates, defined as starches plus non-starch polysaccharides, rather than 'fibre', was chosen as the title and subject of the Report for various reasons:

(i) The US Senate Select Committee on Nutrition and Human Needs (1977) had concluded that the intake of complex carbohydrates should be increased as one of its Nutritional Goals.
(ii) The DHSS Committee on Medical Aspects of Food Policy (1984) had recommended that a reduction in total fat in the diet could be achieved by an increased consumption of 'fibre-rich' carbohydrates (eg bread, cereals, fruit, vegetables).
(iii) It had recently been shown that some forms of starch could resist digestion in the small intestine (Englyst et al., 1987a). These resistant starches could act as

substrates for fermentation in the colon and thus exhibit similar properties to the non-starch polysaccharides.

The variety of chemical entities that constituted what was colloquially called dietary 'fibre' needed definition and it was felt that a greater understanding could be achieved if the effects of the starches, the resistant starches and the non-starch polysaccharides were examined together.

Increasing consumer awareness of the relationship between diet and health has led to demands for more widespread nutrition labelling. How 'fibre' should appear on the label, which method of analysis should be used and whether one single value is appropriate are all current issues which are addressed in the Report. The potential ability of complex carbohydrates to prevent, or alleviate various diseases is also relevant to the validity of health claims which are starting to appear on food products.

The Report begins by classifying the different compounds that make up complex carbohydrates and describes where they are found in the UK diet (Chapters 2 and 3). It goes on to look at how the form and physical properties of both starches and non-starch polysaccharides determine their effects in the small intestine (Chapters 4 and 5) and the subsequent outcome on the digestion and absorption of macronutrients and micronutrients (Chapters 6 and 7). The effects of complex carbohydrates on the glycaemic response are considered in Chapter 10. The interaction of complex carbohydrates that pass into the large intestine with bacteria is discussed in Chapter 8, and their dietary energy values are considered in Chapter 9.

The role of complex carbohydrates in the aetiology of a number of diseases is critically reviewed (Chapters 11 to 19) and the conclusions reached are pertinent to whether starches and non-starch polysaccharides are essential components of the diet. If so, how much should the diet provide and can a recommendation applicable to various groups of the population be determined? The various arguments for and against quantitative recommendations are outlined in Chapter 20 and labelling implications are discussed in Chapter 21.

The popular term, dietary 'fibre', previously defined as 'any substance of plant origin which is undigested by human alimentary enzymes' (Trowell *et al.*, 1972), has been avoided as far as possible in the Report. This Task Force felt that it would be helpful to identify the particular polysaccharide responsible for the observed effects, in the hope that some clarification of the confused state of the literature could be achieved.

This Report provides an objective and timely assessment of the current state of knowledge in what is an exciting area. It points the way ahead to the further research that is required and, more importantly, indicates how this can be done most effectively.

CHAPTER 2
CHEMISTRY OF COMPLEX CARBOHYDRATES AND THEIR ORGANISATION IN FOODS

2.1 INTRODUCTION

This chapter provides an introduction to the chemical and physical structure of the complex carbohydrates as a background to the later chapters on physiological and nutritional properties of this group of substances. In preparing the chapter much use has been made of a number of detailed reviews, and reference to these is essential for the detailed discussion of the primary literature on these substances.

2.1.1 Definition of complex carbohydrates

The term 'complex carbohydrates' was used in the McGovern report (US Senate Select Committee on Nutrition & Human Needs, 1977) without formal definition. In the context of the report, it was used to distinguish the simple sugars from the polysaccharides. This definition is the one most suitable for use in the context of the work of this Task Force so that 'complex carbohydrates' is effectively a synonym for polysaccharides and a reasonable delineation of polysaccharides would be all carbohydrate polymers that contain *twenty* or more monosaccharide residues.

The simple carbohydrates on this basis will include the mono, di-, tri-, and tetra-saccharides and sugar alcohols present in food and other oligosaccharides containing up to 19 residues. This somewhat arbitrary definition is a convenient one pragmatically, because oligosaccharides with more than four residues are rare in foods, except as fragments of polysaccharides produced by enzymatic or acid hydrolysis, eg they are present in starch hydrolysates (glucose syrups). It is also a definition which has some basis in terms of physical structure since some form of tertiary structure has usually developed with a molecule of this size.

The complex carbohydrates, therefore, display a wide range of chemical and physical properties. Furthermore many of them are organised into physical structures in foods, for example, starch granules and cell wall structures, that confer other properties on them.

It is therefore not possible to discuss them as an entity since they share a limited range of common properties, principally that of being polysaccharides and not simple sugars. In general they are insoluble in aqueous alcohols at about 80% v/v but this is not an absolute distinction since many fructans and glucofructans and some arabinans are soluble in aqueous ethanol.

2.1.2 Terminology of complex carbohydrates

Formal rules for the systematic terminology of polysaccharides have yet to be established but one can forecast that such nomenclature will be very complex and too unwieldy for general use. There is, however, a reasonable series of generic terms that can be systematised and these will be used to discuss general classes of polysaccharide structures:

Homopolysaccharides are polysaccharides containing only one monosaccharide or uronic acid residue. They form the largest proportion of polysaccharides. In a strict sense, it is probable that pure homopolysaccharides are uncommon; the terminology relates to polysaccharides that are virtually all composed of only one type of residue.

Homopolysaccharides are named using the prefix of the constituent residue and the suffix *an* – thus starch, glycogen and cellulose are glucans, inulin is a fructan.

Heteropolysaccharides are polysaccharides containing more than one monosaccharide or uronic acid residue.

Heteropolysaccharides are named using the substituent side chains as the prefix followed by the backbone constituent with the suffix *an*. Thus, xyloglucans have a glucose backbone with xylose side chains, arabinoxylans have a xylose backbone with arabinose side chains, galactomannans have a mannose backbone with galactose side chains, uronans are uronic acid polymers.

Glycan is the general systematic terminology for polysaccharides.

2.1.3 Classification of complex carbohydrates

It is possible to construct a number of different systems for classifying the complex carbohydrates (Table 2.1). None of the systems is entirely satisfactory in that the boundaries between categories are not absolute, either structurally or functionally, nor are the boundaries susceptible to precise analytical demarcation. This is due to the fact that the range of reactions that various polysaccharides undergo is limited and non-specific. Many reactions are common to one or more, and usually several, polysaccharides.

The majority of the complex carbohydrates in the human diet are derived from foods of plant origin and classification according to the major functional role in plants is a convenient basis for discussion of their chemistry, properties and organisation (Selvendran, 1984).

Polysaccharide food additives of plant origin are widely used in foods. Many of these are of cell wall origin and closely related to the analogous cell wall polysaccharides.

They are, however, present in foods as the isolated polysaccharides with, or without, further chemical modification and therefore are considered separately.

A range of polysaccharides is present in animal tissues. Animal foods therefore contribute small amounts of complex carbohydrates to the average UK diet. There are no reliable estimates, but the amounts may reach significant levels in extreme carnivorous diets. These polysaccharides, although quantitatively insignificant, are available in large quantities as by-products of meat, fish and, especially, crustacea processing. They have been suggested as possible food additives because of their specific properties.

The complex carbohydrates are therefore discussed under the following headings:

- Storage Polysaccharides
- Cell Wall Polysaccharides
- Isolated Polysaccharides
  i) naturally occurring
  ii) polysaccharide food additives
- Polysaccharides of Animal Origin

Within each category, structure and chemical properties are considered.

2.2 STORAGE POLY-SACCHARIDES

The major storage polysaccharides in foods of plant origin are the starches, although a range of fructans is found in many roots, tubers, and some cereal seeds. Some members of the legume family have variously substituted mannans as the major storage polysaccharide, as do some nuts. In virtually all human diets, starches form

Table 2.1 Alternative classifications of food polysaccharides

Role in the plant/food	Types of polysaccharides	Analytical classification	Site of digestion	Products of digestion	Physiological classification
Storage polysaccharides	Starch amylose amylopectin	α-glucans	Small intestine (enzymatic)	Mono and di saccharides	Available carbohydrates
	Fructans				
	Galactomannans	Non α-glucans			
Structural components of the plant cell walls	Non-cellulosic Pectins Hemicellulose Cellulose	Non-starch polysaccharides	Large intestine (Microbial)	Short chain fatty-acids: acetate propionate butyrate	Unavailable carbohydrates
Isolated polysaccharides Naturally occurring	Gums Mucilages Pectin			Carbon dioxide, hydrogen, methane	
Polysaccharide food additives	Gums Algal polysaccharides Modified celluloses Modified starches				

the major, and often only, storage polysaccharides. In some diets, where tubers form a major part of the diet, the intakes of other storage polysaccharides may be significant.

Glycogen, the storage polysaccharide in animal tissues is rapidly hydrolysed and metabolised *post-mortem*, and is not a significant contribution to complex carbohydrate intakes unless the liver is consumed fresh and raw. In practical nutritional terms, it is therefore only necessary to discuss the storage polysaccharides of plant origin.

2.2.1 Starches

It is preferable to use the plural form because a number of distinct chemical structures and physical levels of organisation are seen. This usage emphasises the fact that starch cannot be considered as a homogeneous component of foods and the diet.

2.2.1.1 Structure

The starches are α-glucans, containing both 1–4 and 1–6 linkages. Two major structural types are present in most foods: Amylose is a linear 1–4 molecule and amylopectin is a branched molecule with both 1–4 and 1–6 linkages. Many food starches contain some intermediary structures where an essentially linear 1–4 molecule contains some 1–6 linkages. The starches are characteristically polydisperse and most preparations isolated using mild conditions contain a range of molecular sizes.

Amyloses are the minor component of starch (15–20%) and typically have molecular weights up to around 60,000 Daltons. The stereochemistry of the 1–4 α-linkage confers a helical conformation on amylose. The interior of the coil can be occupied to form inclusion compounds with, for example, monoglycerides and notably iodine to give the very delicate and characteristic blue colour of the iodine–starch reaction.

Amylopectins are the major components of starch. They are usually larger molecules

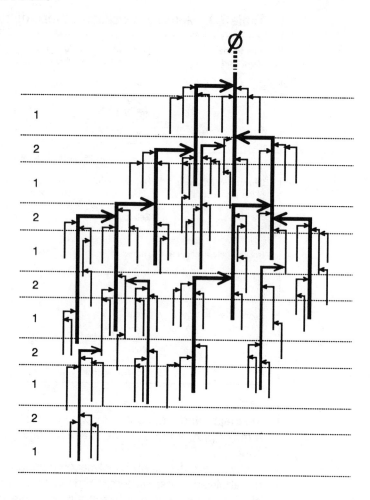

Figure 2.1 Structure of amylopectin. 1 minimal branching region; 2 maximum branching region.

with molecular weights of over 1 million Daltons (greater than 10,000 glucose residues). They have a considerably more complex structure and the details of this fine structure are still the subject of debate and research. Most recent observations give general support to the tree-link structure (Figure 2.1) (French, 1972; Würsch, 1990). The side chains of the molecule are 1–4 linked and are therefore potential helical structures within the steric constraints of the molecule as a whole.

2.2.1.2 Properties

2.2.1.2.1 Effect of heating
The starches are characteristically insoluble in cold water, but disperse on heating to produce colloidal sols. The linear amylose molecules readily associate and form hydrogen bonds. This produces precipitates from dilute solutions and gels from more concentrated ones; a process known as retrogradation. Amylopectins associate less readily, but retrogradation occurs when the side chains associate.

2.2.1.2.2 Effect of group substitution
The hydroxyl groups of the molecule can be substituted with methoxy, acetyl and related constituents to produce a range of modified starches. Organic ester and phosphate ester can also be generated and these are also used as modified starches. Some native starches contain phosphate groups. The modified starches exhibit

a range of physical properties; for this reason they are wholly used to control or modify the textural characteristics of food products (Kearsley and Sicard, 1989).

2.2.1.2.3 Acid hydrolysis

The starches are readily hydrolysed by acids and enzymes. Acid hydrolysis, combined with selective enzymatic hydrolysis, is used to produce a range of food products, ranging from starches which have been partially depolymerised to glucose syrups where extensive hydrolysis has taken place. The extent of hydrolysis can be closely controlled to produce hydrolysates with specific physical properties and levels of sweetness for use in food products.

Acid hydrolysis involves the addition of water to the glucosidic bond, the attack being generally random. The mechanism of acid hydrolysis is such that the inter-mediates could rearrange to produce furfural derivatives, be released as free glucose, or recombine to form dextrins. Under strong acid conditions, the dehydra-tion of the intermediate to furfural is favoured. Dilute hydrolysis and low initial concen-trations of starch favour the formation of free glucose.

Acid hydrolysis forms the basis of many methods for measuring starch in the absence of other hydrolysable polysaccharides. Theoretical yields of glucose are achieved with 1M sulphuric acid with initial concentrations of starch around 100–200 mg/litre (Southgate, 1976). In the presence of other polysaccharides, a glucose specific method, such as glucose oxidase is required for accurate measurements. This is not adequate if β-glucans, branched 1-2 and 1-3 polymers as found in many cereals especially oats and barley, are present. Most specific procedures for starch rely on enzymatic hydrolysis.

2.2.1.2.4 Enzymatic hydrolysis

A number of different α-glucosidases (α glucan hydrolysases EC 3.2.1.n) are known. They are present in salivary and pancreatic secretions of many mammals and also produced by many fungi, bacteria and protozoa. They were originally classified into α and β amylases according to the basis of their mode of attack on the starch molecule (see Figure 2.2).

α amylases (1, 4 α-D-Glucan-glucanohydrolases, EC 3.2.1.1.) are endoenzymes which hydrolyse the 1–4α glucosidic bonds at random producing a range of fragments. The action terminates at 1,6 linkages and therefore, the hydrolysis products of amylopectin include α-limit dextrins and isomaltoses. In vivo, these are hydrolysed further by the isomaltases (EC 3.2.1.10.) in the brush borders of the mucosal cells.

β amylases (1, 4 β-D-Glucan maltohydrolases EC 3.2.1.2) hydrolyse alternate α–1, 4 linkages to give maltose. The hydrolysis products from amylopectin include β-limit dextrins and isomaltoses. A number of glucoamylases (1, 4 α-D-Glucan glucano hydrolases, EC 3.2.1.3) are found in fungi and other microorganisms. These are exoenzymes and hydrolyse the polymers from the reducing ends producing glucose. Some 1,6 activity is usually present and the enzymes can give virtually complete hydrolysis of starches provided that the material is free from retrograded amylose.

2.2.1.2.5 Factors affecting hydrolysis

In vitro studies of the kinetics of hydrolysis of starch show differences in susceptibility to α-amylase hydrolysis. Both the rate and extent of hydrolysis show differences that are dependent on the plant source of the starch and physical properties such as parti-cle size. A major factor in determining both rate and extent of hydrolysis is the state of the granule, and particularly the type of physical treatment that the starch has received (Würsch, 1990). These are particularly important in determining the behaviour of starch physiologically because most starchy foods are consumed after some kind of heat treatment.

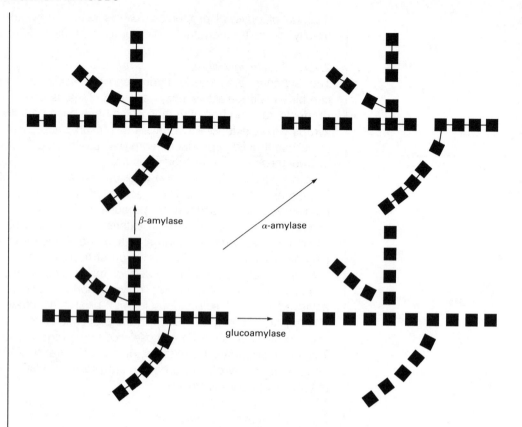

Figure 2.2 Enzymatic hydrolysis of starch. α-amylases hydrolyse α1–4 glucosidic bonds at random. They terminate at α1–6 linkages. β-amylases hydrolyse alternate α1–4 linkages. Glycoamylases hydrolyse α1–4 and α1–6 linkages sequentially.

The detailed organisation of the starch granule is still an active topic for research and most of the current knowledge comes from studies of wheat and other cereal starch granules. The native granule shows a characteristic x-ray diffraction pattern indicating an element of crystallinity in its organisation. The native granule has a phospholipid coat that acts as an initial barrier to enzymatic attack. On treatment with heat in an aqueous environment the granule absorbs water and swells, and when the granule ruptures amylose is leached out, but the x-ray pattern is still evident indicating that the amylopectin plays a major role in the actual structure of the granule.

Most heat treated foods contain a range of granular structures ranging from relatively intact granules such as those in the crust of bread, to starches where the granular structure has virtually disappeared such as those in the breadcrumb. In relatively few foods (eg the unripe banana), the granule is consumed in its native crystalline state.

Englyst *et al.* (1982) has developed a scheme for classifying the starch in foods according to its physical state in relation to susceptibility to enzymatic hydrolysis *in vitro* and its imputed hydrolysis *in vivo* (see Chapter 4 and Table 4.1).

However, at the present time, the range of factors that determine starch hydrolysis *in vivo* cannot be predicted from chemical and physical analysis of foods. It is clear that retrograded amylose is very resistant to enzymatic hydrolysis *in vitro* but this *in vitro* resistance does not necessarily predict behaviour in the gastrointestinal tract (see Chapter 4).

2.2.2 Fructans and glucofructans

Many cereals and tubers contain fructan and glucofructan polymers. In cereals, the levels are low compared with starch, whereas in some tubers (eg Jerusalem artichoke), the fructan, inulin, is the major storage polysaccharide. These substances are not present in ordered granules as is the case with starch.

2.2.2.1 Properties
They are readily soluble in hot water and are precipitated by the addition of ethanol. Precipitation is, however, not complete at 80% v/v ethanol and some lower molecular weight fructans require higher concentration of ethanol. The fructans are very readily hydrolysed by dilute acid eg slow hydrolysis of inulin occurs at pH's of water saturated with carbon dioxide. The analysis of these polysaccharides requires very careful control of pH during extraction as the organic acids present in most plants will hydrolyse them to glucose and fructose. The fructose molecule is very susceptible to dehydration and formation of furfural derivatives. Treatment with strong acid solutions invariably reduces the recovery of the monosaccharide in hydrolysates.

2.2.3 Mannans and galactomannans

These polymers are the major storage form for many plants, galacto and galacto-glucomannans being the more widely distributed and more important in relation to the human diet. They are not usually eaten as components of plant foods *per se* but as the food additives, guar gum (E412) and locust bean gum (E410).

 These polysaccharides are also components of the plant cell wall in some plants. In many plants where these polymers are the major storage polysaccharide, storage occurs as thickened cell walls. This illustrates the comment made earlier that the boundaries between the categories of polysaccharide are arbitrary.

2.2.3.1 Structure
The side chains of gluco and galactomannans are usually only one galactosyl or glucosyl residue in length. The pattern distribution along the mannan backbone is responsible for the physical properties of the molecule and forms 'hairy regions' where substitution is virtually complete and 'bare' regions where side chains are virtually absent.

2.2.3.2 Properties
The mannan backbone is a β1–4 linear molecule which has some direct analogies with cellulose. Pure mannans are very insoluble and chains can link to each other with hydrogen bonds in a directly analogous way to cellulose. The galactomannans are slowly dispersible in cold water and more readily in hot to produce viscous solutions; the property that is the reason for their use as additives.

 Dilute acid hydrolysis progressively removes the substituent side chains thus freeing the mannan core; the molecule tends to become less soluble in the process. Complete hydrolysis can be achieved with 2M sulphuric acid.

 No mammalian enzymes hydrolyse these types of molecules but a number of bacterial and plant enzymes are known.

2.3 STRUCTURAL POLY-SACCHARIDES

2.3.1 Range of structural polysaccharides in the diet

The diet typically contains a very wide range of structural polysaccharides derived from the plant cell walls in foods. The range of plant organs consumed and the different tissues within these organs, produces considerable variation in the types of polysaccharides and their quantitative contributions to the total intake. The

Table 2.2 Principal causes of heterogeneity of structural polysaccharides in the diet

Major variable	Examples	Outcome
Proportions of plant food sources consumed	Cereals Vegetables Fruits	Determine types of polysaccharide present in the diet
Preparation and processing	Grinding Sieving Heat treatment (wet and dry)	Physical properties of ingested polysaccharides Physical structure of foods
Types of plant organ consumed	Roots/tubers Stems Petioles Leaves Flowers/flower buds Seeds	Types of polysaccharides present Organisation within cell wall architecture

Types of plant cell wall structures consumed	Parenchyma
	Conducting tissues
	  phloem
	  xylem
	Supporting tissues
	  collenchyma
	  schlerenchyma
	Epidermal tissues
		Presence of associated proteins, lignins, cutins, suberins and inorganic materials

(From Southgate, 1988)

polysaccharides are organised into a range of cell wall structures and the molecular organisation of the cell walls also shows considerable variation (see Selvendran, 1984).

The major causes of variation in the range of structural polysaccharides in the diet are summarised in Table 2.2.

The principal types of polysaccharide present are given in Table 2.3 which gives an indication of the distribution of the substances in the principal types of plant foods.

2.3.2 Cellulose

2.3.2.1 Structure
Cellulose is the characteristic polysaccharide which is present in all cell walls, although it is usually not the major component of the wall. Cellulose is a linear glucan polymer with 1–4 linkages. The molecular weights are usually very high, about 0.5–1 million Daltons. The conformation of the 1–4 glucan molecule permits strong hydrogen bonding between chains producing the highly organised crystalline fibrils which characterise the cellulose in the wall.

2.3.2.2 Properties
Native celluloses, isolated by mild extraction procedures, contain non-crystalline as well as crystalline regions. The hydrogen bonded crystalline fibrils are resistant to chemical treatment; the non-crystalline regions are more susceptible to enzymatic and acid hydrolysis. Most cellulose preparations, particularly those derived from

Table 2.3 Major types of non-starch polysaccharides in plant foods

Primary source	Major groups	Components present	Summary of structures	Distribution in foods
Structural materials of the plant cell wall	Cellulose		Long chain β-glucans	All cell walls
	Non-cellulosic polysaccharides	Pectic substances	Galacturonans	Mainly in fruits
			Arabinogalactans	and vegetables
		Hemicelluloses	Arabinoxylans	Cereals
			Glucurono-arabinoxylans	Cereals
			Glucurono-xylans	Fruits/vegetables
			Xylo-glucans	Fruits/vegetables
			β-glucans	Cereals
Non-structural polysaccharides	Gums Mucilages		Wide range of hetero-polysaccharides	Seeds and fruits

wood, have been exposed to vigorous oxidative chemical treatments to remove lignin. This introduces acidic groups and produces some depolymerisation.

2.3.2.2.1 Hydrolysis of non-crystalline regions
Cellulose is only slowly hydrolysed by dilute acids (1–2M) unless first dispersed in strong acid (12M sulphuric acid). Most analytical procedures rely on the Saeman hydrolysis, (ie dispersion in 12M sulphuric acid at low or ambient temperature followed by dilution to 1M and heating at 100°C for 2–2½ hours). Such conditions lead to virtual complete hydrolysis to glucose with only minor hydrolytic losses.

No cellulytic enzymes are secreted by the mammalian digestive tract, but a range of cellulases (EC 3.2.1.4) is produced by fungi and some protozoa. These produce the disaccharide cellobiose, and some weak cellobiase activity can be detected in the mucosal brush border disaccharidases.

2.3.2.2.2 Effects of substitution
Cellulose undergoes a range of substitution reactions involving the hydroxyl groups. These modify the properties of the cellulose in changing the virtually insoluble cellulose into more readily dispersible forms. These produce viscous sols. The modified celluloses such as methyl and carboxymethyl-cellulose are used as food additives.

2.3.2.2.3 Water absorption to crystalline regions
Although the cellulose fibril is relatively inert, water absorption does occur and adsorption of cations to the fibrils is frequently observed. Direct covalent binding is usually artefactual: it is either due to traces of non-cellulosic polysaccharides in the preparations or to functional groups introduced during isolation of the cellulose.

2.3.3 Non-cellulosic polysaccharides (NCP)

2.3.3.1 Terminology
In the plant cell wall, the cellulose fibrils are present within a matrix formed by a range of non-cellulosic polysaccharides and protein. In some mature tissues, the aromatic polymer lignin is also present.

In the early classical studies of the plant cell wall, these polysaccharides were characterised by their solubility in water and in alkali of increasing strength. It is clear that these fractions were largely the consequence of the fractionation procedures used which progressively degraded the polysaccharides actually present in the mature cell wall. This terminology persists and it is therefore necessary to comment on it.

Pectic substances were isolated by extraction with hot water, often containing a chelating agent such as oxalates or EDTA. Prolonged extraction was used and recent work using mild techniques suggests that degradation was quite extensive. Nevertheless, it is useful to use *pectic substances* to describe polysaccharides that are primarily soluble.

Hemicelluloses was a name given to the polysaccharides that were insoluble in water, but could be solubilised by dilute alkali. Hemicellulose fractions A, B and C were characterised by their behaviour on acidification of the extract or by the increasing strength of alkali required to solubilise them. Under carefully controlled conditions, these fractionation schemes can give valuable information on the fine structure of the cell wall polysaccharides. For nutritional purposes, however, it is convenient to consider the non-cellulosic polysaccharides as a spectrum of polymers ranging from water-soluble (pectic substances) often rich in uronic acids to insoluble substances with very small amounts of uronic acid.

2.3.3.2 General properties of the non-cellulosic polysaccharides (NCP)

2.3.3.2.1 Solubility
Solubility is very much a function of the specific polysaccharides, but in general, the more highly branched or substituted molecules are more water-soluble than the backbone components.

2.3.3.2.2 Acid hydrolysis
The NCP are hydrolysed by dilute acid. (eg 2½ hours in 1M sulphuric acid at 100°C produces complete hydrolysis of the neutral monosaccharide components with little degradation). Some side chains, particularly the arabinofuranosyl ones, are hydrolysed by very dilute acid (0.1M) at room temperature. Partial hydrolysis by dilute acid is a procedure that has been used in structure analysis where component oligosaccharides are studied.

The NCP containing uronic acid are not completely hydrolysed under the above conditions, which usually produce a range of aldobiuronic acids (disaccharides with one uronic acid component). These cannot be hydrolysed further under acid conditions without degradation. This property of uronic acid containing polysaccharides poses constraints on the quantitative analysis of the NCP.

2.3.3.2.3 Enzymatic hydrolysis
A number of specific enzymes hydrolyse the NCP. Bacterial and fungal sources provide a wide range of both exo and endo glycanhydrolases.

2.3.3.3 Individual classes of non-cellulosic polysaccharides

2.3.3.3.1 Galacturonans
Polymers of galacturonic acid, linked 1–4α, are characteristic of the water soluble pectic substances; commercial pectin preparations are characteristically galacturonans. The homopolysaccharide is rare in nature and most NCP in this category are rhamnogalacturonans containing rhamnose residues at intervals in the backbone. There is evidence of partial regularity in the distribution of rhamnose residues and the configuration of the linkage confers 'kinks' to the otherwise linear chain.

The carboxyl group of the uronic acid residues may be esterified with methyl groups, and the proportion of methoxylation has important effects on the physical properties of the polysaccharide; high methoxyl polymers form gels with acid at high solute concentrations whereas low methoxyl polymers require calcium ions for gelation. In some plants, the polymer may be acetylated, which further alters physical properties; acetylated polymers have poor gelling capacity.

Rhamnogalacturonans are found in most parenchymatous (undifferentiated) cell walls and therefore fruits and vegetables provide the major source of those components in the diet. They also play a major role in cell adhesion and in the middle lamella, a region between plant cells formed when cells divide.

2.3.3.3.2 Arabinogalactans

In the cell wall, it is probable that the galacturonan chains are highly substituted and that the arabinogalactans which form the other major component of the water soluble pectic fraction are covalently linked in the wall and hydrolysed during extraction. These substances are present in the immature cell walls of most fruits and vegetables which provide the major sources.

2.3.3.3.3 β-Glucans

A range of branched (1–2, 1–3) β-glucans can be extracted from the walls of many cereals, especially oats and barley. These polysaccharides are often among the major components of the endospermal cell wall. The degree of polymerisation of these glucans is much lower than cellulose, being typically between 400 and 250 molecules with the more polymerised forms being more soluble in water.

2.3.3.3.4 Arabinoxylans

These are a range of highly branched xylans which are characteristic of the cell walls of cereals. The backbone is D-β (1–4) xylose with arabinosyl side chains of variable length. A substantial proportion of them are water-soluble. Complete extraction requires alkali extraction so the arabinoxylans are present in both classical pectic and hemicellulosic fractions.

It is probable that the insolubility is due to phenolic acid linkages in the wall itself, since most isolated arabinoxylans are water-soluble. Dilute acid hydrolysis leads to the production of the xylan core which has many conformational analogies with the cellulose chain; these xylan cores are insoluble in water.

2.3.3.3.5 Glucuronoxylans

These are a range of xylans which are found in many mature lignified walls. The xylan backbone is β-(1–4)D xylose with glucuronic acid or 4-0-methylglucuronic acid side chains linked to C-2. The polymers have degrees of polymerisation of around 150–250 molecules. They are insoluble in water and thus fall within the hemicellulosic fractions.

2.3.3.3.6 Xyloglucans

These are found in many cell walls. They are insoluble in water and the D-β (1–4) glucose backbone has D-xylopyranose side chains on C-6 of at least 50% of residues. The polymers are insoluble in water and require strong alkali (4M potassium hydroxide) to solubilise them, indicating very strong hydrogen bonding to the cellulose fibrils. For this reason, these polymers are often found as contaminants in cellulose preparations.

2.3.3.3.7 Galactomannans

These form components of the endospermic cell walls of some leguminous seeds eg guar, locust bean. Functionally, they are storage polysaccharides, but they are stored in the wall. The backbone β-(1–4)D-mannopyranose has single galactosyl side chains (ratio of gal:man ranges from 1:1 to 1:5). The polymers are extracted with hot water.

2.4 SUBSTANCES ASSOCIATED WITH PLANT CELL WALL POLY-SACCHARIDES

A number of non-carbohydrate substances are associated with the polysaccharides in the plant cell wall. Some are integral parts of the wall structure, others are closely associated with the wall on external surfaces of the plant. Quantitatively they are minor components but they modify the properties of the polysaccharides and their nutritional and physiological effects when eaten.

2.4.1 Integral parts of wall structure

2.4.1.1 Protein
Proteins are present in all cell wall structures and form up to 10% of the wall dry matter in immature cell walls. The proportion falls as the wall increases in thickness and matures. The proteins seem to be intimately involved with the wall structure and glycoproteins covalently linked to the polysaccharides are present. The wall proteins are less digestible than most dietary proteins and are included in the dietary 'fibre' complex by Saunders and Betschart (1980).

2.4.1.2 Lignins
These are a group of aromatic polymers formed by the condensation of the aromatic alcohols (cinnamyl, guaicyl and syringyl). The lignin infiltrates into the polysaccharide matrix expanding the wall volume as the wall matures. In most foods, lignification is confined to the vascular elements, mature seed coats and some special lignified structures.

Covalent links between lignin and polysaccharides have been identified and the lignification creates hydrophobic regions in the wall and confers resistance to bacterial degradation. However, less polymerised polyphenolic materials form covalent bonds with polysaccharide in many plant tissues and this is one reason why the tissues must be treated with alkali to give good extraction of hemicelluloses. Analytical procedures for lignin are non-specific and the precise measurement of lignin is a matter of some difficulty.

2.4.2 Non-integral parts of wall structure

2.4.2.1 Cutin, subeun and plant waxes
These complex lipids are found in many external surfaces and are closely associated with the polysaccharides, they also create hydrophobic, less digestible, regions in the tissue.

2.4.2.2 Inorganic constituents
Most plants contain inorganic constituents which are present in the wall. Some walls are rich in silica which seems to be involved in the wall structures. In others, calcium, potassium and magnesium salts are deposited as inclusions; these frequently contain phytate as the anion.

2.5 ISOLATED POLY-SACCHARIDES

In addition to structural polysaccharides, many foods contain isolated polysaccharides that are present naturally and others contain polysaccharide food additives.

2.5.1 Naturally occurring polysaccharides

The naturally occurring materials are usually considered as *gums and mucilages*. Many gums, for example cereal gums (a mixture of β-glucans and arabinoxylans) are water extracts of cell wall components. So are guar and locust bean gum. Other gums, the exudate gums, are formed in response to damage to the plant.

Many mucilages are contained within specialised cells, for example ispaghula is often found in cells surrounding seeds.

Table 2.4 Major types of polysaccharide food additives

Source	Examples	Structural features
Plant exudates	Arabic, Ghatti Tragacanth	Complex, highly branched, heteropolysaccharides
Plant seeds	Guar, Carob Psyllium	Galactomannans Arabinoxylan
Plant extracts	Pectin	Galacturonorhamnans
Algal polysaccharides	Alginates Agar, Carrageenan	Uronans Galactans, SO_4
Modified polysaccharides	Starches Pectins Cellulose	Ethers, esters etc. Amidated Esters, ethers
Fermentation gums	Xanthan	Heteropolysaccharides

The range of structures present in these polysaccharides is very diverse and they are usually complex highly branched heteropolysaccharides. They are all soluble and may form viscous solutions. Some examples are given in Table 2.4.

2.5.2 Polysaccharide food additives

A wide range of polysaccharides are used in processing foods at low concentrations, usually less than 1% by weight. (Glicksman, 1969, Whistler and BeMiller, 1974). The principal technical reason for their use is in the control of physical properties and texture of the product, but some use is made of their bulking and low-energy value properties in calorie-reduced products. Many of these are derived from cell wall polysaccharides and they may be used as the unmodified isolated polysaccharide or after chemical modification. The main types are listed in Table 2.4.

The algal polysaccharides share some features not found in higher plants. Thus agar and the carrageenans have deoxygalactose residues and sulphated residues, the latter conferring special cation binding properties. The alginates are uronans with variable ratios of guluronic and mannuronic acid residues. The carboxyl groups also produce specific cation binding effects and the properties of the gels are modified by specific cations. Calcium produces elastic gels which are used in special products.

A range of modified starches and celluloses fall into this category. The modifications to the starches involve the introduction of esters or ether cross links which control retrogradation in starch products that are heated and cooled before consumption. The introduction of a small number of methyl and carboxymethyl groups into the cellulose molecule produces soluble viscous polysaccharides (Kearsley and Sicard, 1989).

Modified celluloses are also produced by selective depolymerisation using physical procedures leading to products which have technical value as emulsifiers and more recently as low-caloric bulking agents.

2.5.3 Semi-synthetic polysaccharides

Glucose, under certain conditions, can be induced to polymerise into a series of random structures producing a range of glucans. These contain only very small numbers of glucosidic bonds and are therefore not available as carbohydrate in the small intestine. Polydextrose is an example of this type of polysaccharide which is technically a non-starch polysaccharide. Polydextrose is approved as a food additive under the 'bulking agent' category although the levels of use, up to 10% in a yoghurt, for example, indicate that it is being used as an ingredient. The molecular size of polydextrose is such that it is soluble in 80% v/v ethanol and thus is not currently measured with the NSP's in the Englyst procedure. It is not hydrolysed by α-amylase. Effectively then, it is not measured as available carbohydrate either.

2.6 POLY-SACCHARIDES OF ANIMAL ORIGIN

A number of polysaccharides are found in animal tissues. Glycogen is found in liver and muscle and is a branched α1–4 α1–6 glucan having some similarities to amylopectin. The branching is more fan-like and the molecular weights are not usually so high. While the amounts of glycogen in raw liver and muscle (especially from horse flesh) are significant, post-mortem metabolism usually reduces the levels considerably so that the concentrations are low in liver and meat as normally eaten.

Animal tissues also contain a range of aminoso amino glycans (mucopolysaccharides) which play a structural role in extracellular tissues. The concentrations in most meats and animal products are low. These polysaccharides are polymers of galactose, N-acetyl-glucosamine, N-acetyl galactosamine, and glucoronic and iduronic acid. The N-acetyl galactosamine residues are often sulphated. In most diets the intakes of these are low with intakes probably of the order of a few hundred milligrams a day.

In the phylum Arthropoda, the exoskeleton contains chitin – a polysaccharide containing N-acetyl D-glucosamine and galactosamine. The polymer forms crystalline arrays of parallel chains and is insoluble in water. The intake of chitin in most human diets is quite low because most people separate the exoskeleton before eating insects and crustacea. However, chitin has attracted commercial interest because of the large amounts available from the processing of crustacea and a number of possible polysaccharide additives have been proposed. Alkaline deacetylation of chitin produces chitosan – a polysaccharide that is soluble in acid solution (pH < 5.5) giving a viscosity comparable to guar. It has been shown to be a strong binder of inorganic ions and there were some concerns about its use at high levels of intake. It has yet to be accepted as a food additive (Furda, 1983).

Chitins also occur in the hyphal walls of some fungi. They are regarded as normal constituents of the human diet but little is known of their physiological properties.

2.7 ORGANISATION OF COMPLEX CARBO-HYDRATES IN FOODS

The majority of complex carbohydrates in foods are organised into physical structures that confer properties over and above those present in the isolated polysaccharide. Even the polysaccharide food additives produce specific physical states within the food; these may involve interactions between different polysaccharides or proteins in the food. As a general principle therefore, when trying to relate the physiological effects of a specific food or mixture of complex carbohydrates in the diet to the polysaccharides present, it is essential to consider the physical organisation and state of the polysaccharides. The physical properties are discussed at length in Chapters 4 and 5 and this Chapter is therefore limited to the overview of the types of physical organisation seen in foods.

2.7.1 Starches

In uncooked foods, the starches are present in the form of discrete granules within the cell. The microscopic appearance of the granules is characteristic of the food and the range of sizes of granules seen is often characteristic of the plant. Wheat starch granules have been studied in great detail, but remain a topic of research. The crystalline character of the starch granules is due to the amylopectin since the amylose in the granule is largely amorphous and lies between the amylopectin clusters. On heating in an aqueous environment to 50°C, the amorphous phase swells and disrupts the granule leading to a melting of the crystalline structure – a process known as gelatinisation. On cooling, the amylose crystallises and retrogrades to an insoluble aggregated or crystalline state (Würsch, 1990).

In many products which are heat treated with limited amounts of water the granules do not swell completely and limited disruption and solubilisation occurs. Many cooked foods may therefore exhibit a range of granules, from those that are substantially unaltered to those that are completely solubilised.

2.7.2 Structural polysaccharides

These are present in a range of cell wall types derived from the range of plant organs and component tissues in foods (see section 2.3).

Although the detailed organisation of the cell walls are characteristic of specific plants, it is possible to make some generalisations based on the major types of plant tissues in foods.

Parenchyma These undifferentiated tissues form the major part of fruits and vegetables. The typical cell is polygonal. The intra-cellular middle lamella is rich in rhamnogalacturonans and these are highly methoxylated. In the primary wall, the cellulose fibrils are formed as a network in a predominantly rhamnogalacturonan and arabinogalactan matrix. Subsequent layers of the wall show highly orientated cellulose fibres and insoluble xyloglucans are deposited. The wall always contains some protein, usually glycoproteins. In immature cereal walls, the matrix is mainly arabinoxylan or β-glucan.

Vascular tissues In the conducting tissues, phloem and xylem differentiation involves a thickening of the wall by the formation of layers of cellulose fibrils surrounded by the matrix NCP. In xylem tissue, lignin infiltrates the carbohydrate matrix, producing progressively rigid walls. In woody tissues with completely lignified walls, the nucleus and cytoplasm have been lost.

Supporting tissues These may have thickened unlignified walls (collenchyma) or become lignified sclerides.

Epidermal tissues These are characterised by the development of wax cutinised or cutilicularised surfaces. In these cells, the cutin is apparently very intimately attached to the wall itself.

Seeds – coats These may be relatively simple cutinised structures, one or a few cells thick, or complex many layered lignified structures such as seen in cereals.

Seeds – endosperm The endospermal walls in cereals are thin structures which are often mainly NCP, either arabinoxylans or β-glucans with low concentrations of cellulose.

2.8 ANALYSIS OF COMPLEX CARBO-HYDRATES

2.8.1 Primary considerations

The analysis of the complex carbohydrates in foods usually requires the separation of the various polysaccharides present; a single total value is only appropriate when only one species of polysaccharide is present. Virtually all foods require a combination of fractional extraction followed by a chromatographic separation on the basis of polymer size and/or active groups. The individual polysaccharides are usually determined by analysis of the mixture of neutral sugars and uronic acids after hydrolysis by either GLC after derivitisation, or HPLC. Colorimetry can be used but the results are less informative (Southgate and Englyst, 1985).

Research on the plant cell wall is the major source of techniques and this research shows that it is usually necessary to modify the actual procedure for each particular matrix. One major problem is caused by the presence of lignin and other phenolic substances which prevent complete extraction of the matrix non-cellulosic polysaccharides. The removal of lignin, in particular, without altering the carbohydrates, is very difficult.

The structural identity of the polysaccharides is obtained by the use of a combination of methylation analysis and selective partial hydrolysis using dilute acid and specific enzymes. These procedures are time-consuming and because specific techniques have to be used for each food matrix, complete analyses for foods are very few in number and in most nutritional studies a compromise has been made in the types of methods used. This is particularly true for the analysis of dietary 'fibre' and equally so for the non-starch polysaccharides. The pressures from regulatory bodies for 'fibre' values to be used in nutritional labelling has produced additional constraints by seeking a single value which in view of the complexity of the mixtures present in most foods is of little value to the consumer (see Chapter 21).

2.8.2 Measurement of total non-starch polysaccharides

The main features of the procedure are summarised in the figure (Figure 2.3), the principal stages are as follows:

(i) *Extraction of free sugars and lipids*. This is usually achieved with aqueous alcohols and suitable lipid solvents. Care is essential to avoid losses of soluble polysaccharides and the hydrolysis of labile polymers such as the fructans.

(ii) *Removal of starch*. Specific extractants for starch are virtually unknown and most procedures use enzymatic hydrolysis; alpha-amylase combined with a debranching enzyme such as pullulanase give near theoretical yields of glucose, as do glucoamylases if the starches do not contain retrograded starch. Most analytical procedures use treatment with dimethyl sulphoxide (DMSO) to disperse the starch prior to hydrolysis.

(iii) *Recovery of non-starch polysaccharides*. After enzymatic hydrolysis, the NSP are precipitated with ethanol by adjusting the concentration to 80% v/v and recovering the polysaccharides by filtration or centrifugation. This can sometimes lead to losses and dialysis and freeze-drying may be preferable.

(iv) *Hydrolysis of non-starch polysaccharides*. Two approaches are adopted; hydrolysis of the non-cellulosic polysaccharides by dilute 1M or 2M sulphuric acid for 2.5h at 100°C; or Saeman hydrolysis, 12M sulphuric acid at ambient (or below) followed by dilution to 1M and heating at 100°C for 2.5h. The difference between the two values for glucose is a measure of the cellulose present (Figure 2.4).

(v) *Measurement of neutral sugars and uronic acids*. Total sugars can be measured colorimetrically. Individual sugars can be measured, after separation, by HPLC. Measurement by GLC requires derivitisation; reduction to the alditols and acetylation to give the alditol acetates is a widely used procedure. Uronic acids cannot be analysed in this way and colorimetry is usually adopted (Figure 2.4).

2.8.3 Measurement of individual polysaccharides

The above procedures provide total values, together with some idea of the major types of polysaccharide present. The measurement of the individual polymers requires a procedure of the type illustrated in Figure 2.3(vi).

Water-soluble components are extracted with a solution of a chelating agent to facilitate the release of uronans. The residue is then extracted sequentially with alkali of increasing strength under nitrogen to give a range of 'hemicellulosic' fractions. These are further fractionated by gel-permeation to give a range of polymer fractions.

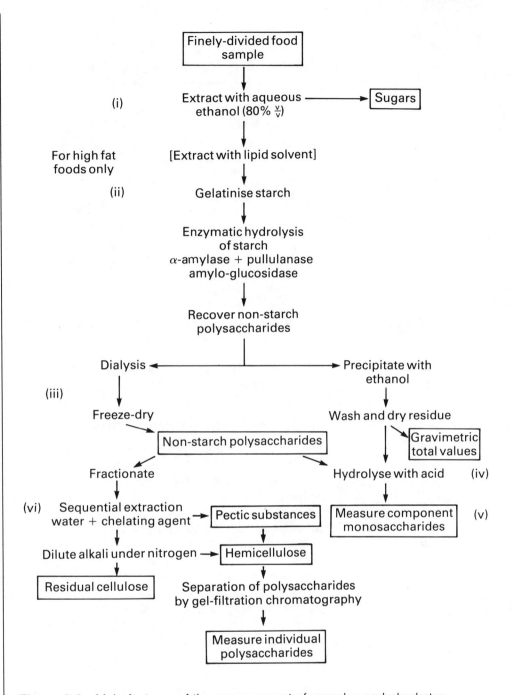

Figure 2.3 Main features of the measurement of complex carbohydrates.

The fractions are isolated by neutralisation and precipitation, or dialysis and freeze-drying, to give the polysaccharides which may be analysed as described above. As mentioned earlier, removal of lignin may be necessary to get complete extraction.

2.8.4 Gravimetric procedures

The precipitated fractions can be filtered off and weighed to give either total values or values of the components. The fractions are rarely pure carbohydrates and correction for contaminating protein and minerals is usually essential. Some simplified

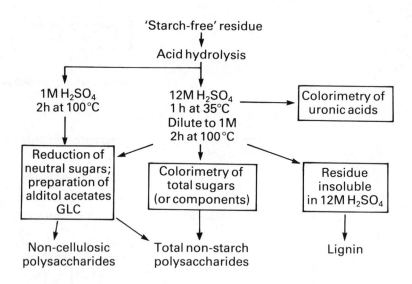

Figure 2.4 Direct measurement of polysaccharides in non-starch polysaccharides.

procedures incorporate a proteolytic enzyme with the amylases but protein contamination is still seen and correction is still necessary.

2.8.5 Choices of analytical procedure

The principles for the measurement of non-starch polysaccharides and dietary 'fibre' have been the subject of considerable debate. Southgate and Englyst (1985) have reviewed the features of the various analytical approaches. In the analysis of food carbohydrates some compromise is always required of the analyst in choosing between the ideal of complete separation and measurement of the isolated components and achieving a practicable procedure (Southgate, 1969).

The gravimetric procedure developed collaboratively by the Association of Official Analytical Chemists (Prosky *et al.*, 1984) measures the residue after enzymatic removal of protein and starch – the residue weight is corrected for protein and ash and provides a value for total dietary 'fibre'. It includes all non-starch poly-saccharides, lignin and enzymatically resistant starch.

The Englyst enzymatic method (Englyst, Wiggins and Cummings, 1982) measures the non-starch polysaccharides (NSP) as their component monosaccharides and uronic acids after hydrolysis; the values exclude lignin and resistant starch (Englyst and Cummings, 1987).

For many heat processed cereals, the NSP values are substantially less than the values obtained by the gravimetric method. For fruits and vegetables, the two procedures give substantially the same values.

Both procedures are reasonable indices of plant cell wall material (Asp and Johansson, 1984), but the gravimetric method tends to over-estimate at the lower end of the scale, because it includes insoluble artefacts. At the higher end of the scale, the values obtained from the enzymatic method are lower because lignin is not included. Figure 2.5 illustrates how the different ways of measuring dietary 'fibre' are related to each other.

The enzymatic method is preferable, especially for research purposes, because it provides some limited characterisation of the polysaccharides present. Both methods can be modified to measure soluble and insoluble components, but since solubility is highly method dependent, different values are obtained. Establishing the role of

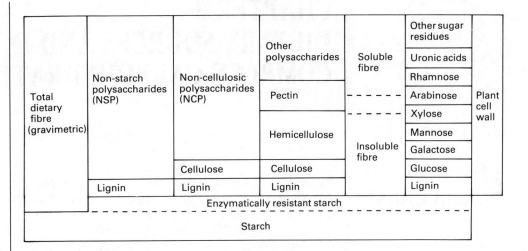

Total dietary fibre (gravimetric)	Non-starch polysaccharides (NSP)	Non-cellulosic polysaccharides (NCP)	Other polysaccharides	Soluble fibre	Other sugar residues	Plant cell wall
					Uronic acids	
					Rhamnose	
			Pectin	– – – – –	Arabinose	
				– – – – –	Xylose	
			Hemicellulose		Mannose	
				Insoluble fibre	Galactose	
		Cellulose	Cellulose		Glucose	
	Lignin	Lignin	Lignin		Lignin	
	Enzymatically resistant starch					
	Starch					

Figure 2.5 The relationship between the different ways of measuring dietary 'fibre'. Broken lines indicate boundaries that are not absolute. (Modified from Asp and Johansson, 1984)

individual complex polysaccharides in the diet can only be achieved by more detailed procedures where fractionation of the individual polysaccharides has been included.

CHAPTER 3
DIETARY SOURCES AND INTAKE OF COMPLEX CARBOHYDRATES

3.1 INTRODUCTION

Epidemiological evidence for the benefits of complex carbohydrates has so far been based upon a limited knowledge of people's intakes. If the roles of complex carbohydrates are to be better defined, it is essential to have accurate estimates of the different kinds of complex carbohydrates, as well as of the total amount available, in different countries and in different population groups within countries.

The main reason for the paucity of data on intakes is that few tables of food composition other than those used in Britain (Paul and Southgate, 1978; Holland *et al.*, 1988, 1989) give values for anything but total carbohydrate (including sugars). Furthermore, even these values are of limited accuracy because they are usually derived 'by difference'; that is to say, the foods are analysed for their water, fat, protein (N x 6.25), ash and possibly 'crude fibre' contents, and the residue (which includes any errors in these determinations and varying amounts of minor constituents as well as sugars, starch and other polysaccharides) is taken as the carbohydrate content of the food.

3.2 COMPLEX CARBOHYDRATES IN FOOD SUPPLIES OF DEVELOPED COUNTRIES

Table 3.1 shows estimates of the national supplies of starch and other complex carbohydrates in a number of developed countries. The values are based on food supply statistics published by the Organisation for Economic Cooperation and Development (OECD, 1988), which record the amounts of basic agricultural commodities (plus imports and minus exports) destined for human consumption in each country. Similar statistics are available for most countries of the world from the Food and Agriculture Organisation of the United Nations (FAO, 1988), but they are unfortunately not directly comparable with those from the OECD. These calculations

Table 3.1 Estimated (complex) carbohydrate content of cereal and vegetable supplies in selected countries in 1985 (g/person/day)

	From cereals	From vegetables	Total 'starch'	% energy from 'starch'
United States	135	30	165	19
Australia	120	35	155	20
Germany	150	45	195	22
Ireland	190	65	255	26
United Kingdom	170	60	230	27
Finland	150	45	195	27
Spain	160	70	230	28
France	165	50	215	30
Italy	235	35	270	32
Japan	230	60	290	44
Turkey	395	85	480	57

(Derived from food supply statistics in OECD, 1988)

assume that all of the carbohydrate in the supplies of cereals and vegetables, including potatoes, nuts and pulses, is starch and other complex carbohydrates, and ignore the comparatively small contributions from all other foods.

Apart from any errors in carbohydrate analysis, these quantities will still be substantially greater than the amounts of complex carbohydrate actually eaten – perhaps by as much as 30 per cent, which is the amount by which the energy content of national food supplies in most developed countries exceeds estimates of their populations' energy requirements (FAO, 1983). Although losses in storage, distribution and processing would be different in developing countries, where starch commonly provides 75 per cent of the energy (FAO, 1980), they are likely to be similar in most of the countries shown in the table. The order in which they are given here should be broadly correct.

3.3 AVERAGE INTAKES OF DIFFERENT TYPES OF COMPLEX CARBO-HYDRATES IN BRITAIN

3.3.1 Food Supply Data

It has long been possible to make better estimates of complex and other carbohydrate intakes in Britain because, in the 1920s, McCance and his co-workers started to analyse the carbohydrate content of foods directly (McCance and Lawrence, 1929). Since then, tables of food consumption in this country have shown the true carbohydrate content of foods, and indeed have given separate values for the amounts of sugars and starches. They have also presented estimates of unavailable carbohydrates where appropriate, and, more recently, show the amounts of specific types of non-starch polysaccharides. Using the food tables (Paul and Southgate, 1978), estimates have been made by Southgate *et al.* (1978) of the amounts of unavailable carbohydrates in the national food supplies in this country since 1880. The values vary only between about 22g and 24g per person per day except during the Second World War, when they may have been as high as 40 g per person per day. Intakes of starch and many other complex carbohydrates were higher during the War because of the large amounts of brown bread and of potatoes and root vegetables that were eaten. But apart from this time, there has until recently been a steady decline in the amounts eaten. A general decline in food intakes in an increasingly sedentary population accounts for part of this, but a halving of cereal consumption has also been important, for carbohydrate intakes from fruit and vegetables have remained steady or even increased.

3.3.2 Food Consumption Data

More accurate estimates of nutrient intakes by different groups of people in this country can be obtained from the National Food Survey (Ministry of Agriculture, Fisheries and Food, 1989). This survey records the quantities of almost all foods brought into homes throughout Britain, and detailed nutritional evaluations are provided. Southgate *et al.* (1978) also made estimates of unavailable carbohydrate intakes at this level too, and their values are summarised in Table 3.2. In addition to intakes in the home, there will of course be carbohydrates in foods obtained away from the home, but these are not recorded in the survey.

There is now new information on the amounts of the major components of complex carbohydrate in cereals, vegetables and fruit (Englyst *et al.*, 1988; Holland *et al.*, 1988). These values have been applied to the quantities of food recorded in the National Food Survey since 1988, and a summary of the results for that year is given in Table 3.3.

The total amount of 'available carbohydrate' in the British household diet in 1988 was 237.5g per person per day, of which 138.5g was starch and 99 g was sugars (Lewis and Buss, 1990). There was also an indeterminate amount of 'resistant starch' (quantification of which awaits a clearer definition) and 12.5g of non-starch polysaccharides. The main contributors to this starch intake were cereal products (73 per

Table 3.2   Trends in unavailable carbohydrate in household intakes in Britain in selected years, g/person/day

Year	Cellulose	NCP (including some starch)	Total unavailable carbohydrate
1951	7.3	19.7	28.4
1961	5.6	15.1	21.7
1971	5.2	14.8	21.2
1982	5.7	14.9	22.2

NCP = Non cellulose polysaccharides, with as much starch as possible removed (From Southgate *et al.*, 1978 and Wenlock *et al.*, 1984).

cent), potatoes (13 per cent) and other vegetables including pulses (8 per cent). Almost all the remainder came from the cereals in meat and fish products such as pies, sausages and fish fingers. Of the non-starch polysaccharides, there was a slightly greater amount of insoluble 'fibre' (cellulose and insoluble non-cellulosic polysaccharides) than of soluble 'fibre' (ie the soluble non-cellulosic polysaccharides). Cereals and vegetables were both important, and made complementary contributions to most types of complex carbohydrate.

Table 3.3   Household intakes of major types of complex carbohydrates in Britain in 1988 (g/person/day)

Food group	Starch	Resistant starch	Cellulose	Insoluble NCP	Soluble NCP	NSP	Unavailable carbohydrate
Dairy products	0.10	0	0.04	0.02	0.02	0.08	0.12
Meat and meat products	4.54	–	0.05	0.07	0.09	0.20	0.72
Fish and fish products	0.80	–	–	0.01	0.02	0.03	0.04
Eggs, fats, sugar and preserves	0.15	0	0.01	0.01	0.03	0.04	0.06
Potatoes	18.56	–	0.46	0.11	0.73	1.31	1.79
Other fresh vegetables	0.35	–	0.54	0.24	0.75	1.42	1.92
Processed vegetables	10.18	–	0.87	0.42	1.04	2.31	4.03
Fruit and fruit products	0.38	0.16	0.38	0.33	0.59	1.33	1.80
Bread and flour	65.80	1.01	0.37	1.56	1.51	3.36	6.89
Cakes and biscuits	13.07	0.10	0.13	0.24	0.30	0.64	1.06
Other cereal products	22.86	0.25	0.24	0.76	0.51	1.51	2.30
Other foods	1.72	–	0.07	0.03	0.08	0.23	0.31
Totals	138.5	1.5+	3.2	3.8	5.7	12.5	21.0

NCP = Non cellulose polysaccharides, excluding starch too. The total NSP (non-starch polysaccharides) is the sum of the cellulose, the soluble and the insoluble NCP, while 'unavailable carbohydrate' also includes 'resistant starch', some other starch, and 'lignin' as well.
(From Annual Report of the National Food Survey, Ministry of Agriculture, Fisheries and Food, 1990)

3.4 VARIABILITY IN COMPLEX CARBOHYDRATE INTAKE

The data from the National Food Survey show little variation in household intakes between income groups or between England, Scotland and Wales as a whole (Lewis and Buss, 1988). A wide range of individual intakes was found in the recent Government study of the diets and health of more than 2000 people throughout Britain (Gregory *et al.*, 1990). In 7-day weighed diets, the median intake of starch by men was 155g per day, but the 5th centile was 84 g and the 95th centile was 237g. For women, the median was 106 g and the 5th and 95th centiles were 54 g and 160 g per day. Unavailable carbohydrate intakes varied similarly: for men, the median the intake was 24g per day (5th and 95th centiles, 12 and 41 g respectively), while for women the median intake was 18g and the 5th and 95th centiles were 9g and 30g.

CHAPTER 4
HOW DO THE FORM AND PHYSICAL PROPERTIES OF STARCHES INFLUENCE THEIR BIOLOGICAL EFFECTS?

4.1 INTRODUCTION

Starch is the major storage polysaccharide in the human diet, the main sources being cereals, legumes and tubers – particularly the potato. As a consequence, the conditions that govern its digestion are of considerable importance. Starch is present within plant cells as discrete microscopic granules enclosed in phospholipid membranes. The size and form of a granule is often characteristic of the plant of origin. Within each granule, amylopectin forms a branched, helical, crystalline system with the linear amylose dispersed within the amylopectin structure. The chemical structures of amylose and amylopectin have already been described in Chapter 2.

The digestibility of raw starch depends on the accessibility and crystalline structure of its starch granules. The granules are gelatinised during cooking and freshly cooked starchy foods are easily digestible. However, when cooled, starch may recrystallise into forms which are less susceptible to pancreatic amylase.

4.2 FACTORS AFFECTING STARCH DIGESTION

4.2.1 Physical accessibility

The degree of milling of grain has a major influence on its digestibility and it has been demonstrated that whole grains, or coarsely milled grains provoke smaller plasma insulin responses after ingestion than does finely ground flour (Heaton *et al.*, 1988). This is probably due to the retarded release of glucose from the starch by digestive enzymes. Similarly, the extent of mastication may be important. In exceptional cases it has been shown that after meals of sweetcorn, peas and beans, up to 20% of faecal solids may be starch in undigested food particles (Englyst, 1985). These effects depend on the extent of the physical disruption of the plant structures as they enter the small intestine.

4.2.2 Structure of the granule

The crystalline structure of the starch granule has been studied by X-ray diffraction (Katz, 1934). Three types of structure have been identified which depend partly on the chain lengths making up the amylopectin lattice, the density of packing within the granule and the presence of water (Wu and Sarko, 1978 a and b; Gidley, 1987: Hizukuri, 1985).

Type A – chain lengths of 23–29 glucose molecules with further crystalline structures interspersed, the usual pattern for cereals.

Type B – chain lengths of 30–44 glucose molecules with water interspersed, the common pattern in raw potato and banana.

Type C – chain lengths of 26–29 glucose molecules – a combination of types A and B, typical of peas and beans.

In general, types B and C tend to be more resistant to enzyme degradation.

4.2.3 Response to heat treatments

When heated to about 50° C in the presence of water, the amylose in the granule swells, the crystalline structure of the amylopectin disintegrates and the granule ruptures. The polysaccharide chains take up a random conformation, causing swelling of the starch and thickening of the surrounding matrix (gelatinisation) – a process which renders the starch easily digestible. The extent of gelatinisation is dependent on the amount of water present and the duration of the heat treatment, so that various cooking techniques result in foods with a wide range of susceptibility to pancreatic amylase.

On cooling or drying, recrystallisation occurs. This takes place very fast for the amylose moiety because the linear structure facilitates cross linkages by means of hydrogen bonds. The branched nature of amylopectin inhibits its recrystallisation to some extent and it takes place over several days (eg this is responsible for the staling of bread).

In addition, temperature and water content are important. Higher temperature and less water result in a Type A configuration and lower temperature and high water content result in a Type B configuration (Wu and Sarko, 1978 a and b).

This process is known as retrogradation and retrograded starch is less soluble and less susceptible to enzymic hydrolysis. The rate and extent to which a starch may retrograde after gelatinisation essentially depends on the amount of amylose present.

4.2.4 Other factors

Digestion of starch also depends on the availability of amylase in the gut, the time available for digestion – that is the transit time in the small intestine – and the presence of other compounds, some derived from foods, which might impede access of the enzyme to the starch.

4.3 NUTRITIONAL CLASSIFICATION OF STARCHES

4.3.1 Classification into digestible and resistant starches

Starches have been classified according to their behaviour when incubated with enzymes without prior exposure to dispersing agents (eg. for wheat products, see Berry, 1986a). Englyst and Cummings (1987a) were the first to propose a nutritional classification of starches based on the rapidity with which glucose is released from a food source under specified laboratory conditions.

First, the total starch (TS) content of a food source is required. This is measured as the yield of glucose from a finely milled or homogenised sample of the food in which the starch is completely gelatinised at 100° C, treated with potassium hydroxide to ensure complete dispersion of the starches to an amorphous, digestible form and then enzymatically digested with pancreatin and amyloglucosidase.

Three subfractions of starch can then be identified by controlled periods of enzymic digestion of homogenised and non-homogenised food samples:

(i) Rapidly digestible starch (RDS) consists mainly of amorphous and dispersed starch. It is typically found in high amounts in starchy foods which have been cooked by moist heat eg bread and potatoes. It is measured chemically as the starch which is converted to the constituent glucose molecules in 20 minutes of enzyme digestion.

(ii) Slowly digestible starch (SDS), like RDS is expected to be completely digested in the small intestine but, for one reason or another, it is digested more slowly. This category consists of physically inaccessible amorphous starch and raw starch with Types A and C crystalline structures, eg cereals and some Type B starch, either in granule form or retrograded in cooked foods. It is measured chemically as the starch converted to glucose after a further 100 minutes enzyme digestion.

(iii) Resistant starch (RS) is the starch which may potentially resist digestion in the small intestine. It is measured chemically as the difference between total starch obtained from the homogenised and chemically treated sample and the sum of rapidly digested and slowly digested starch generated from non-homogenised food samples by enzyme digestion.

Thus: $RS = TS - (RDS + SDS)$

4.3.2 Classification of different types of resistant starch

Resistant starch can be subdivided into three fractions:

(i) RS_1 represents starch which is resistant because it is in a physically inaccessible form such as partly milled grains and seeds and in some very dense types of processed starchy foods.

It is measured chemically by comparing the glucose released by the enzyme digestion of a homogenised food sample with that released from a non-homogenised sample.

(ii) RS_2 represents starch which is in a certain granular form which is particularly resistant to enzyme digestion.

It is measured chemically by comparing the glucose released by the enzyme digestion of a boiled, homogenised food sample with that from an unboiled, non-homogenised food sample.

(iii) RS_3 represents the most resistant starch fraction and is mainly retrograded amylose formed during the cooling of gelatinised starch. Most moist heated foods will therefore contain some RS_3.

It is measured chemically as the fraction which resists both dispersion by boiling and enzyme digestion. It can only be dispersed with potassium hydroxide or dimethyl sulphoxide.

Thus:

$$RS_1 = TS - (RDS + SDS) - RS_2 - RS_3$$
$$RS_2 = TS - (RDS + SDS) - RS_1 - RS_3$$
$$RS_3 = TS - (RDS + SDS) - RS_2 - RS_1$$

RS_1 and RS_2 represent the residues of starch forms which are digested very slowly and incompletely in the small intestine. RS_3, however, is entirely resistant to digestion by pancreatic amylases.

The resistant starches are fermented by colonic bacteria to produce short chain fatty acids, carbon dioxide, and methane. The rate and extent of fermentation is related, in part, to the degree of crystallinity of the starch (Englyst and Macfarlane, 1988). It is not yet certain whether the fermentation of retrograded amylose is complete. Factors affecting this will probably include the nature of the colonic bacterial population and its capacity to adapt to its substrates (see Chapter 8).

4.3.3 Variation in types of starches present in foods

Although the above classification is based on experimental manipulation it may be used to broadly classify food sources according to the type of starch contained and to indicate the likely site of digestion in the gut (Table 4.1).

The amounts of RDS, SDS and RS in foods are highly variable. They depend partly

Table 4.1 *In vitro* nutritional classification of starch

Type of starch	Example of occurrence	Probable digestion in small intestine
Rapidly digestible starch	Freshly cooked starchy food	Rapid
Slowly digestible starch	Most raw cereals	Slow but complete
Resistant starch		
1. Physically inaccessible starch	Partly milled grain and seeds	Resistant
2. Resistant starch granules	Raw potato and banana	Resistant
3. Retrograded starch	Cooled, cooked potato, bread and cornflakes	Resistant

(From Englyst and Kingman, 1990)

on the source of starch, but largely on the type and extent of processing the food has been given. It should be noted that, for most starchy foods, cooking converts the starch to a readily digestible form, and even when retrogradation occurs on cooling, the amounts are small in terms of overall consumption of starch. Table 4.2 shows the *in vitro* digestibility of starch in a variety of foods. The values are derived from the analyses of Englyst and Kingman (1990) and are in accordance with the rates of starch hydrolysis shown in a range of common foods which were subjected to a simulated digestion (Gee and Johnson, 1985).

Table 4.2 *In vitro* digestibility of starch in a variety of foods

			% RS		
	% RDS	% SDS	RS_1	RS_2	RS_3
Flour, white	38	59	–	3	t
Shortbread	56	43	–	–	t
Bread, white	94	4	–	–	2
Bread, wholemeal	90	8	–	–	2
Spaghetti, white	55	36	8	–	1
Biscuits, made with 50% raw banana flour	34	27	–	38	t
Biscuits, made with 50% raw potato flour	36	29	–	35	t
Peas, chick, canned	56	24	5	–	14
Beans, dried, freshly cooked	37	45	11	t	6
Bean, red kidney, canned	60	25	–	–	15

The values are expressed as a percentage of the total starch present in the food. RDS = rapidly digestible starch; SDS = slowly digestible starch; RS = resistant starch; t = trace. Values taken from Englyst and Kingman (1990)

4.4 BIOLOGICAL EFFECTS OF STARCHES

4.4.1 Effects via Glycaemic index

Apart from the range of essential nutrients associated with starchy foods, starch itself is the major source of glucose in the diet and after consumption of a starchy meal, the blood glucose concentration is increased. The extent of this effect is measured by the glycaemic index which compares the extent and duration of the increase with that observed after ingestion of 50 g of glucose (see Chapter 10). A rise in blood glucose stimulates the secretion of insulin causing temporary relative hyper-insulinaemia until the blood glucose returns to normal levels. The magnitude of hyperinsulinaemia is related to the rapidity of absorption of glucose and is probably important in two conditions, namely diabetes and coronary heart disease.

4.4.1.1 Diabetes (see Chapter 11)

This is due either to a failure to secrete insulin in response to glucose absorption or to a relative insensitivity of the tissues to circulating insulin. In each case it is an important therapeutic consideration to limit the glucose challenge by reducing the rapidity of glucose absorption, an effect achievable by meals that include a proportion of starch of reduced digestibility. In general, foods that exhibit a reduced glycaemic index tend to be foods low in free glucose content and with an increased content of slowly digestible starch or resistant starch.

4.4.1.2 Coronary Heart Disease (CHD) (see Chapter 14)

There is some evidence that there is an association in males between elevated fasting plasma insulin and the development of CHD which is independent of other risk factors. The association exists whether the high plasma insulin level occurs in fasting individuals or in response to glucose loading. Although it cannot be claimed that the CHD is due to raised insulin levels it remains possible that the avoidance of episodic hyperglycaemia might be of value in the prevention of CHD.

4.4.2 Effects via Fermentation

As mentioned already, a small proportion of starches resist digestion in the small intestine and are available for fermentation in the large intestine. Very little is known about the specific effects of the fermentation products from resistant starches, but it is assumed that the end-products of fermentation, gases and short chain fatty acids have the same potential effects on the host as those from non-starch polysaccharides. There has been a suggestion that fermentation of starch results in a higher proportion of butyrate to acetate (Englyst *et al.*, 1987b) and this difference might have important consequences (see Chapter 8).

CHAPTER 5
HOW DO THE FORM AND PHYSICAL PROPERTIES OF NON-STARCH POLYSACCHARIDES INFLUENCE THEIR BIOLOGICAL EFFECTS?

5.1 INTRODUCTION

Amongst the physical properties of non-starch polysaccharides which may influence their function are their interaction with other components of cell walls, their viscosity, water holding capacity, particle size, their cation exchange capacity, and their ability to bind molecules such as bile acids and minerals. These properties can all be altered during the preparation, cooking and mastication of foods.

This chapter will discuss each of these physical properties in turn. Table 5.1 provides a summary.

5.2 INCORPORATION INTO PLANT CELL WALLS

Plant polysaccharides can be ingested in their natural state, as part of plant cell walls, or as purified or semi-purified forms. The physiological actions of non-starch polysaccharides have largely been investigated using purified or semi-purified material. It is difficult to extrapolate from the results of experiments using purified material to predict the action of ingested plant material containing these polysaccharides (Eastwood *et al.*, 1986).

5.2.1 Effects of other components of cell walls

The physical and chemical environment of polysaccharides within the plant cell has a large influence on their action in the gastrointestinal tract. The plant cell wall is a complex physical structure with a detailed molecular architecture which is dependent on its type and maturity (Selvendran, 1985). The parenchymatous cells of fruits, vegetables and dicotyledonous seeds contain mainly pectic polysaccharides such as pectin and hemicellulose with very little polyphenol (lignin) or protein cross-linkage. Partially lignified non-parenchymatous cells contain fewer pectic polysaccharides and mainly cellulose, hemicellulose and galactomannans (Selvendran, 1985). The lignin content is usually low but increases as the plant matures. Cereal grains contain a matrix of hemicellulose (arabinoxylans and β-glucans) some cross-linked with phenolic esters and proteins, and cellulose closely associated with glucoxylans. Lignified tissues are a more important component of cereal 'fibre' than of fruit and vegetable 'fibre'.

The lignin and protein cross-linkages reduce the solubility of polysaccharide components of cell walls, strengthen the cellular structure and are resistant to fermentation. The strength of intercellular adhesion also reduces polysaccharide solubility and fermentation.

5.2.2 Physical structure of plant walls

The physical structure of the plant cell wall may also trap starch and other nutrients (O'Dea *et al.*, 1980). Thus, lignification of the plant material will decrease its

Table 5.1 The modulation of biological effects by the physicochemical properties of non-starch polysaccharides

Physicochemical properties	Possible biological effects
Incorporation into plant cell wall	Increases resistance to digestion Increases resistance to fermentation Reduces carbohydrate availability
Increased viscosity	Slows nutrient absorption Reduces post-prandial glycaemia Resists effects of gastrointestinal motility Slows gastric emptying Prolongs small bowel transit Reduces interaction with enzymes and epithelial surface Alters hormone profiles
Increased water holding capacity	Induces propulsion in small intestine Increases faecal bulking (non-fermentable) Decreases faecal bulking (fermentable)
Increased particle size	Increases water holding capacity Increases faecal bulking Reduces post-prandial glycaemia Direct action of particles on mucosal mechano-receptors
Increased susceptibility to bacterial fermentation	Reduces faecal bulk Accelerates transit time Increases faecal bile acid excretion

disruptibility and hence starch availability (Southgate, 1986). Most of the lignin occurs in the outer layers of the wheat grain, whereas the soluble non-starch polysaccharides occur in the endosperm and hence the solubility of non-starch polysaccharides in wheat is influenced by the degree of milling.

Starch granules may be intimately associated with a protein matrix that can impair digestion. Thus gluten-free flour is more rapidly digested and absorbed than gluten-containing flour though the addition of gluten to purified starch does not impair its digestion (Jenkins *et al.*, 1987a).

5.3 ASSOCIATION OF NON-STARCH POLY-SACCHARIDES WITH WATER

Non-starch polysaccharides form sols or gels with water. This association of non-starch polysaccharides with water is essential to our understanding of physical properties and physiological effects.

5.3.1 Viscosity

Soluble non-starch polysaccharides may form viscous solutions.

5.3.1.1 Chemical determinants of viscosity
Viscosity is imparted to a sol by the polymeric structure of the polysaccharide and also by the cross linkages between the polymeric structures. This is a consequence of the internal molecular associations of the polysaccharide resulting in non Newtonian flow.

Some chemical determinants of viscosity are as follows:

(i)   A low methoxy content makes pectins less viscous.
(ii) Clustering of side chains along each polymer molecule can alter viscosity eg carboxymethylcellulose (CMC) and locust bean gum.
(iii) Hydrophilic polymers become more viscous than hydrophobic polymers.

5.3.1.2 Physical determinants of viscosity

Viscosity is affected by concentration, temperature, ionic concentration, pH, hydrophilic or hydrophobic properties, particle size, and association with protein (coacervation) (Morris, 1986).

The size of fibrous polysaccharides has very important effects on viscosity; the size of spherocolloids does not.

Cooking can alter the viscous nature of a polysaccharide solution by rearranging the physical configuration. Locust bean gum has to be heated to 70°C before maximum viscosity is obtained and starch gelatinises on cooking. Some polysaccharides form true gels at high concentration. Unlike viscous solutions, the more solid gels can be completely disrupted by large shear forces which may occur during chewing and during grinding in the stomach.

5.3.1.3 Physiological effects of viscosity

The addition of purified viscous polysaccharides to meals or drinks of glucose reduces the rate of absorption and decreases post-prandial plasma glucose concentrations. It seems likely that the effect is brought about by the resistance of the viscous sols to the flow induced by gastrointestinal motility (Blackburn et al., 1984; Edwards et al., 1990).

The changing ionic environment and pH during passage of a meal through the gastrointestinal tract can alter the properties of some polysaccharides (Edwards et al., 1990). Because of this and incomplete knowledge of shear rates in the gut lumen, it is difficult to predict the effect of non-starch polysaccharides in vivo from their properties in vitro.

The viscosity of most polysaccharide sols is lost in the colon when the colonic bacteria ferment the polysaccharide and produce short chain fatty acids (see Chapter 8). However, the bacterial enzymes necessary for the fermentation of the more closely packed substances, such as xanthan gum, are not present in all people, and there may be insufficient time available for the fermentation of others to take place. Thus the viscous nature of the luminal contents may influence colonic mixing and transit.

5.3.2 Water holding capacity

5.3.2.1 Determinants of water holding capacity

The water holding capacity of non-starch polysaccharides is a measure of the ability of a polysaccharide to immobilise water within its matrix. Such water will influence the metabolic activity of the polysaccharide along the gut.

The amount of trapped water present in non-starch polysaccharide will depend on the source of non-starch polysaccharides, the mode of preparation and the method of measurement. Wheat bran holds 2–6g water per gram of bran, whereas fruit and vegetables hold 18–30g water per gram of non-starch polysaccharide.

Water holding capacity may be measured by centrifugation or by dialysis methods (McConnell et al., 1974) or by glass columns (Anderson and Eastwood, 1987). All these methods yield different results for water holding capacity because each measures different phases of water.

Water can exist in three phases in relation to non-starch polysaccharides:

(i)   tightly bound water which can only be removed with disruptive methods such as freeze drying,
(ii) firmly held water which is removed by pressure but not by centrifugation,
(iii) loosely associated water which is readily removed by filtration.

5.3.2.2 Physiological effects of water holding capacity

Depending on how water is held in association with non-starch polysaccharides in the gut, the measured water holding capacity of a food source may bear little relationship to the water holding capacity of the polysaccharide in the gut.

Viscous polysaccharides have the greater water holding capacity, and may dilute and disperse intestinal contents causing distension and encouraging propulsive motor activity. In the case of highly viscous solutions this effect would be counterbalanced by the inhibitory effect of an increased luminal viscosity on propulsion.

In the colon, the correlation between the water holding capacity and the biological effect of the polysaccharides on faecal bulking is affected by the fermentation of the polysaccharide. Polyphenolic materials in polysaccharides make them resistant to fermentation by virtue of the cross linkages. Faecal bulking of minimally fermented non-starch polysaccharide sources such as wheat bran can be predicted, in general, by the water holding capacity (Eastwood, et al., 1983; Stephen and Cummings, 1979). For the fermentable non-starch polysaccharides it seems that the greater the in vitro water holding capacity, the smaller the effect on faecal weight (McBurney et al., 1985).

Non-fermented polysaccharides are the most effective stool bulkers because they retain a proportion of their structure and are thus still able to bind water. However, polysaccharides that are fermented may accelerate colonic transit time. The mechanism of this effect is not known, but may be related to the effects of the products of fermentation such as short chain fatty acids and gases. Ispaghula is one of the most effective laxative agents; this non-starch polysaccharide does not lose its viscous properties upon exposure to colonic bacteria, but is partially fermented to gases and short chain fatty acids (Tomlin and Read, 1988a).

5.4 PARTICLE SIZE

5.4.1 Evidence for an effect of particle size

- Ingestion of ground rice resulted in a greater postprandial glycaemia than ingestion of grains of rice (O'Dea et al., 1980), presumably because the increased surface area of the ground rice leads to a more rapid digestion.
- Chewing foods thoroughly caused a much greater increase in post-prandial glycaemia than when the same foods were swallowed whole (Read et al., 1986).
- Plasma insulin responses varied according to the degree of refinement of isocaloric wheat-based meals. Cracked grains and fine flour gave bigger responses than whole grains and coarse flour. (Heaton et al., 1988).
- Bran was a more effective stool bulker when it was administered as large rather than small particles (Brodribb and Groves, 1978; Heller et al., 1980; Smith et al., 1981). The coarser the bran the greater its water holding capacity and the greater its effect on stool weight.

5.4.2 Possible reasons for an effect of particle size

It is likely that the effect of coarse bran on stool weight is a simple function of the retention of water within a polysaccharide matrix. This would result in an increase in water holding capacity.

Another possibility is that the particles themselves may stimulate propulsive motor activity. Tomlin and Read (1988b) have shown that inert polyvinyl pellets cut to the same size as coarse bran increase stool weight and frequency and accelerate colonic transit to the same extent as coarse bran. Perhaps the edges of the plastic particles, and by implication, the coarse bran, induce secretion and propulsion by stimulating mucosal mechanoreceptors?

5.5 INCREASED SUSCEPTIBILITY TO BACTERIAL FERMENTATION

The physical properties of non-starch polysaccharides may change significantly in the colon. Those polysaccharides that are not immediately fermented and so removed from the lumen may be chemically modified by the bacteria in a way that changes their physical structure; very little is known about the impact of bacterial metabolism on these plant materials.

The more acidic colonic environment will reduce the ionisation of uronic and phenolic acid radicals present in some polysaccharides and lignin, increasing the binding of bile acids and reducing the binding of minerals.

The bacterial mass itself will be altered by ingestion; fermentable polysaccharides will increase the numbers and possibly the types of bacteria and it may be that some of the properties attributed to the polysaccharides, eg, cation exchange capacity, and stool bulking, may in fact be properties of the bacterial mass.

5.6 EFFECT OF COOKING

5.6.1 Effects of heating

Heating can have several important actions on plant constituents.

- Heating expands and splits starch granules, rendering the starch more accessible to digestive enzymes and increasing the absorption of carbohydrate (Collings et al., 1981).
- Heating disrupts plant cell walls, allowing access of digestive secretions to the enclosed substrate and the solubilisation of viscous polysaccharides (Selvendran, 1985).
- Heating can reduce intercellular adhesion, eg pectins in cooked vegetables are more soluble in intestinal fluids than those in uncooked vegetables (Sevendran, 1985).
- Heating can alter the properties of the polysaccharides; eg, it leads to starch gelatinisation which results in the swelling or eventual bursting of the granules.
- Heating can facilitate chemical reactions between the nutrient molecules. Maillard reactions which are non-enzymic browning reactions between sugars and nitrogenous components forming undigestible products can occur. Protein digestibility is reduced and the apparent polysaccharide content is increased.
- Heating can cause caramelisation, the scorching or browning in a polysaccharide due to a partial breakdown of carbohydrate (especially sucrose) yielding dehydration pyrolysis products.

5.6.2 Effects of food processing

Food processing can also result in the production of starch that is resistant to human enzymic digestion (see Chapter 4). Retrograded starch is an aggregated form which is not readily digested by pancreatic amylase. This form of starch is commonly associated with the cooking, cooling and reheating of starchy foods (Englyst and Cummings, 1987). Cooking and recooling increase the amount of retrograded starch in potato (Englyst and Cummings, 1987b) and high temperature can form retrograded starch in cornflakes (Englyst and Cummings, 1985) and wheat and flour products (Theander, 1987; Asp et al., 1987). The conditions selected for this processing such as the hydration of the plant material at high temperature and shear stress may have an important influence on the physical and chemical nature of the polysaccharides in the final product.

Cooking wheat bran to form All Bran yields a product that is a less effective stool bulker than whole bran (Wyman et al., 1976). In a long term study, six slices of commercial wholemeal bread only increased stool weight by 16% compared to stool weight in the same individuals eating white bread (Eastwood et al., 1984).

5.7 CHEMICAL BINDING OF BILE ACIDS AND MINERALS

5.7.1 Effect on bile acids

Some non-starch polysaccharides contain reactive groups – phenolic acids and uronic acids – which can adsorb bile acids and lipids. The binding is highest at low pH and is probably hydrophobic (Eastwood and Hamilton, 1970).

The polysaccharides which influence sterol metabolism, eg, pectin and gum arabic (McLean Ross et al., 1983) are substantially fermented and probably reduce serum cholesterol by increasing faecal bile acid excretion but via a mechanism different from adsorption.

5.7.2 Effect on minerals (see Chapter 7)

Non-starch polysaccharides, rich in uronic and phenolic acids and sulphated residues, also have cation exchanger properties and bind minerals such as zinc, calcium and iron (Southgate, 1987). Minerals may adsorb onto less purified plant material, but much of this binding is due to the presence of non-polysaccharide components associated with the cell wall. Phytic acid, a plant phosphorus storage compound found in cereals, legumes, nuts and a few fruits and root vegetables, is believed to be the major binding agent in plant material (Davies, 1982). Oxalates, lignins, tannins and silicates may also be involved (Vahouny, 1985; Southgate, 1987). Mineral binding occurs readily at neutral pH and is inhibited in acid conditions, by protein and by agents such as ascorbate and citrate (Kelsay, 1986; Hallberg, 1987).

5.8 MODULATION OF PHYSICAL PROPERTIES BY OTHER DIETARY COMPONENTS

Each of the physical properties discussed so far may modulate the biological effect along the gastrointestinal tract. However, non-starch polysaccharides are not eaten on their own. They are also accompanied in the diet by other substances which may modulate their effects on events along the gastrointestinal tract. Examples are: phytate, tannin, saponins; modified starch; resistant starch; ungelatinised starch; amylase inhibitors; oligosaccharides; vegetable and animal proteins; protein: carbohydrate maillard reactions; undigestible proteins; and amylose:lipid complexes.

CHAPTER 6
EFFECTS OF COMPLEX CARBOHYDRATES ON THE DIGESTION AND ABSORPTION OF MACRONUTRIENTS

The actions of non-starch polysaccharides on digestion and absorption depend on whether or not they form viscous solutions. Most experiments involve the addition of purified substances to meals or solutions of glucose and it is important to exercise some caution when extrapolating these results to the ingestion of foods which naturally contain complex polysaccharides.

6.1 VISCOUS POLY-SACCHARIDES

6.1.1 Overall effect and importance of viscosity

The addition of viscous polysaccharides to meals reduces postprandial hyperglycaemia and insulinaemia (Jenkins *et al.*, 1978a) (see Chapter 10). These results suggest that viscous polysaccharides reduce the rate of carbohydrate absorption. This phenomenon could be explained by several different mechanisms and probably all are implicated in the net reduction in absorption.

The putative effects of viscous polysaccharides on slowing gastric emptying, reducing pancreatic digestion and limiting access of nutrients to the absorptive epithelium can all be explained by the action of viscous substances in resisting the flow of solutions.

The gut can be regarded as a conveyor belt along which ingested food is first processed by digestive secretions and then absorbed. The contractile activity of the upper gut controls the rate of digestion and absorption by:

(i) regulating the progress of food and digestive secretions
(ii) mixing food with digestive enzymes and
(iii) exposing the nutrients to the absorptive surface.

The viscous solutions formed by certain polysaccharides would resist the effects of gastrointestinal contractions on mixing and propulsion.

6.1.2 Effects on gastric emptying

The addition of viscous polysaccharides to a meal slows the emptying of liquids from the stomach (Holt *et al.*, 1979). In contrast, the rate of emptying of solids is often accelerated and the size of the solid particles that pass through the pylorus may be increased (Meyer *et al.*, 1986). The lack of solid/liquid discrimination in the presence of viscous solutions may be caused by the failure of the solids to settle in the gastric sump so that they remain in the axial stream and are swept with the liquids through the pylorus (Meyer 1987).

The slowing of gastric emptying of liquids by viscous polysaccharides limits the delivery of contents to the absorptive site. This, however, may not necessarily be the dominant factor in reducing postprandial glycaemia since the rate of gastric emptying does not correlate with the reduction in plasma glucose levels after the administration of guar gum (Blackburn *et al.*, 1984a). Indeed, at low concentrations some viscous polysaccharides such as locust bean gum accelerate gastric emptying but these still depress postprandial glycaemia (Edwards *et al.*, 1987). Locust bean gum could accelerate gastric emptying by limiting the access of glucose to the duodenal receptors that regulate gastric contractility.

6.1.3 Effects on pancreatic digestion

There is little evidence that polysaccharides reduce the rate of digestion of food in the gut; although several studies have demonstrated an inhibition of digestion *in vitro* presumably due to impaired interaction with enzymes (Dunaiff and Schneeman, 1981). The effect on mixing *in vivo* may be compensated by other factors such as an adaptive increase in pancreatic enzyme secretion (Ikegamu *et al.*, 1982) or impaired enzyme degradation (Percival and Schneeman, 1979).

6.1.4 Effects on intestinal absorption

The rate and degree of absorption from the small intestine depends upon delivery from the stomach, the efficiency of digestion and epithelial transport and the degree of contact with the epithelium.

6.1.4.1 Reduced absorption
Mixing viscous polysaccharides with glucose solutions reduces absorption of glucose from intestinal loops of experimental animals and man, and strongly suggests a direct effect on the small intestine. (Johnson and Gee, 1981; Blackburn *et al.*, 1984a). However, it may be difficult to extrapolate the results of these experiments to the *in vivo* situation. Dilution of some complex polysaccharides with acid and alkaline digestive juices can result in a dramatic reduction in their viscous properties (Edwards *et al.*, 1987) which could attenuate their effects on absorption.

There is no evidence that viscous polysaccharides can influence epithelial transport mechanisms directly. Instead, it seems likely that their effects on absorption can be explained by their actions on epithelial contact.

6.1.4.2 Increased epithelial contact
Two mechanisms bring nutrients into contact with the epithelium:

(i) Intestinal contractions create turbulence and convective currents. These mix the luminal contents and bring material from the centre of the lumen close to the epithelium (Macagno *et al.*, 1982).
(ii) Nutrients then have to diffuse across the thin layer of relatively unstirred fluid layer adjacent to the epithelium (Blackburn *et al.*, 1984a).

Viscous polysaccharides have been shown to increase measurements of the apparent thickness of the intestinal unstirred layer (Johnson and Gee, 1981).

The unstirred layer, however, is not an anatomical reality but a functional concept which has been invented to explain the changes in absorption that occur under stirred or less stirred conditions. An increase in functional unstirred layer thickness could be caused by reduction in luminal convection causing an actual increase in the unstirred regions. Studies which claim to show an effect of viscous polysaccharides on diffusion have not eliminated the effect of convection.

The results of *in vitro* studies to investigate the action of viscous polysaccharides are more consistent with the hypothesis that the way they reduce epithelial access depends on molecular size:

• Small molecules and ions are denied epithelial access by resistance to the convective effects of intestinal contractions (Edwards *et al.*, 1988).

- Large molecules or complexes, such as micelles, are denied access through reductions in diffusion coefficients (Phillips, 1986).

6.1.4.3 Slowing transit

Viscous polysaccharides tend to delay mouth to caecum transit (Jenkins et al., 1978a, Blackburn et al., 1984b). This effect is partly related to the delay in gastric emptying but there is also a direct effect on small intestinal transit (Blackburn et al., 1984a). Slowing of small bowel transit by viscous polysaccharides may be due not only to the increased resistance of the luminal contents to propulsion. The delay in absorption of nutrients in the jejunum may result in a greater delivery of nutrients to ileal receptor sites, resulting in a reflex slowing of transit (Read et al., 1984).

In theory, the delay in the transit of a meal down the small intestine, caused by viscous polysaccharides, could reduce the rate of nutrient absorption by limiting the spread of luminal contents along the intestine, and hence the area of mucosa in contact with the nutrients (Blackburn et al., 1984b). A delay in small bowel transit would also be expected to increase the degree of absorption by prolonging contact time. However, the increased expulsion of fat from an ileostomy in the presence of viscous polysaccharides suggests that the predominant effect of these substances may be on luminal mixing (Isackson, 1983).

6.1.5 Changes in intestinal morphology

6.1.5.1 Increased cell turnover

Ingestion of viscous polysaccharides by experimental animals increases cell turnover by enhancing cell proliferation and cell destruction in both proximal and distal small intestine (Brown et al., 1979; Vahouney, 1986).

6.1.5.2 Jejunalisation of the distal intestine

Experiments in animals have shown that reduced absorption of nutrients in the jejunum results in an increased delivery of nutrients to the distal small intestine. Feeding viscous polysaccharides to animals has been reported to increase the number of cells per villus in the distal small intestine (Imaizumi and Sugaro, 1986) to increase small intestine length (Brown et al., 1979) to increase the weight of distal intestinal segments (Brown et al., 1979; Imaizumi and Sugaro, 1986; Vahouney, 1986) and to increase mucosal levels of sucrase in the distal small intestine (Johnson and Gee, 1986).

The morphological adaptation is probably due to a direct trophic effect of the luminal nutrients on the intestinal mucosa (Williamson, 1978). Putative trophic hormones, such as gastrin, enteroglucagon and peptide YY, may also be involved (Williamson et al., 1978).

6.2 NON-VISCOUS POLY-SACCHARIDES

6.2.1 Overall effect

Although not as effective as the viscous polysaccharides, there is some evidence that ingestion of supplements of non-viscous polysaccharides reduces absorption in the small intestine (Bijlani et al., 1986). Gallaher and Schneeman (1986) found that ingestion of cellulose increased the amount of triacylglycerol in the lumen and mucosa of the distal small intestine. Unlike viscous polysaccharides, this reduction in absorption is related more to sequestration of nutrients or binding of enzyme inhibitors than to effects on motor activity.

6.2.2 Sequestration of nutrients

The effects of non-viscous polysaccharides differ according to whether they are added to food or given as supplements.

Release of nutrients from intact plant material is slower than from structurally disrupted plant components (O'Dea *et al.*, 1981) and may result in a reduction in the rate of absorption in the small intestine.

6.2.3 Enzyme inhibitors

Some plant materials contain enzyme inhibitors (Mistunaga, 1974) such as anti-α-amylase in legumes (Griffiths, 1979) and cereals (Sharma *et al.*, 1978), and lipase inhibitors in bran (Lairon *et al.*, 1985). Adsorption of the enzymes by non-viscous polysaccharides may also inhibit digestion (Isaksson *et al.*, 1983). Wheat bran, oat bran, solka floc-cellulose and alfalfa decreased pancreatic enzyme activity *in vitro* (Dunaiff and Schneeman, 1981).

Studies of the effects of non-viscous polysaccharides on pancreatic output (Stock-Damage *et al.*, 1983; Zebrowsky and Low, 1987; Isaksson *et al.*, 1983) are conflicting. Some show increased output, some show no change (Calvert *et al.*, 1985).

6.2.4 Intestinal morphology

Morphological adaptation of the distal small intestine after non-viscous polysaccharide ingestion is not well supported by experimental evidence. Ingestion of Tryfiba (enriched wheat bran) and an elemental diet by fasted rats increased cellular proliferation in the distal small intestine (Goodlad *et al.*, 1987), and mucosal weight was increased by cellulose (Imaizumi and Sugaro, 1986). However, other workers found that non-viscous polysaccharides had little effect on intestinal morphology (Vahouney, 1986).

It is important to note that the studies described above may not reflect the effect of a mixed high 'fibre' diet. Here sequestration of nutrients in the plant matrix may be the most important determinant of absorptive site, and other plant components (proteins such as gluten, lectins or saponins) may affect mucosal morphology (Maxton *et al.*, 1987).

CHAPTER 7
EFFECTS OF COMPLEX CARBOHYDRATES ON THE DIGESTION AND ABSORPTION OF MICRONUTRIENTS

7.1 INTRODUCTION

Very little is known about the effects of starches or resistant starch on the digestion and absorption of micronutrients. This Chapter will focus, therefore, on non-starch polysaccharides.

Foods rich in non-starch polysaccharides, such as unrefined cereal grains, generally contain higher levels of inorganic elements than their refined counterparts. This is because minerals are concentrated in the germ and outer layers of grains. Thus, increasing the dietary intake of non-starch polysaccharides may result in an increased intake of minerals, for example iron and zinc. The bioavailability of many minerals may be reduced in the presence of foods rich in non-starch polysaccharides, due to binding to the carbohydrate structures and closely associated substances (such as phytate, tannins, and oxalate), resulting in lower mineral absorption. Some of the minerals trapped in the lumen of the small intestine may be released and absorbed in the colon if the 'fibre' is fermented (James, 1980).

The reduction in absorption of minerals and vitamins could, in theory, have adverse nutritional consequences, particularly in poor people in developing countries where diets may be marginal in micronutrients but high in 'fibre'; in children whose zinc intake may be deficient (James, 1980); in anorexic patients who may be consuming a diet containing large amounts of dietary 'fibre', (Sculati et al., 1987); in women who are iron deficient and in people who are consuming high 'fibre' slimming diets.

Evaluations of the mineral status of groups of long-term vegetarians whose diets generally contain more non-starch polysaccharides, do not show any adverse effects (Freeland-Graves, 1988). The fact that new vegetarians had lower iron stores, serum B_{12} and thiamin levels than their omnivore counterparts (Helman and Darnton-Hill, 1987) suggests however that even if vegetarians encounter lower bioavailability of minerals in their diet, given sufficient time, they are able to adapt to the situation by increasing their efficiency of absorption.

This is not necessarily true for children, where meeting physiological iron requirements is a very real problem that requires careful planning of diets (Dwyer, 1982). The shortfall in meeting mineral and vitamin requirements, in some instances, can reflect the effect that eating diets rich in bulky non-starch polysaccharides can have on limiting total energy intake.

7.2 TECHNIQUES USED TO INVESTIGATE EFFECTS ON MICRONUTRIENTS

7.2.1 Balance studies

The traditional method of studying interactions between non-starch polysaccharides and micronutrients is the metabolic balance, in which the intake and excretion of a nutrient are measured in order to calculate whole body retention. In practice, properly controlled experimental conditions are difficult to achieve because replacing a low with a high-'fibre' food (e.g. wholemeal bread for white bread) also changes the intake of micronutrients. Time is required for adaptation to the new level of intake before attempting metabolic balance work, but this is a luxury that is rarely affordable in today's research climate, especially in view of the fact that the length of the adaptive period has not yet been established for most dietary changes.

7.2.2 Isotopic methods

Alternative approaches to estimate mineral absorption have been made using radio or stable isotopes to label minerals in foods. Although this is an improvement on the balance method, in that specific foods can be studied in isolation, there is still the problem of differentiating between unabsorbed isotope and that which has been absorbed and re-excreted. For this, double label techniques are necessary, as developed, for example, for calcium (Fairweather-Tait et al., 1989).

7.2.3 Assessment of nutritional status

The final test for a specific food or type of diet is its effect on nutritional status. This will reflect the level of intake of a micronutrient, absorbability, and metabolic efficiency of utilisation. The latter two are affected by a number of physiological factors, and also the length of time of consumption. Unfortunately, sensitive measures of status have not yet been developed for many micronutrients.

7.2.4 Studies using isolated polysaccharides

In vitro studies have shown that plant cell wall materials can act as weak cation exchangers and therefore have the capacity to bind divalent ions. These include pectins (in which there is a negative association with the degree of acetylation or esterification), alginates, hemicelluloses, and lignin. However, results of animal and human studies have shown that mineral absorption is often higher than would be predicted from in vitro experiments. This disparity reflects the complex nature of the absorption processes within the intestine and the interactions that occur with other food components.

7.3 THE EFFECTS OF NON-STARCH POLY-SACCHARIDES ON MINERALS

7.3.1 Mineral-binding substances associated with foods rich in non-starch polysaccharides

7.3.1.1 Phytate

Phytate (myoinositol hexaphosphate) is found in many foods which are rich in non-starch polysaccharides. It is therefore difficult to dissociate the effects of the two on mineral bioavailability. The pioneering work of McCance and Widdowson (1942) ascribed the deleterious effects of unrefined foods on calcium and iron balance to the high phytate content of unrefined foods. Most recent research continues to support the concept that phytate rather than non-starch polysaccharides, impairs mineral bioavailability. During food processing and digestion in the gut, phytate is degraded to inositol phosphates with a lower degree of phosphorylation. It has been suggested that for iron, at least, absorption is reduced in the presence of hexa and penta but not the lower inositol phosphates (Sandberg et al., 1989). It is therefore important to determine the exact nature of the phytate compounds present in a food or diet, as illustrated by the finding that monoferric phytate, found in wheat bran, is relatively well absorbed (Morris et al., 1982).

The use of phytate:mineral molar ratios to evaluate adequacy has become more widespread, particularly in the case of zinc where ratios above 10 reliably predict zinc deficiency in man and animals (Oberleas, 1975). The inhibitory effect is more pronounced with high calcium intakes, due to the formation of insoluble calcium-zinc-phytate complexes. It has therefore been suggested that the (calcium x phytate/zinc) ratio would be a more accurate predictor of available zinc absorption (Sandstrom & Lonnerdal, 1989).

7.3.1.2 Tannins

Tannins (polyphenols) are present in vegetables and fruit, notably spinach, lentils, aubergines and bananas. These form insoluble iron tannates, thereby markedly reducing iron availability. The effect may be ameliorated, however, by consuming organic acids (ascorbic, citric, and malic) at the same time (Gillooly et al., 1983).

7.3.1.3 Oxalates

Oxalates are organic acids found in cauliflower, spinach, rhubarb and chocolate. They bind calcium, magnesium and zinc, and in the presence of complex carbohydrates probably form a carbohydrate-mineral-oxalate complex which is thought to be less easily broken down in the digestive tract than the oxalate-mineral complex alone.

7.3.2 Direct interactions of non-starch polysaccharides and minerals

Non-starch polysaccharides, particularly those that possess uronic and phenolic acid groups such as pectins and alginates, can bind calcium, iron, zinc and magnesium.

7.3.2.1 Calcium

Many inconsistencies exist among the results of human and animal studies on the effects of non-starch polysaccharides on calcium nutrition (Allen, 1982). These may be attributed to differences in the chemical composition of foods under study, and the experimental conditions, particularly the length of time allowed for adaptive responses to occur in the intestine. In general, there is good evidence that diets rich in non-starch polysaccharides increase faecal calcium excretion, partly due to phytate, but also to calcium binding to components of the diet that are resistant to digestion (British Nutrition Foundation, 1989).

7.3.2.2 Iron

Iron deficiency is probably the most common nutrient deficiency world-wide, even occurring in countries where the food supply is plentiful. There is little doubt that wheat bran is one of the most potent inhibitors of iron absorption. Levels as low as 12g per meal have been reported to significantly reduce iron absorption (Simpson et al., 1981a). On the other hand, diets high in fruits and vegetables do not appear to influence iron balance (Kelsay et al., 1979). Much of the evidence linking low absorption of iron with diets high in non-starch polysaccharides points towards phytate as the most powerful inhibitory component.

7.3.2.3 Zinc

Zinc deficiency was first described in populations in the Middle East consuming diets high in non-starch polysaccharides. It is now clear that the deficiency was caused by a very low bioavailability of zinc, primarily due to high intakes of unleavened bread, which contain substantial levels of phytate (see Section 7.3.1.1). Non-starch polysaccharides themselves, and purified fractions such as cellulose and pectin, appear to be relatively inert as regards any effect on zinc absorption.

7.4 THE EFFECTS OF NON-STARCH POLY-SACCHARIDES ON VITAMINS

7.4.1 Fat soluble vitamins

The absorption of both water soluble and fat soluble vitamins may be reduced by ingestion of non-starch polysaccharides, either because they are trapped within the plant matrix, or because they are bound by specific 'fibre' components, or in the case of fat soluble vitamins, because lipid absorption is reduced. Diets high in non-starch polysaccharides tend to contain higher levels of vitamins. The absorption of β-carotene from vegetables was higher when they were finely chopped (Van Zeben and Hendricks, 1948). Faecal fat and vitamin A excretion is increased in humans fed a mixed 'fibre' diet compared with a low-'fibre' diet supplemented with β-carotene to contain equivalent amounts of Vitamin A (Kelsay, 1982). Several investigations have shown that the rickets occurring in Asians, associated with the consumption of unleavened bread, is related to high phytate intakes. Not only does this bind calcium, but it has been suggested that Vitamin D becomes attached to 'fibre'-bile acid complexes and is thereby transported unabsorbed through the gut (Kasper, 1986).

7.4.2 Water soluble vitamins

Studies of the effect of non-starch polysaccharides on water-soluble vitamins have provided mixed results. Wheat bran and cellulose adversely influence vitamin B_{12} status, have a variable effect on folate, and enhance the absorption of riboflavin, nicotinic acid and ascorbic acid (Kasper, 1986). Experimental pellagra is more easily induced with diets containing whole corn than diets containing milled corn indicating that the niacin was trapped within the plant matrix (Goldsmith *et al.*, 1956).

7.5 *IN VITRO* AND *IN VIVO* CONSIDER-ATIONS

Although the results of many *in vitro* studies demonstrate quite marked mineral binding by non-starch polysaccharides, these effects do not appear to be confirmed in human studies. However, the *in vitro* procedures used are not necessarily appropriate models for the *in vivo* situation, and require further development and validation. Furthermore, although the ability of the body to adapt in response to changes in mineral bioavailability is a largely unexplored area, it could explain some of the differences seen between *in vitro* and *in vivo* studies.

CHAPTER 8
INTERACTIONS BETWEEN COMPLEX CARBOHYDRATES AND BACTERIA

8.1 INTRODUCTION

Non-starch polysaccharides and a small proportion of starches are poorly digested by host enzymes in the small intestine, but are extensively metabolised by the bacteria in the large intestine. The physiological effects of complex carbohydrates in the colon can be related, in part at least, to the interaction between the carbohydrates and the bacteria. This interaction can be in both directions and so this chapter will discuss three aspects of that interaction:

i) the metabolism of complex carbohydrates by the bacteria.
ii) the effect of complex carbohydrates on the composition, ecology and metabolic activity of the bacteria.
iii) the implications for the host of the bacterial metabolism of complex carbohydrates.

First, it is necessary to review some essential facts about the gut bacteria.

8.2 HUMAN GUT BACTERIA

In contrast to the rumen, where ciliates, protozoa, yeasts and fungi are all metabolically important, the healthy human colonic microbial flora is dominated by bacteria; other microbes have not been reported to have any roles in the metabolic activity of the flora and need not be considered further.

8.2.1 Classification on the basis of oxygen tolerance

The major types of bacteria in the intestine can be divided on the basis of their oxygen-tolerance and requirements for carbon dioxide into strictly aerobic, facultative, microaerophilic and strictly anaerobic genera. There is, however, a continuous spectrum of sensitivity to oxygen.

Strictly aerobic organisms are defined as those which will only grow in the presence of oxygen and die in its absence. The definition is not an absolute one, since there are special circumstances where many of these organisms can grow in the absence of oxygen. (eg *Pseudomonas* spp can grow anaerobically provided that nitrate is present).

Facultative organisms, like the strict aerobes, use oxidative pathways to generate energy in the presence of oxygen but, in its absence, can equally well use (anaerobic) fermentative pathways.

Micro-aerophilic organisms are facultative organisms which are unable to detoxify the oxygen radicals produced during oxidative metabolism (such as superoxide, peroxide etc). In consequence, they die in the presence of high oxygen levels unless protected by a source of scavengers of oxygen-radicals *per se*. In general, they grow best in the presence of high concentrations of carbon dioxide, reputed to be beneficial to 'membrane tone'.

Strictly anaerobic organisms are not only unable to use oxygen or to carry out oxidative metabolism, but are killed by its direct action on sensitive components such as their enzymes, transport systems etc. They vary in their sensitivity, from the 'very

Table 8.1 Principal genera of bacteria in the human digestive tract

Organisms	Description	Comments
Strictly aerobic		
Pseudomonas	Gram-negative, rods	
Bacillus	Gram-positive, spore-forming, rods	
Neisseria	Gram-negative, cocci	Mouth
Staphylococcus	Gram-positive, cocci, in clusters	Nose
Micro-aerophilic		
Lactobacillus	Gram-positive, rods, in chains	All gi tract
Streptococcus	Gram-positive, cocci, in chains	All gi tract
Enterococcus	Gram-positive, cocci, in chains, bile-resistant	Large bowel
Campylobacter	Gram-negative, short spirals	Pathogen
Facultative		
Escherichia	Gram-negative, ferment lactose	Large bowel
Klebsiella	Gram-negative, produce butanediol from glucose	Large bowel
Proteus	Gram-negative, rods, hydrolyse urea	Large bowel
Salmonella	Gram-negative, rods, non-lactose fermenter	Pathogen
Shigella	Gram-negative, rods, non-lactose fermenter	Pathogen
Strictly anaerobic		
Bacteroides	Gram-negative, ciger shaped, rods	All gi tract
Actinomyces	Gram-positive, rods	Mouth
Bifidobacterium	Gram-positive rods, bifurcating, produce acetic and lactic acids from glucose	Colon
Eubacterium	Gram-positive, rods	Colon
Propionibacterium	Gram-positive, rods, produce propionic acid	Colon
Fusobacterium	Gram-negative, rods, produce butyric acid	All gi tract
Veillonella	Gram-negative, cocci	All gi tract
Peptostreptococcus	Gram-positive, cocci, in chains	Colon
Clostridium	Gram-positive, spore-forming rods	Colon

oxygen-sensitive', which are consequently very difficult to grow, to the more robust anaerobes that are able to cause human disease.

8.2.2 Further classification

By the use of just two other criteria, the cell morphology and the Gram stain, most of the gut bacteria can be tentatively identified. This simple classification to genus level is given in Table 8.1; it uses the presence of spores, the fermentation of a few simple sugars, and some end-products of fermentation, to complete the tentative identification.

The end-products of fermentation are sufficiently characteristic of the anaerobic species of bacteria that they can be used in bacterial identification and taxonomy; they are summarised in Table 8.1.

Table 8.2 The normal human faecal bacteria

Organisms	Number per gram of faeces
Bacteroides spp.	10^{11}
Fusobacterium spp.	10^5–10^8
Bifidobacterium spp.	10^{10}–10^{11}
Propionibacterium spp.	10^9–10^{10}
Eubacterium spp.	10^9–10^{10}
Veillonella spp.	10^4–10^6
Peptostreptococcus spp.	10^5–10^9
Clostridium spp.	10^5–10^8
Lactobacillus spp.	10^6–10^8
Escherichia group	10^6–10^8
Streptococcus spp.	10^6–10^8
Enterococcus spp.	10^5–10^6

8.2.3 Factors affecting bacterial populations in the human large intestine

Table 8.2 gives an indication of the normal human faecal bacterial flora. Within the digestive tract, the bacteria live in mixed populations or communities, the composition of which depends on a wide range of factors including nutrient supply, physico-chemical conditions (pH, redox potential (Eh) oxygen tension etc) and host-microbe interactions (eg, surface attachment sites, host enzymes, bile concentrations, mucin secretion etc).

Furthermore, different substrates favour a different balance of fermenting organisms, with some favouring butyric acid producing strains and others favouring, for example, acetate producers.

8.2.4 Types of bacterial catabolic enzymes

Catabolic enzymes produced by bacteria may be extracellular or intracellular:

i) Extracellular enzymes have ready access to their substrates but the products of their action are also extracellular and so are potentially available to other (competing) organisms in the ecological niche. There is a loss of competitive advantage to the producer-strain if the environment allows free diffusion of metabolites.

ii) Intracellular (cell-bound) enzymes retain the products of their metabolism within the cell, thereby giving maximum competitive advantage to the producer strain.

For large molecular weight substrates, such as complex carbohydrates, the cell-bound enzymes are irrelevant and the extracellular enzymes are much more important. Recent studies using scanning electron microscopy show that the bacteria form microcolonies on the surface of particles of plant material in the colon. There is no loss of competitive advantage in having the products of metabolism produced outside of the cell, since there is no free diffusion and the metabolites are not available to competitors.

Having said this, most of the studies of the enzymes responsible for the degradation of complex carbohydrate in the colon have been on cell-bound enzymes. This is in part because they are very much easier to isolate and to purify. Betian et al. (1977) reported the isolation of a strain of Bacteroides spp able to degrade cellulose. Salyers et al. (1977) studied the degradation of a number of polysaccharides including the algal storage polysaccharide laminarin – a polymer of glucose molecules not dissimilar to some found in plant cell walls. Laminarinase was detected in strains of *B fragilis*, *B distasonis* and *B thetaiotaomicron* as a cell-bound enzyme. The enzyme was induced in the presence of laminarin.

In some of the few studies of extracellular enzymes, Hoskins (1968) showed that the carbohydrate blood group substances on intestinal mucin were degraded by extracellular enzymes produced by gut bacteria but did not isolate any of the organisms responsible. Reddy *et al.* (1983) showed that bacteria of the genus *Bacteroides* were able to ferment the hemicellulose of wheat starch.

8.3 THE METABOLISM OF COMPLEX CARBO-HYDRATES BY THE GUT BACTERIA

8.3.1 Historical background

Early studies showed that faeces contained volatile fatty acids (VFAs): mainly acetic with smaller amounts of propionic and butyric acid and trace amounts of formic acid (eg Brieger, 1878; Hecht, 1910; Fischer, 1913). Fischer (1913) recognised these as the principal volatile fatty acids produced *in vitro* by bacterial fermentation of carbohydrate. In support of this, Roux and Goiffon (1921) and Grove *et al.* (1929) showed that the faecal VFA concentration was higher on a high starch or high cereal diet and lowest on a high protein diet. They also noted that most of the VFAs produced by carbohydrate fermentation in the colon were absorbed during intestinal transit, and estimated that 1–4% of the total dietary carbohydrate reached the colon to be fermented by the gut bacterial flora.

Williams and Ormstedt (1936) studied the digestibility of various fractions of complex carbohydrate from 10 different food items including cabbage, canned peas, sugar beet pulp, carrots, wheat bran, corn germ meal, agar, cellulose flour and cotton seed bulbs. They showed that hemicellulose was extensively degraded during colonic transit, cellulose less so and lignin almost totally undegraded. A high lignin content in foods also inhibited the metabolism of hemicellulose and cellulose.

Similar studies of the 'disappearance' of cellulose and hemicellulose from the digestive tract were carried out by Hummel *et al.* (1943) in children. The average daily faecal excretion (as a percentage of daily intake) showed a very wide range for both cellulose and hemicellulose. There was no relationship between the digestibility of the complex carbohydrate and the age or sex of the child or the amount of complex carbohydrate consumed.

8.3.2 Recent studies

8.3.2.1 Metabolism according to type of complex carbohydrate

Interest in the colonic degradation of complex carbohydrate, was revived in the 1970s, largely as a result of the propagation of the ideas of Burkitt, Trowell and Painter. Key investigations were carried out by Stephen and Cummings (1980). As part of their studies of the mechanisms of stool-bulking by high carbohydrate foods they demonstrated that almost all of the 'indigestible' complex carbohydrate of dietary cabbage or a pectin supplement was degraded during transit through the colon but that the complex carbohydrate of wheat bran was recovered largely undegraded from faeces. Whereas the colonic digestion of cellulose was dependent on a range of factors and varied from 7% to 82 %, the breakdown of non-cellulosic polysaccharide was almost complete in the human colon, varying from 73% to 93% degraded. Some typical measurements of complex carbohydrate degradation are listed in Table 8.3.

8.3.2.2 Metabolism according to physiological state

People who have had a total colectomy exhibit little degradation of complex carbohydrates (Holloway *et al.*, 1980). Similarly, in germ-free rats complex carbohydrates are excreted virtually undegraded. This supports the hypothesis that complex carbohydrates are normally degraded by the colonic bacteria.

Table 8.3 Degradation of complex carbohydrate during colonic transit

Carbohydrate Source	Subjects	Number	Intake (g/day)	Percentage degraded
Wheat bran				
unspecified	Young men	3	14.3	35
coarse	Young men	8	9.0	50
fine	Young men	8	9.0	54
unspecified	Adults	14	21.4	42
	Ileostomists	6	–	< 10
Carrot	Young men	3	7.8	84
Peas	Young men	3	2.4	84
Cabbage	Young men	3	6.9	80
Pectin	Adults	4	39.6	93
	Ileostomists	6	5.1	31
	Adults	12	5.1	96
Ispaghula	Adults	4	37.4	87
Hemicellulose	Adults	7	12.2	96
	Ileostomists	4	12.2	74
Cellulose	Young men	8	2.7	6

(From Cummings, 1982)

8.3.3 Possible consequences of end products of fermentation

The major end-products of fermentation are the short chain fatty acids principally acetic, propionic and butyric acids, which acidify the proximal colon and which result in bulking of the stool. Water is removed from the colon by osmotic equilibration with the mucosal blood; one molecule of complex carbohydrate yields 10–200 molecules of monosaccharide, each of which yields 2 molecules of short-chain fatty acids, (SCFA). Although much of this is absorbed, the potential role in stool bulking is great simply by the osmotic action of the fermentation products.

There is a group of colonic bacteria – the so called end-chain metabolisers, that use the end products of fermentation in further energy-yielding reactions. Thus, the methanogenic bacteria use the CO_2 and hydrogen to produce the odourless gas methane; sulphate-reducing bacteria (SRBs) in contrast, utilise colonic hydrogen to produce the highly odorous hydrogen sulphide. These two sets of end-chain reactions compete for the colonic hydrogen, with people carrying SRBs tending not to produce large amounts of methane in the colon and vice versa. This little-understood competition has obvious social implications and hydrogen sulphide production is increased in SRB carriers by diets known to increase colonic fermentation and hydrogen production. The major consequences for the rest of colonic fermentation are discussed later in this Chapter in Section 8.5.

8.4 THE EFFECTS OF COMPLEX CARBOHYDRATES ON THE GUT BACTERIA

8.4.1 Effects on the composition of the bacteria

The supply of essential nutrients is recognised to be a major determinant of the composition of mixed bacterial populations *in vitro* (Marsh *et al.*, 1983; Carlson and Griffiths, 1974). For example, the bacteria grown from an inoculum of dental plaque were much more complex when the medium was deficient in glucose than when it was rich in glucose. Similarly, it has been demonstrated that the flora of the rumen is dependent on the diet (Hungate, 1985). In consequence, it has been assumed that this is also true for the human large intestine and that the major influences would come from the complex carbohydrates.

In practice it has not proved easy to document and to identify the nature of these effects, but evidence has been sought from three main sources:

(i)   the effects of feeding specific foods or supplements to normal people.
(ii) the effect of abnormal diets that are either residue-free or are known to be rich in complex carbohydrates, and
(iii) the effect of any dietary manipulation on the bacteria of ileostomy effluents.

8.4.1.1 Evidence from feeding specific foods or supplements

The mechanism of stool-bulking by a range of complex carbohydrates was studied by Stephen and Cummings (1980) who noted that, for carrot and cabbage, the contribution of undegraded dietary complex carbohydrate to the faecal mass was small and could not account for the increased stool bulk. By the use of sieves of varying pore size they were able to fractionate faeces and to show that most of the increase in stool mass was due to increased bacterial numbers. They postulated that the stool bulking effect of these particular plant materials was the result of bacteria thriving on the carbohydrate energy source, leading to the synthesis of new bacterial mass.

Studies of the action of supplements of various complex carbohydrate sources (Hill, 1982) have shown no change in concentration of bacteria per gram; the increased stool mass therefore implied an increase in daily output of bacteria, in agreement with the observations of Stephen and Cummings (1980).

8.4.1.2 Evidence from comparing groups with gross dietary differences

8.4.1.2.1 Residue-free diets

Residue-free (elemental) diets, in addition to containing no complex carbohydrates, differ from normal control diets in a wide range of respects (eg very low fat). However, since these differences are in components that would not normally reach the large intestine it has been assumed that any effects on the gut bacteria are due to the differences in the complex carbohydrate content. Table 8.4 summarises the results of a number of studies of various formulations of elemental diets. In all the studies there was a massive decrease in stool bulk and, therefore, in total bacterial excretion rate. However, studies of the relative proportions of organisms within the overall bacterial community revealed only changes in the proportions of the minor components of the bacteria such as enterococci, veillonellae and lactobacilli. The exception to this was the study by Winitz *et al.* (1970) who showed a marked decrease in the concentration of all organisms, particularly the numerically dominant non-sporing anaerobic genera.

8.4.1.2.2 Vegans

Crowther *et al.* (1973) studied the faecal bacteria of adult vegans and compared them with those from matched controls who were consuming a normal mixed diet. No differences were seen in the composition of the faecal bacteria except that *Sarcina ventriculae*, was isolated from the vegans and absent from the bacteria of the controls.

8.4.1.3 Evidence from ileostomy patients

In contrast to the investigations of the faecal bacteria, the studies of the effect of dietary change on the bacteria of ileostomy effluent have demonstrated major effects which are highly statistically significant. The rationale for transferring attention to the terminal ileum/proximal colon was that the carbohydrate concentration is very much higher in the proximal colon than in the rectosigmoid region (where the fermentable material is almost entirely exhausted).

Table 8.4 The effect of elemental diets on the composition of the faecal bacteria of healthy volunteers

Diet	Time on diet (days)	n	Faecal output per day	Effect on the faecal bacteria	
				organisms per gram faeces	specific organisms
CDD6-G (glucose base)	14	8	Marked decrease	Marked decrease	Decrease in all organisms
CDD7-S (sucrose-base)	14	8	Marked decrease	Decrease	Marked decrease in enterococci and lactobacilli
CDD6-O (oligosaccharide)	14	3	Marked decrease	None	Marked decrease in enterococci and lactobacilli
3200AS (oligosaccharide)	12	14	Marked decrease	None	Decrease in enterococci
Cambridge diet (oligosaccharides)	7	6	Marked decrease	None	Decrease in enterococci, lactobacilli and veillonella

n = number of people in study
(From Hudson *et al.*, 1981)

There have been few such studies. Fernandez *et al.* (1985) investigated the effects in ileostomists of supplements of protein and of fat and showed large effects of diet *per se*, particularly on specific bacteria. These results confirmed the ecological advantage gained by the possession of specific and intracellular degradative enzymes.

Berghouse *et al.* (1984) compared the bacteria of ileostomists on a diet rich in complex carbohydrate and low in simple sugars with those of ileostomists on the converse diet. The diet rich in complex carbohydrates promoted a large (20–30 fold) increase in the total number of organisms per gram of fluid; the increase was general with no specific species being preferentially favoured. This suggests that the degradation of complex carbohydrates to small oligomers must be carried out by extracellular enzymes that leave the products available for further fermentation by other bacteria. Most gut bacteria have the enzyme systems for the catabolism of small oligomers and this results in the general increase in bacterial counts.

8.4.2 Effects on the colonic ecology

8.4.2.1 Effect on pH

The major demonstrable effect of the metabolism of complex carbohydrates on the ecology of the colon is to cause a fall in the pH of the luminal contents.

A radiotelemetry device can measure the pH along the human gastrointestinal tract. The normal terminal ileum is slightly alkaline (pH 7.0–7.5), the pH then falls in the caecum and ascending colon to approximately 6.5 but returns to neutrality during transit through the remainder of the colorectum. The magnitude of the initial fall in pH is therefore related to the ease with which the substrate is fermented. A substrate that is slowly fermented might be expected to have an effect on the pH of a longer segment of the colon.

The consumption of lactulose, which is not absorbed from the small intestine but is rapidly fermented to SCFAs in the caecum, causes the caecal pH to fall to 4.0–4.5. The pH soon returns to neutrality during transit through the distal colon and rectum because the SCFAs are slowly absorbed from the colon (Bown *et al.*, 1974). On the other hand, consumption of ispaghula or other plant cell wall preparations causes a decrease in caecal pH that is smaller than that seen with lactulose but which is still detectable in the distal colon (Pye *et al.*, 1987). Fadden *et al.* (1985) investigated the effect of dietary change on the pH of the terminal ileum, the caecum, the mid-colon and on faeces in pigs fitted with multiple canulae. They observed effects on pH similar to those seen in humans; lactulose caused a large decrease in caecal pH and wheat bran caused a smaller decrease; neither substrate had any effect on the faecal pH.

Acidity is one of the major factors determining the *in vitro* composition of a mixed bacterial population. Bacteria differ in their ability to tolerate acidic conditions: the lactic acid bacteria (lactobacilli, streptococci, bifidobacteria) are tolerant of acid conditions and are able to multiply and thrive at pH values as low as 5.0; the ureolytic bacteria (eg, *Proteus* spp) are able to multiply at alkaline pH values. The lactic acid bacteria would, therefore, be expected to be favoured by the low pH values generated in the proximal colon in people eating diets rich in complex carbohydrates.

8.4.2.2 Effect on attachment surfaces

Bacteria tend to flourish most when growing on surfaces; they produce adhesion processes to make it easy to stick to a particular spot in which ecological conditions are favourable. Adhesion is a major virulence determinant in enteric disease. The major surfaces available to the bacteria of the colon are the gut wall, shed mucosal cells and undigested food particles.

Attachment of bacteria to particles of wheat bran has been demonstrated using scanning electron microscopy. It is clear that the attached organisms form microcolonies and these appear to be responsible for local digestion of the food particles. A diet containing large amounts of complex carbohydrate would, therefore, provide a large increase in the surface area of the colon available for bacterial colonisation.

8.4.3 Effects on bacterial metabolic activity

8.4.3.1 Effects on enzyme profiles

Enzyme assays are more precise than bacterial counts and so smaller changes should be detectable. The selection of enzymes for inclusion in the profile is important; those which are ubiquitous are unlikely to change greatly when the bacteria change whilst those that are rare will only change when the change in the composition of the bacteria happens to affect producer-species. There are limited human studies, particularly where the product of a particular enzyme activity has been measured in faeces or in urine. Goldin *et al.* (1980) studied the effects of diet on a range of human faecal bacterial enzymes. In short-term interventions (4 weeks) supplements of wheat bran had no effect on faecal β-glucuronidase, azoreductase and nitroreductase but resulted in decreased steroid 7-dehydroxylase activity. However, when American omnivores were compared with American vegans or Seventh Day Adventists, all four enzymes were at lower activity in the vegetarians and this was thought to be the result of long-term diet change. Cummings *et al.* (1979) showed that people eating a diet supplemented with wheat bran showed a decrease in the rate of metabolism of phenolic amino acids to the urinary volatile phenols.

8.4.3.2 Effects on the bile acid pool

Numerous studies (reviewed by Hill, 1982) have failed to show any effect of wheat bran on the metabolism of bile acids or of cholesterol by assaying the products and substrates in the faeces. An alternative method of studying bile acid metabolism in the proximal colon is to assay the composition of the bile acid pool, which contains that deoxycholic acid produced by bacterial action on cholic acid and then absorbed from the colon whilst the luminal contents are still sufficiently fluid to permit free diffusion of the bile acid to the colon wall. The results of such studies showed that wheat bran causes a decrease in the rate of production of deoxycholic acid by a mechanism still to be determined (Low-Beer, 1979). In the cannulated pigs studied by Fadden *et al.* (1985), there was a similar decrease in the rate of cholic acid dehydroxylation (measured by analysis of caecal contents obtained through the canula) and this was due to a decrease in enzyme activity.

8.5 EFFECTS ON THE HOST

The major effects on the host are the results of stool bulking and the various effects of the products of metabolism from the short chain fatty acids.

8.5.1 Positive effects

8.5.1.1 Changes in stool bulk and consistency

Stephen and Cummings (1980) have demonstrated that the metabolism of complex carbohydrates in the colon results in the increased rate of synthesis of bacterial mass and a consequent increase in stool bulk. Such an increase has been advocated both in the treatment and in the prevention of a number of 'diseases of Western civilisation' including diverticulitis, irritable bowel syndrome and constipation. The evidence that the consumption of complex carbohydrate either prevents or ameliorates the symptoms of these diseases has been discussed elsewhere (see Chapters 15 and 16). Here it is relevant to note that increased bacterial mass alone cannot be the mechanism of any such relationship; stool softness and consistency are likely to be at least as important as stool bulk.

8.5.1.2 Effects of short chain fatty acids

The products of fermentation of carbohydrate in the large bowel are likely to have a number of direct and indirect effects. The major SCFA metabolites are absorbed from the colon and contribute to the energy balance of the host; this is discussed in detail in Chapter 9. Butyrate from the colonic lumen has been shown to be the major energy source to the colonic mucosal cells *in vitro*, (Roediger, 1982). A high butyrate supply should therefore be of importance to colonocyte welfare. Roediger has suggested that a low intake of complex carbohydrate causes 'butyrate starvation' in the colonic mucosa and might be one of the factors in the causation or maintenance of inflammatory bowel disease (IBD). However, it has not been possible to repeat and verify this work and IBD is not a major complication in patients treated with low-residue diets.

Mixed bacterial communities exhibit 'colonisation resistance' ie they can protect their ecosystem from invading organisms such as bacteriophages. Fermentation products from complex carbohydrates can favour 'colonisation resistance' by increasing the numbers and variety of bacteria.

There are many examples of decreased 'colonisation resistance', (always being manifest following suppression of the gut bacteria, such as traveller's diarrhoea and antibiotic-associated diarrhoea). SCFA end products of fermentation are likely to be major factors in increasing 'colonisation resistance' and aiding recovery.

Fermentation of carbohydrate in the caecum results in acidification of the caecal contents and this has effects on bacterial metabolism (see Section 8.4). Inhibition of cholate conversion to deoxycholate has been cited as a possible cause of the low

Table 8.5 The major end products of fermentation of various species of human gut bacteria

Organism	Acid products	Gas production
Facultative anaerobes		
Streptococcus spp.	Lactic, acetic	None
Enterobacteria	Lactic, acetic, formic	CO_2, H_2
Micrococci	Lactic, acetic, formic	CO_2
Lactobacilli	Lactic	None
Strictly anaerobic		
Bacteroides	Acetic, propionic, butyric	CO_2, H_2
Fusiforms	Acetic, butyric	CO_2, H_2
Bifidobacteria	Acetic, lactic	None
Eubacteria	Little acid	H_2
Propionibacteria	Acetic, propionic	CO_2 (little)
Veillonella	Little acetic and propionic	H_2
Clostridia	Acetic, propionic, butyric, caprioc, lactic, valeric	CO_2, H_2

incidence of gallstones in vegetarians and of the beneficial effect of complex carbohydrate on the formation of gallstones (Low-Beer, 1979), (see Chapter 13). Similarly, a decrease in the rate of production of secondary bile acids in the caecum could result in a decreased rate of colorectal cancer (see Chapter 17).

8.5.1.3 Effects on nitrogen balance

Metabolism of complex carbohydrates in the colon has an important effect on nitrogen balance. Urea undergoes enterohepatic circulation and is hydrolysed in the colon to release ammonia. This is then absorbed from the colon and returned to the liver to re-enter the host biosynthetic system. The fermentation of complex carbohydrates is used to generate new bacterial mass. This, of necessity, involves the incorporation of large amounts of colonic ammonia (Stephen & Cummings, 1980). The utilisation of ammonia in the colon can be of importance in the amelioration of the protein sensitivity of patients with liver or renal failure (Rowland *et al.*, 1985).

8.5.2 Negative effects

There are also negative effects. The products of bacterial fermentation of carbohydrate vary greatly between species (Table 8.5), with some organisms (particularly the lactic acid bacteria such as streptococci, lactobacilli and bifidobacteria) producing little or no gas, and others (such as the Gram-negative coliforms and bacteroides) producing large volumes of hydrogen and carbon dioxide. In consequence, when people with bacteria rich in gas-producing species are placed on a diet rich in complex carbohydrates, the resultant pain and discomfort caused by the excessive amounts of flatus can be very distressing. If the bacteria are rich in putrefactive organisms, active on the sulphur amino acids, then the embarrassment of the release of pungent sulphur-containing gases is added to the physical discomfort.

The problem of flatus can possibly be decreased by gradually increasing the intake of complex carbohydrate from low levels. The bacteria of the proximal colon are thought to undergo an adaptive change from a gas-producing population to one which produces little gas. Since the latter organisms are also acid-tolerant they are likely to be favoured by the low pH generated in the colon by such a diet. There is no evidence for or against such a change, but no alternative explanation has ever been proposed.

CHAPTER 9
ENERGY VALUES OF COMPLEX CARBOHYDRATES

9.1 BACKGROUND

9.1.1 The value of energy conversion factors

The energy intakes of individuals or populations can be devised from two assessments: the amount of food eaten (a measurement fraught with difficulty) and the energy value of that food. Energy values of foods can be predicted from the proximate nutrient composition of the food using energy conversion factors for each nutrient. The principle of deriving energy conversion factors for nutrients is based on making assessments of the factors which account for the *difference* between the heat of combustion for that nutrient and the energy which is ultimately lost to the body, usually in urine and faeces (metabolisable energy). It has to be recognised that all energy conversion factors are approximations and represent estimates based on many assumptions. This fact must be remembered in all interpretations of energy value data.

The energy value of food components has been the subject of many reviews over the years. (eg Food and Agricultural Organisation, 1947; Widdowson, 1955; Merrill & Watt, 1973; Life Sciences Research Office, 1983)

9.1.2 Reasons for the slow progress in development of energy conversion factors for complex carbohydrates

Acceptance of energy conversion factors for complex carbohydrates has made slow progress in comparison with those for other nutrients. There are three main reasons for this:

(i) a diversity of experimental approaches has been used to determine energy values for poorly defined complex carbohydrate fractions
(ii) a complicated situation exists whereby unknown proportions of complex carbohydrates resist digestion and absorption in the small intestine and are fermented to various degrees in the large intestine.
(iii) a variety of methods has been used to determine the proportion which escapes digestion and absorption in the small intestine.

9.1.3 Explanation of Terminology

9.1.3.1 Unavailable complex carbohydrates

In other parts of this Report, the terminology used to describe the different fractions of complex carbohydrates has followed the outline described in Chapter 2 and the usual division has been into starch and non-starch polysaccharides. In discussing energy values, the division has to be into available complex carbohydrates which are virtually only starches, and unavailable complex carbohydrates (UCC) which are non-starch polysaccharides and resistant starches, since all energy values are derived from dietary energy balance experiments. None of these have ever measured digestible energy from carbohydrate expressed per unit of non-starch polysaccharide as measured by the Englyst procedure (Englyst *et al.*, 1982). Several of the diets which will be mentioned in the following section have used the methodology of Southgate

(1969), so the energy values of UCC can probably be considered to apply to Southgate's unavailable carbohydrate.

It is also pertinent to note that the term 'unavailable carbohydrate', as used by Southgate, refers to the unavailability of the carbohydrate moiety to the normal metabolic pathways and not to the unavailability of the energy in the molecule (Widdowson, 1960).

9.1.3.2 Energy components

- The Gross Energy (GE) refers to the energy of a food component or a mixed diet which would be measured by bomb calorimetry, ie the heat of combustion.
- Digestible Energy (DE) refers to the difference between the gross energy and the energy lost in the faeces.
- Metabolisable Energy (ME) refers to the difference between digestible energy (DE) and the energy lost in the urine (UE).
- The Net Energy for Maintenance of Man (NEm) refers to the *useful* energy that man can acquire from the food; it takes account of energy losses during the metabolism of the nutrients.

It is important to note that, in the case of complex carbohydrates, urinary losses (or gains) are usually assumed to be negligible. This is generally true (Southgate & Durnin, 1970; Kelsay *et al.* 1978) so that digestible energy will equate to metabolisable energy.

9.2 ENERGY VALUES OF STARCHES

Chapter 4 reviews the current state of knowledge on the fate of starches in the diet as they pass through the gastrointestinal tract.

Virtually no starch escapes into the faeces (Southgate and Durnin, 1970); it is all digested in the small intestine (probably about 90%) or fermented in the large intestine (probably about 15 g a day or 10% of total starch intake).

9.2.1 Energy value of available starch

Starch has a heat of combustion of 4.2 kcal/g. In the UK, starch is analysed chemically as free glucose, the form in which it is used in metabolism. Starch is therefore given an energy value of 3.75 kcal/g monosaccharide, ie Atwater and Bryant's (1900) heat of combustion for glucose. Modern tables give a value of 3.72 kcal/g glucose (Weast *et al.*, 1984). This value can now only be truly applied to the fraction of starch which is fully digested and absorbed in the small intestine.

9.2.2 Energy value of starches measured as unavailable carbohydrate

As explained in Chapter 4, starch may resist digestion for several reasons and has been categorised accordingly as resistance due to physical form (RS_1), resistance due to crystallinity (RS_2) and resistance conferred by retrograde amylose formation on heating and cooling (RS_3).

Any carbohydrate that can be fully oxidised by human tissues will deliver less energy to man if it is first fermented. Estimated losses of energy due to fermentation range from 20 to 50%, the precise value being dependent on many assumptions, as will be described in Section 9.3.

The energy values of α-amylase resistant starches have not been studied in man. Studies in the rat with two resistant starches produced by cooking, cooling, hydrolysis with α-amylase and dialysis, showed digestible energy values in dietary energy balance experiments of 2.9 kcal/g resistant starch from peas and 3.7 kcal/g resistant starch from maize (Livesey, 1990) compared with 4.2 kcal/g as gross energy. The lower value for resistant starch from peas probably reflects less digestion and greater fermentation than that from maize.

9.3 ENERGY VALUES OF UNAVAILABLE COMPLEX CARBOHYDRATES (UCC) IN FOODS

9.3.1 Hypothesis that digestible energy value is about zero based on faecal bulking effect of UCC

It was once thought that faeces were mostly the remnants of plant material. Increased ingestion of plant foods cause increased faecal bulk (Williams and Olmstead, 1936). Thus, it was often thought that no useful energy could be derived from 'roughage'. This hypothesis ignored the early literature suggesting that energy could be obtained by fermentation of plant cell wall material (eg McCance & Lawrence, 1929) and that plant cell wall material was partially used in the intestinal tract (Williams and Olmstead, 1936).

9.3.2 Alternative hypothesis that digestible energy value is about zero, based on ability of UCC to increase faecal losses of fat and protein as well as providing energy from fermentation

Even with the recognition that a certain proportion of non-starch polysaccharides could be fermented in the large intestine (see Chapter 8), the energy value of these substances was still considered to be zero, (Widdowson, 1960; Southgate & Durnin, 1970). It was reckoned that the energy gained from the end products of bacterial fermentation was more or less compensated for by the loss of energy brought about by increased faecal losses of fat and protein.

Some energy balance studies produced results which were consistent with this hypothesis, namely Southgate & Durnin, (1970) and Miles et al., (1988). Other studies cast doubt upon the hypothesis: two have suggested that losses of faecal fat and protein are small in relation to the energy gained from fermentation (Goranzon et al., 1983; Goranzon and Forsum, 1987) and two have suggested that the faecal energy losses far exceed the energy gained from fermentation (Judd, 1982; Wisker et al. 1988).

9.3.3 Factors which might affect digestible energy (DE) values for UCC

9.3.3.1 Level of intake
As levels of intake of UCC in mixed diets increase, energy balance data show that the determined DE values also increase (Livesey, 1990).

9.3.3.2 Association of UCC with other food components
Very low energy values can be obtained for whole or kibbled grains (Judd, 1982; Wisker et al. 1988). This is probably because the UCC in the plant cell wall fraction protects some starch against digestion, thus reducing its effective energy contribution.

9.3.3.3 Apparent digestibility or fermentability
This is probably the most important factor influencing energy values of UCC; a value for apparent digestibility is needed to account precisely for the energy losses in the faeces.

9.3.4 Derivation of equation relating factors

Analysis of published data on 19 mixed diets enabled Livesey (1990) to derive the following relationship:

$$\frac{1}{S} = 2.6D + 6.2B - 0.96 \ (r = 0.98, \ p < 0.001)$$

where $S = \dfrac{\text{additional loss of faecal energy}}{\text{additional gross energy intake from UCC}}$

D = apparent digestibility of UCC
B = intake of UCC as a proportion of total dietary gross energy intake

The value of D (the apparent digestibility) for UCC has shown to approximate to 0.7 in Livesey's analysis of mixed diets (ie 30% of the gross energy from UCC escapes into the faeces as undigested, unfermented material).

It should be noted that this equation applies D to the apparent digestibility of the UCC in the whole diet and not to the individual components of UCC in the diet. The dependence of energy losses in the faeces on the amount of UCC ingested (B) in this equation might be because small, but not larger, amounts of UCC displace bacteria from the large intestine; this bacterial population (which is presumed to have been developed on energy sources other than the measured UCC in the diet), would otherwise have consumed itself by 'autodigestive processes'.

9.3.5 Proposed hypothesis that the average digestible energy value of UCC is about 2 kcal/g in mixed diets

There are three pieces of evidence to suggest the average digestible energy value of unavailable complex carbohydrates in most mixed diets is about 2 kcal/g.

9.3.5.1 Evidence from a comparison of food energy assessment systems

The two systems often used to assess food energy assessment show bias if increasing amounts of UCC are consumed. The Atwater general factor system (Atwater, 1910) and the British factor system (Southgate and Durnin, 1970) each make the same assumptions about the caloric conversion factors for dietary protein and dietary fat. The important difference between them is for carbohydrate. The UCC is included with the carbohydrate in the Atwater system (4 kcal/g) and excluded from the British system (0 kcal/g). With increasing amounts of UCC in the diet, the Atwater system overestimates the metabolisable energy of the whole diet and the British system underestimates it (see Figure 9.1). It is clear that an appropriate general factor for UCC is one about midway between the values of 4 and 0 kcal/g applied in these two systems; ie, about 2 kcal/g (Livesey, 1990).

9.3.5.2 Evidence from making the assumption that 70% of energy released in the colon is available to the host

The second piece of evidence is drawn from what is known to occur in the colon. Unavailable complex carbohydrates provide substrate for the growth of colonic bacteria which are largely eliminated in the faeces. This represents a conversion of energy in the UCC to energy in bacteria eliminated in the faeces.

The efficiency of this conversion in humans is not known precisely and probably varies. There are several studies which show an increased loss of energy to faeces with increased consumption of UCC. Those which have involved only small increments in UCC intake are difficult to interpret. Two studies (Calloway and Kretsch, 1978; Goranzon et al., 1983) with very high intakes of UCC of 85.6 and 93 g/day, show an efficiency of conversion of UCC to faecal energy, other than unfermented UCC, of 0.30 and 0.39 respectively. A lower value, approximately 0.2, has been obtained when feeding the disaccharide alcohol lactilol which escapes digestion and absorption in the small intestine. Cummings (1983) had earlier suggested that

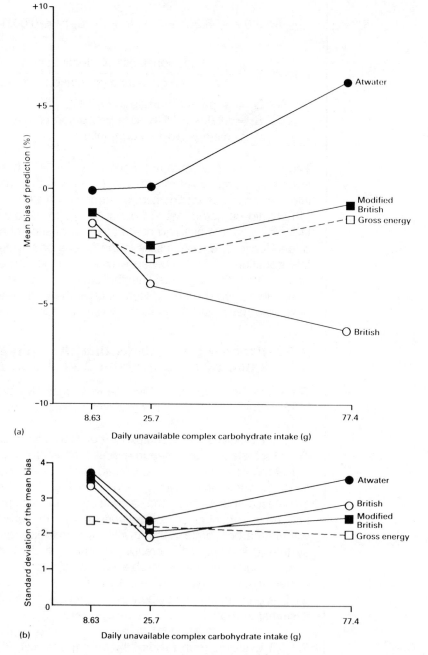

(a)

Daily unavailable complex carbohydrate intake (g)

(b)

Daily unavailable complex carbohydrate intake (g)

Figure 9.1 Bias in the prediction of the digestible energy in whole diets based on different caloric factors. Comparison with the prediction of gross energy contents.

The following equations have been used to derive this figure:

Atwater DE for diet	=	5.25P + 9F + 4C
British DE for diet	=	5.25P + 9F + 3.75Cm
Modified British DE	=	5.25P + 9F + 3.75Cm + 2UCC
Gross dietary energy	=	5.65P + 9.4F + 3.75Cm + 4.1UCC

where P = Protein (g), F = fat (g), C = carbohydrate by difference (g), Cm = available carbohydrate as monosaccharide (g) and UCC = unavailable complex carbohydrate (g)

The lower, middle and upper levels of UCC intake are means for 7,7 and 3 diets respectively. Data from Livesey (1990).

Table 9.1 The digestible energy value of unavailable complex carbohydrate from mixed diets and diets high in fruit and vegetables based on a 70% efficiency of conversion of fermented energy to digestible energy

UCC intake		Apparent digestibility		0.7 × D	Digestible energy (0.7 × D × 4.1)		
(g/day)	(sd)	(D)	(sem)		(kcal/g)	(sem)	
8.6	(3.0)	0.75	(0.16)	0.52	2.1	(0.4)	(n = 7)
25.7	(6.3)	0.66	(0.09)	0.47	1.9	(0.3)	(n = 7)
77.4	(21.0)	0.69	(0.11)	0.49	2.0	(0.3)	(n = 3)

sd = standard deviation; sem = standard error of the means; n = number of diets. (From Livesey, 1990)

20–30% of the energy in fermented carbohydrate was utilised by bacteria, which is in general agreement with the other values referred to here. In experiments with rats consuming large amounts (8% of gross dietary energy) of an α-amylase resistant pea starch, a value of 0.2 was obtained (Livesey, 1990) whereas a value of 0.4 has been obtained for guar gum (Davies et al., 1987). All these values range between 0.2 and 0.4, so that the efficiency of conversion of fermented UCC to faecal energy can be considered to be approximately 0.3. Thus, the efficiency of conversion of fermented energy to digestible energy becomes 0.7 or 70%.

Table 9.1 shows how digestible energy values of UCC can now be estimated on the basis of knowing the apparent digestibility and taking the efficiency of conversion of fermented energy as 70%. On this basis, the digestible energy value of UCC in mixed diets approximates to 2 kcal/g. Assuming no changes in urinary energy losses, this evidence again predicts that, on average, digestible energy for UCC is about 2 kcal/g.

9.3.5.3 Evidence obtained from multiple regression analysis of a large number of studies

The third piece of evidence comes from a further analysis of data in the published literature. Information on 35 diets of varied UCC intake ranging from 6 to 93 g/day from several published studies has been collected (for details of studies, see legend to Figure 9.2). A multiple regression equation was obtained using data from thirty of these diets, to relate faecal energy losses (FE) to the intake of UCC (g) and the ingested energy of the whole diet (IE). The equation was:

FE (kcal) = 0.05 × IE + 2.2 × UCC − 45

This corresponds to an equation for the prediction of digestible energy in the whole diet as follows:

DE (kcal) = 0.95 × IE (kcal) − 2.2 × UCC + 45

So, for a diet with a gross energy value of 2000 kcal and including 20 g UCC, the DE works out at 1900 − 44 + 45 ie 1901 kcals.

The relationship between the variate DE (or FE) and the independent variables IE and UCC is not strictly linear but for simplicity it has been considered to be so.

These equations also suggest that the digestible energy value of UCC is, on average, about 2 kcal (ie, 4.1 minus 2.2).

The predicted digestible energy for each of the thirty diets obtained using the

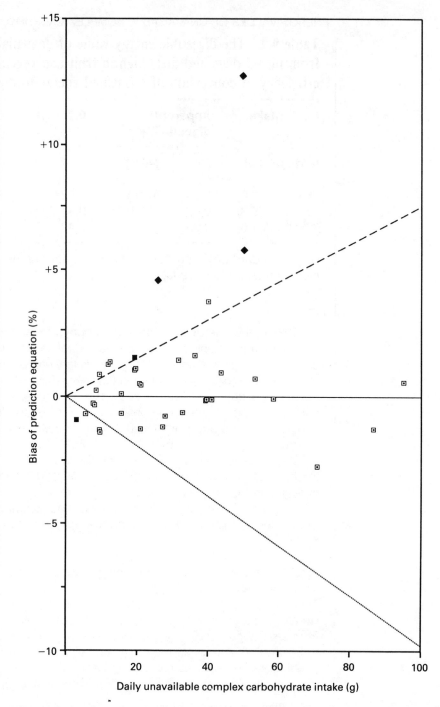

Figure 9.2 Prediction of the dietary digestible energy in 35 diets based on a prediction formula, DE (kcal) = 0.95 × IE − 2.2 × UCC + 45 where IE = ingested energy (kcal), and UCC = ingested unavailable complex carbohydrate (g). Data points marked ◆ or ■ have been excluded from the analysis because they were diets with a high content of whole grain cereal (◆) or with a high content of fruit or fruit juice (■). The bold line indicates the line of identity between the predicted and the experimentally determined value for DE. Other lines indicate the mean course of the data expected had the digestible energy value of the UCC been 4 kcal/g (---) and 0 kcal/g (·····). Data has been taken from the following papers: Southgate and Durnin, (1970); Judd (1982); Kelsay *et al.*, (1978); Farrel *et al.*, (1978); Calloway and Kretsch (1978); Goranzon *et al.*, (1983); Goranzon and Forsum (1987); Mills *et al.*, (1988); Stevens *et al.*, (1987); Slavin and Marlett (1980).

above equation is shown in Figure 9.2, with a bold line showing the line of identity between experimentally determined values and the predicted values for DE. Figure 9.2 also shows the lines expected for the prediction equation had the digestible energy value of the UCC been either 0 or 4 kcal/g and shows them to be inappropriate. The five diets eliminated for the purposes of deriving the regression equation are indicated in Figure 9.2 by the closed symbols. They are eliminated either because of their abnormally high content of cereal or because inconsistent analytical procedures had been used to estimate UCC.

9.3.5.4 Variance in digestible energy values of UCC

While average values for mixed diets seem to be about 2 kcal/g UCC, the individual components are likely to supply different amounts of energy. The literature offers too little data on different types of diets to enable an analysis of the energy contributed from the different types of UCC which they would contain. Variation in the apparent digestibility of the fractions of UCC is consistent with values ranging from 1 to 3 kcal/g (Livesey, 1990). The regression analysis for the thirty diets mentioned above indicated a mean digestible energy value of 2 kcal/g, and had an associated standard deviation of only 0.2 kcal/g. The energy values of UCC in a diet are more varied if isolates from single sources are considered.

9.4 DIGESTIBLE ENERGY VALUES OF INGREDIENTS, SUPPLEMENTS AND ADDITIVES

9.4.1 Poorly fermentable sources

From the few available studies in man, digestible energy values have been calculated (Livesey, 1990; Harley et al., 1989) for the poorly fermentable UCC in sources such as wheat bran, psyllium gum (Stevens et al., 1988), and cellulose (Solka-floc) (Slavin & Marlett 1980). The values are about 1, 1, and 0 kcal/g UCC respectively (Prosky et al., 1984). They are probably suitable for application when these supplements are added to a diet already containing moderate amounts of UCC (about 20 g), but not necessarily for diets with little or no UCC content.

Unpublished dietary energy balance studies in the rat (Davies, 1990), where gum karaya and hydroxypropyl-methyl-cellulose were administered at a level of 8% of gross dietary energy intake, are consistent with a zero digestible energy value.

9.4.2 Easily fermentable sources

Apart from a small study on 'Isogel' which produced conflicting results (Prynne & Southgate, 1979), there appears to be no substantial energy balance study in man in which more readily fermentable sources of UCC have been added to a basal diet with moderate UCC content. There is, however, no convincing evidence to suggest that, with supplements added to a diet of moderate UCC content, the DE value of the supplementary UCC should depart substantially from what might be expected. It will be approximately 4.1 x 0.7 x its apparent digestibility, ie the same equation as that suggested above for the UCC in mixed diets.

On this basis, the DE values of the soluble gum additives such as the readily fermentable guar gum and gum arabic (Nyman et al., 1986; McLean-Ross et al., 1983), can be estimated to be close to 2.9 kcal/g. These values are in accordance with direct measurements obtained in rats (Davies et al., 1987; Harley et al., 1989).

An alternative estimate for the DE values of guar gum based on measurements of faecal bulking in man (Nyman et al., 1986), and assuming a large proportion of the additional bulk to be bacteria, gives a value of 2.4 kcal/g.

9.5 LIMITATIONS OF THE EVIDENCE ON WHICH THE PROPOSED HYPOTHESIS IS BASED

9.5.1 Use of non-human data

In order to derive the equations above, in the main data from human studies has been used. In the absence of human data, information has been taken from similar studies in the rat. The coprophagic nature of rodents casts certain doubts over estimates of faecal energy. However, it is fortunate that apparent digestibilities of UCC for rats are at least similar to those in man (see Nyman *et al.*, 1986). No evidence has been taken, though, from experiments with pigs or with fowl because these species appear to yield apparent digestibilities for UCC that differ substantially from those obtained with similar substances in man (Longland & Low, 1988).

9.5.2 Limitations of methodology

i) In all calculations, urinary losses (or gains) have been ignored. Bacterial fermentation might result in reduced nitrogen loss in the urine (see Chapter 8) and in this case, the energy gains should really be included in the calculation of metabolisable energy. However such gains or losses of urinary energy appear to be negligible (Southgate & Durnin 1970; Kelsay *et al.*, 1978; Miles *et al.*, 1988; Wisker *et al.*, 1988).

ii) Rat studies, which have used the animal growth assay, are not suitable. This is because the growth assay was originally designed for, and validated, using substrates with high digestibility (Rice *et al.*, 1957). Moreover, the growth assay has often been badly applied and can give very conflicting results (see Harley *et al.*, 1989).

9.5.3 New methods

Some of the newer methods which are currently at the development stage include:

(i)   The use of isotopic tracers.
(ii) *In vitro* methods based on microbial enzymatic degradation of glucose polymers.
(iii) *In vitro* methods based on anaerobic fermentation of carbohydrates.
(iv) Various comparative methods looking at either absorption, blood chemistry, calorimetry or body retention of energy from UCC in comparison with simple carbohydrates.

None are sufficiently advanced for application to UCC on a systematic basis.

9.6 THE BALANCE OF ENERGY ACROSS THE COLON DURING FERMENTATION

9.6.1 Routes of energy loss

The digestible energy released in the colon is not fully available as 'useful' energy to man. Other routes of energy loss are known and include:

(i)   The heat of fermentation.
(ii) The combustible energy losses in the gaseous end products hydrogen and methane, and
(iii) The energy lost to the host due to the absorption of short chain fatty acids instead of the monosaccharides because these metabolites generate less ATP in the host tissue per calorie oxidised than does glucose (Livesey & Elia, 1985).

9.6.2 Calculation of the Net Energy of Maintenance for man (NEm) for UCC

To calculate the useful energy, or the Net Energy of Maintenance for man (NEm) some assumptions must be made which are all based on the fermentation of carbohydrates. While much is known about fermentation in the rumen there are

Intake of energy from UCC ----- $IE_{ucc} = 4.1 \times UCC(g)$

↳ Faecal energy

Digestible energy --------- $DE_{ucc} = 4.1 \times UCC(g) \times 0.70 \times D$

↳ Urinary energy (= 0)

Metabolisable energy ------ $ME_{ucc} = 4.1 \times UCC(g) \times 0.70 \times D$

↳ Gas energy and heat of fermentation

Absorbed energy --------- $AE_{ucc} = 4.1 \times UCC(g) \times 0.63 \times D$

↳ Excess heat relative to glucose
during ATP synthesis

Net energy ------------ $NE_{m,ucc} = 4.1 \times UCC(g) \times 0.54 \times D$
for maintenance and physical
expenditure of host
(useful energy)

Figure 9.3 Flow of energy from the unavailable complex carbohydrates (UCC) through humans. 4.1 is the approximate heat of combustion of the UCC (kcal); UCC is the weight of unavailable complex carbohydrate ingested (g); D is the apparent digestibility of the unavailable complex carbohydrates ((ingested UCC − faecal UCC)/ingested UCC). Faecal energy arises from 3 sources: unfermented UCC, bacteria and possible malabsorption of fat and protein.

various reasons why this knowledge is not entirely appropriate in man, eg man produces much smaller quantities of methane (about 150 ml/day) and hydrogen (about 600 ml/day) than those produced in the rumen for an equivalent amount of carbohydrate fermented (see Livesey and Elia, 1985).

Measurements in man suggest that the quantity of the combustible gases produced is about 3% of the carbohydrate fermented and the heat generated accounts for about 4% of the initial energy.

The balance between the carbohydrate fermented (100%) and the faecal energy (30%), heat (4%) and gas produced (3%) is the quantity of energy that is absorbed by the host mostly as volatile fatty acids. The value is about 63% of the energy content of the carbohydrate fermented. This is possibly a slight underestimate, as some of the additional energy in the faeces is expected to be derived from ammonia or urea used in the synthesis of bacterial protein and a small amount may be other endogenous substrates that are reduced, eg, unsaturated fatty acids, bile acids and glucuronides.

Each calorie of short chain fatty acid enables about 15% less energy to be trapped as ATP than does glucose in the mammalian tissues (see Livesey & Elia, 1985). Therefore, the 63% value becomes only 54% after accounting for this inefficiency.

Provided each type of unavailable complex carbohydrate is fermented in roughly the same manner, then Figure 9.3 indicates the flow of energy from the unavailable complex carbohydrates through man and the amounts of energy made available at each stage.

The useful energy (NEm) to the host can thus be calculated as:

4.1 x UCC (g) x 0.54 x D

ie NEm works out to be 77% of the estimated digestible energy or 1.5 kcal/g as D is about 0.7 in man eating a mixed diet.

9.7 PRACTICAL USE OF ENERGY VALUES FOR UCC

While the dietary energy balance procedure provides useful information about the effects of unavailable complex carbohydrates on the availability of dietary energy, the information obtained in this way needs to be considered carefully before applying it to an evaluation of food energy.

Thus, when Southgate and Durnin (1970) found that unavailable carbohydrate had little influence on the digestible energy value of their diets, it could not be assumed that zero digestible energy values for UCC should be appended to the British system of food energy assessment. The zero energy contribution arose from a regression equation which took account of the influence of the unavailable carbohydrates on the faecal loss of protein and fat. However, much, if not all, of this influence would already be accounted for in the calorific conversion factors for the protein and fat that were derived from diets already containing up to moderate amounts of unavailable carbohydrate. Care has to be taken, therefore, not to allow for these energy losses twice. If the current proposal to use the value of 2 kcal/g for the digestible or metabolisable energy value of UCC in mixed diets of conventional foods becomes common practice, then there should be no need for reappraisal of the currently accepted conversion factors of 4 and 9 kcal/g for protein and fat respectively. Moreover, when such foods are supplemented with either readily fermented or poorly fermented isolates of UCC, more specific energy values for the supplementary UCC would be appropriate.

If a net energy system for human foods were to be proposed and adopted, a value of 1.5 kcal/g UCC would apply and corresponds to net energy values for available carbohydrate of 3.75 kcal/g, and 9 kcal/g for fat, ie approximately equal to their metabolisable energy values. However, a reappraisal of the currently accepted value for protein would need to be made. The losses of energy during protein oxidation, due to urea synthesis and gluconeogenesis, are about 0.8 kcal/g (see Livesey, 1984). Thus an equivalent net energy value for protein would be approximately 3.2 kcal/g.

This last point emphasises how important it is to remember that all nutrients are taken as complex foods in mixed diets and that all factors are derived on the basis of many assumptions. Consequently, they must be regarded as 'tools of the trade' rather than accurate values.

CHAPTER 10
EFFECTS OF COMPLEX CARBOHYDRATES ON THE GLYCAEMIC RESPONSE

10.1 WHAT IS THE GLYCAEMIC RESPONSE?

10.1.1 General form of the glycaemic response curve

When a meal containing carbohydrate is consumed, there is a characteristic rise and fall in levels of blood glucose over a period of about 3 hours. This is known as the glycaemic response and is shown schematically in Figure 10.1a.

The bell-shaped form of the glycaemic response curve is dictated by two opposing factors:

(i) The initial rise in blood glucose from its fasting levels reflects entry of glucose from the gut and liver into peripheral blood circulation. Changes in blood glucose, insulin, gut hormones etc, are a manifestation *inside* the body of events occurring within the lumen of the gut, which is really *outside* the body in a strict topological sense.

(ii) The subsequent fall to fasting levels is due to the action of insulin, secreted by the pancreas in response to various meal-related stimuli including glucose, amino acids, gut hormones, and neurotransmitters (Morgan *et al.*, 1988). Insulin produces hypoglycaemia by allowing glucose to enter respiring cells and tissues from the blood. Its site of action is at specialised transporter sites that exist for glucose within the plasma membrane of many cell types, notably in muscle and fat, but not in the liver or the central nervous system. Characterising these sites has proved difficult but is now yielding to modern immunolabelling techniques (James *et al.*, 1989).

The relative, or absolute deficiency, of insulin that characterises diabetes produces the paradox of cells that are metabolically starved, in spite of their being bathed in extracellular fluid with elevated levels of glucose. The influence of insulin in the return phase of the glycaemic response becomes less cryptic in the phenomenon of 'rebound hypoglycaemia' shown schematically in Figure 10.1b. Rapid assimilation of some carbohydrates stimulates secretion of a temporary excess of insulin relative to need, with the result that blood glucose levels 'undershoot' before settling at their normal fasting levels.

10.1.2 The Glycaemic Index (GI)

The measurement of the post-prandial blood glucose response has been placed on a firm quantitative footing, using the concept of 'glycaemic index' (Jenkins *et al.*, 1981). This index compares the rise in blood glucose relative to fasting levels produced by a given amount of available carbohydrate (usually 50g) in a test food, expressed as a percentage of the response produced by the same weight of available carbohydrate in a standard drink or meal in the form of glucose solution or white bread. Figure 10.2 shows the part of the glycaemic response curve used by Jenkins *et al.*, for the determination of GI. Other groups appear to follow different conventions in this respect, although this may not always be apparent. Consequently,

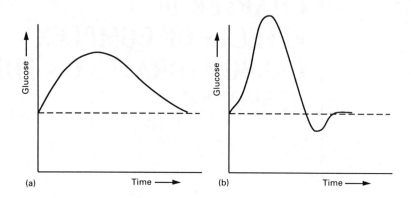

Figure 10.1 Post-prandial glycaemic response (a) without 'rebound hypoglycaemia'; (b) with 'rebound hypoglycaemia'.

Wolever and Jenkins (1986) have emphasised the importance of measuring GI as the *increment* in the area of blood glucose relative to fasting levels, as distinct from the total area under the glycaemic response curve: the latter is a less sensitive measure of differences between foods and may account for failure by some authors to detect differences in foods.

A more questionable feature of Jenkins' methodology is that only those changes *above* fasting blood glucose levels are considered for calculation of GI. A physiologically more complete measure of the glycaemic response would include all changes in blood glucose relative to fasting levels, including 'rebound hypoglycaemia', but summation of areas above and below fasting levels can lead to ambiguities. It may at the present time be preferable to measure GI 'above the line', as a measure of rate of release of carbohydrate from the gut, and to make a separate measurement of rebound hypoglycaemia index (area below the line). Data on blood

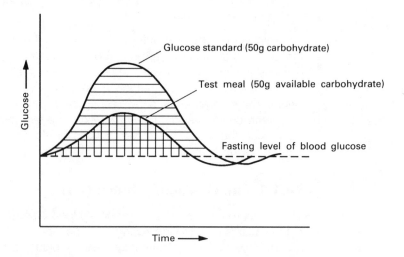

Figure 10.2 Determination of glycaemic index

$$GI = \frac{\text{Area shaded in vertical bars}}{\text{Area shaded in horizontal bars}} \times 100$$

Table 10.1 Glycaemic indices for common foods determined in healthy non-diabetic volunteers

Foods	Glycaemic index	(n)	Foods	Glycaemic index	(n)
Simple sugars			*Flour confectionery*		
Glucose (reference)	100	(35)	Sponge cake	46 ± 6	(5)
Fructose	20 ± 5	(5)	Pastry	59 ± 6	(5)
Maltose	105 ± 12	(6)			
Sucrose	59 ± 10	(5)	*Vegetables*		
			Broad beans		
Bread			(25g (portion)	79 ± 16	(6)
White	69 ± 5	(10)	Frozen peas	51 ± 6	(6)
Wholemeal	72 ± 6	(10)	Beetroot (25g portion)	64 ± 16	(5)
			Carrots (25g portion)	92 ± 20	(5)
Rice			Parsnips (25g portion)	97 ± 19	(5)
White	72 ± 9	(7)	Potato (instant)	80 ± 13	(8)
Brown	66 ± 5	(7)	Potato (new)	70 ± 8	(8)
			Potato (crisps)	51 ± 7	(6)
Spaghetti					
White	50 ± 8	(6)	*Legumes*		
Wholemeal	42 ± 4	(6)	Baked beans (tinned)	40 ± 3	(7)
			Butter beans	36 ± 4	(6)
Breakfast cereals			Haricot beans	31 ± 6	(6)
All Bran	51 ± 5	(5)	Kidney beans	29 ± 8	(6)
Cornflakes	80 ± 6	(6)	Soya beans	15 ± 5	(7)
Muesli	66 ± 9	(6)	Peas (marrowfat)	47 ± 3	(15)
Porridge oats	49 ± 8	(6)	Lentils	29 ± 3	(7)
Shredded wheat	67 ± 10	(6)			
Weetabix	75 ± 10	(6)	*Fruit*		
			Apples	39 ± 3	(6)
Biscuits			Banana	62 ± 9	(6)
Digestive	59 ± 7	(6)	Oranges	40 ± 3	(6)
Oatmeal	54 ± 4	(6)	Raisins	64 ± 11	(6)
Rich Tea	55 ± 4	(6)			
Ryvita	69 ± 10	(7)	*Dairy products*		
Water	63 ± 9	(6)	Milk (skimmed)	32 ± 5	(6)
			Milk (whole)	34 ± 6	(6)
			Ice cream	36 ± 8	(5)
			Yoghurt	36 ± 4	(8)

Tests were performed with 50g carbohydrate except where indicated.
(From Jenkins *et al.*, 1981). Values given are ± sem.

glucose levels are always incomplete: wherever possible, insulin responses should be measured and reported. The use of a glucose drink was originally suggested as the reference standard (Jenkins *et al.*, 1981). Later Jenkins *et al.* (1984) adopted white bread as standard, on the grounds that it is a 'real' food. French nutritionists, however, say that bread is not the same the whole world over, making it unsuitable as an international standard for glycaemic index (Bornet *et al.*, 1987).

10.2 GLYCAEMIC INDICES OF DIFFERENT CARBOHYDRATE CONTAINING FOODS

Tabulations of individual foods according to their GI represents the time-honoured reductionist approach to multi-component systems. The glycaemic indices for a range of food products are shown in Table 10.1 (taken from Jenkins *et al.*, 1981). Whilst these data cover an admirably comprehensive range of foods, it is worth noting that individual test sessions used groups of 5 to 10 subjects from the total pool of 38 subjects, and that no indication was given of the inter or intra-subject variation, or the mean response of each group to the glucose reference. GI values determined in diabetic subjects were similar to those in healthy subjects. Some important conclusions may be drawn from the data in Table 10.1:

- The GI values varied from as little as 15 for soya beans and certain legumes to values of about 80 for potatoes and some other root vegetables
- There is a wide variation within product categories, such as breakfast cereals, root vegetables etc.
- No clear line of demarcation exists between simple sugars and complex carbohydrates. Thus, the value for sucrose is less than that for bread and boiled potatoes.
- The values for white and wholemeal breads are almost identical. Moreover, no correlation was found between GI and 'fibre' (non-starch polysaccharides) across the broad range of foods. The presence of the largely insoluble cell wall polymers of wheat bran appears not to affect immediate post-prandial glycaemic response (although see later reference to long-term effects).
- Values for two oat products (porridge oats and oatmeal biscuits) were low in their respective categories, confirming other data that oat fibre is effective in reducing postprandial glycaemia, in addition to its possible ability to reduce plasma cholesterol (see Chapter 14).

10.3 FACTORS INFLUENCING GLYCAEMIC RESPONSE

GI values are known to be influenced by a whole host of factors, only some of which relate to food. Non-food factors include rate of gastric emptying, insulin secretion and insulin sensitivity, and probably account for the between subject variation seen in Table 10.1. Table 10.2 lists some of the food-related factors which are known to influence the glycaemic response.

10.3.1 Particle size

Cooked rice grains produced a smaller glycaemic response than cooked flour (O'Dea *et al.*, 1981), suggesting an important role for food texture in influencing glycaemic response. Cracking or milling of cereal grains to produce progressively greater disruption and finer particle sizes resulted in increased glycaemic responses (Jenkins *et al.*, 1986; Heaton *et al.*, 1988). Soda bread scones baked from coarsely-milled wholemeal flour evoked smaller insulin and glucose responses than similar scones baked from a more finely-milled flour from the same grist (O'Donnell *et al.*, 1989). Thus baking need not negate differences produced by milling.

Particle size may also be a factor in the low GI of pasta products relative to bread. The physical characteristics of the two, post-mastication, are very different.

Foods of coarse consistency produced smaller glycaemic responses when swallowed without chewing (Read *et al.*, 1986), reinforcing the importance of particle size. Glucose solution, sipped slowly, produced a smaller glycaemic response than when quickly swallowed (Jenkins *et al.*, 1978a).

10.3.2 Disruption of cell wall integrity

Apples, fed as juice, produced a very different glycaemic response compared with apples that were consumed whole (Haber *et al.*, 1977). Whilst both produced almost

Table 10.2 Factors affecting glycaemic response

1. Particle size, texture
2. Disruption of cell wall integrity
3. Starch availability (gelatinisation, retrogradation)
4. Amylose/amylopectin ratios
5. Presence of fat, especially high levels of added fat and protein
6. Presence of non-starch polysaccharides (especially viscous forms)
7. Presence of antinutrients (alpha-amylase inhibitors, phytates, lectins, tannins, etc.)

identical peak values in blood glucose, a marked rebound hypoglycaemia was seen about an hour after consuming juice that did not occur after whole apples. The reason for the later hypoglycaemia was apparent from the insulin response curves. Peak blood insulin levels after juice were approximately twice those after whole apples, reflecting enhanced pancreatic secretion of insulin in response to rapid release of glucose from the gut. Apple pureé produced insulin responses and rebound hypoglycaemia that were intermediate between those of juice and whole apples.

The flesh of an apple may be considered as an approximately 10–15% solution of simple sugars along with salts, etc, which are microencapsulated within a mere 2% by weight or thereabouts of cell wall material. Of the latter, only some, notably cellulose, is 'fibrous' in the physical sense; other components may be more dispersed and viscous (eg, pectins). Carbohydrate in free solution (ie, juice) is clearly absorbed more rapidly than carbohydrate trapped within fibrous cell walls (whole apples) or within a gel or viscous pureé.

10.3.3 Starch availability

Some studies in rats (Holm *et al.*, 1988) have shown a reasonable correlation between GI, *in vitro* digestibility and the degree of starch gelatinisation in products. Starch gelatinisation is influenced by processing factors, particularly moisture content in the case of baked goods. Retrogradation is the re-ordering of starch polymers ('re-crystallisation') that occurs in gelatinised starch on cooling and storage (Collison, 1968). The rapid retrogradation of the linear amylose component that occurs in bread on cooling produces starch with an absolute resistance to digestion by *alpha*-amylase, both *in vitro* and in the small intestine (Englyst *et al.*, 1982; Berry, 1986b). Since resistant starch (RS) is quantitatively a minor fraction of the total starch or carbohydrates in most products, this particular product of retrogradation is unlikely *per se* to affect the GI of a product. However, it is still not certain whether retrogradation influences the rate of digestion of the major (non-RS) component of food starch. Other data from studies with boiled potatoes, stored overnight at low temperature, suggest that at least in this system, retrogradation may alter rates as well as extent of starch digestion (Englyst and Cummings, 1987b). Further research is needed to determine the effects of processing on rates as well as extent of starch digestion *in vitro* and *in vivo*.

10.3.4 Amylose/amylopectin ratio

Amylose/amylopectin ratios have been suggested as a factor in glycaemic response, based on studies with starches from hybrid maizes with very different ratios (approx. 70:30 or 30:70) by Behall *et al.* (1988). However, it is not entirely certain whether these differences arise from linear versus branched structure *per se*, or from differences in retrogradation or enzyme-resistant starch. Most of the common dietary starches contain less than 30% amylose (Morrison and Laignelet, 1983). Legumes are a notable exception, with higher levels of amylose (typically 35–40%), which could partly explain their low GI, but other factors, notably cell wall structure and antinutrients are likely to make a greater contribution (see below).

10.3.5 Presence of fat and protein

Fat and protein, especially fat, appear to be important factors influencing the glycaemic response, as shown in correlation data for 62 foods (Jenkins et al., 1981), and in controlled studies (eg, Collier et al., 1986). Fat has a well known ability to delay gastric emptying whilst protein stimulates insulin secretion. The sizeable differences in GI between bread and biscuits (Ross et al., 1987) are most readily interpreted as differences in fat content rather than reflecting the higher levels of gelatinised starch in bread compared with biscuits. The ability of fat to depress GI may depend on the intimacy with which it is associated with carbohydrate, ie, fat applied as a spread may behave differently from fat that is baked into a product.

10.3.6 Presence of non-starch polysaccharides

Anderson (1986) has produced a valuable summary of data from previous studies, excluding those that did not meet his exacting set of quality control criteria. Diets with high levels of complex carbohydrates from normal foods were associated with lower levels of blood glucose, whilst smaller effects were seen in studies using guar gum.

10.3.6.1 Wheat bran
The correlation studies of Jenkins et al. (1981) showed no significant effect of 'fibre' on GI. However, most of the foods tested contained insoluble complex carbohydrates derived from wheat, which have little effect on postprandial glycaemic response.

10.3.6.2 Legumes
The low GI of legumes has attracted considerable interest. A useful study in which legumes were cooked before or after milling has suggested an explanation, viz. that the cell wall structure in the unmilled material impedes the ability of starch granules to swell and gelatinise on cooking (Würsch et al., 1986). Other factors may also contribute; high amylose content, and antinutrients, with which legumes are well-endowed (alpha-amylase inhibitors, lectins, phytates etc), might inhibit starch digestion or nutrient absorption in the gut.

10.3.6.3 Guar gum
Incorporation of guar gum into food produces a flattening of post-prandial glycaemic response (Jenkins et al., 1978b). Inasmuch as guar gum (a storage polysaccharide of the cluster bean) is not a constituent of the normal diet, except in the small amounts used in food processing as a thickener or stabiliser, it has to be regarded as a model system, albeit one that has found pharmacological application in dietary management of diabetes. Nevertheless the guar effect has important implications for 'real' foods especially for those such as oats, etc, that contain sizeable amounts of glucans, pectins and other viscous non-starch polysaccharides.

The mechanism by which guar gum and other viscous polysaccharides reduce postprandial glycaemic response is not entirely resolved. Initially it appeared that the effects could be accounted for mainly in terms of delayed gastric emptying, but subsequent studies have indicated a role for effects on processes of digestion and/or transport in the small intestine (see Leeds, 1982).

10.3.7 The 'multiple meal' effect

Another physiological factor that complicates or confounds interpretation of GI data is the 'second' or 'multiple' meal effect, ie, the phenomenon whereby a particular meal, eg, breakfast, may modify the response to subsequent meals. Thus a high complex carbohydrate breakfast (based on lentils) resulted in lower postprandial glucose and insulin than an equivalent breakfast based on wholemeal bread. In addition, it produced a flatter response subsequent to a standard bread lunch fed the same day (Jenkins *et al.*, 1982). However, Shaheen and Fleming (1987) using a red kidney bean-based breakfast saw no significant differences between legume and bread, either in immediate postprandial response, or in subsequent response to standard lunches. A possible reason for the conflicting findings was either the type of legumes or their processing (boiling in the case of lentils, autoclaving in the case of kidney beans) which produced differences in starch bioavailability. Separate *in vitro* tests of starch digestibility are desirable in work of this kind. Particular conditions may be needed reliably to see the 'second meal' effect.

10.4 DO GLYCAEMIC INDEX DATA HAVE CLINICAL SIGNIFICANCE?

10.4.1 Criticisms of GI methodology

The question of whether GI values have practical use in the clinical context is one that has been the subject of recent debate and controversy. Criticisms of the GI concept have been voiced by many and are summarised by Coulston *et al.* (1984) as follows:

- GI data are being misinterpreted and recommendations are being made which could result in avoidance of specific foods on physiological grounds, irrespective of their nutritional merit.
- some statements regarding the aetiology of diabetes mellitus are misleading and irresponsible, especially those suggesting that adult-onset diabetes can be caused by overconsumption of high GI carbohydrates.
- the physiological significance of the glycaemic response is questionable since it ignores the insulin response which could be of greater clinical significance in the normal population and might be a greater risk factor for the development of hypertriglyceridaemia and coronary heart disease (CHD). Studies have shown a poor correlation between glucose and insulin responses in both normal and Type 2 diabetics.
- foods will continue to be given different GI values by different research groups unless the test meals are standardised for fat and protein content as well as carbohydrate.

10.4.2 Improvements in technique

Some of these criticisms have already led to improved standard methodology for GI measurement: Collier *et al.* (1986) have now measured GI values under standard conditions of fat and protein, and find that these GI values can accurately predict responses to mixed meals. Chew *et al.* (1988) have tested meals representative of those consumed in different parts of the world (China, India, Greece, Italy, 'The West', Lebanon) and found that their very different glycaemic responses in healthy volunteers were in agreement with those calculated from a knowledge of the individual sources of carbohydrate. Bornet *et al.* (1987) not only found that the GI concept was predictive in the context of mixed meals, but also that insulin index correlated with glycaemic index in meals in which protein content was controlled. They concluded: 'there is no *good* food in terms of GI which becomes bad in terms of insulinaemic index (as far as high insulinaemic index can be regarded as pejorative and vice versa)'.

Nevertheless, the main objection still stands, namely that the GI concept is but one aspect of postprandial physiology which should not be given excessive weight in assessing the long-term dietary needs of diabetics or healthy subjects.

10.5 LONGER TERM EFFECTS OF CONSUMING LOW GI DIETS

Given the intense interest that exists in the therapeutic potential of guar gum and other viscous polysaccharides in reducing hyperglycaemia in diabetics, it was inevitable than clinicians would want to know whether the same effect could be achieved more 'naturally' by encouraging patients to choose low GI foods.

Jenkins *et al.* (1987b) reported effects of metabolically-controlled high and low GI diets fed for two week periods to healthy male volunteers. Among the effects observed were significant reductions (37%) in 12 hr blood glucose profile, and in serum total cholesterol (15%) on the low GI diet, in addition to evidence of reduced insulin secretion (32%), shown by a reduction in urinary C-peptide levels.

A variety of other studies were cited by Anderson (1980) in which complex carbohydrates from a variety of sources produced significant lowering of fasting insulin and/or glucose levels. In some of these studies, levels of plasma lipids were also reduced. However, it is not certain at the present time whether effects were due to reduced GI (which was not always measured) or to longer-term effects of complex carbohydrates that did not affect postprandial glycaemic response. Thus wheat bran, has in most studies, had no significant effect upon glycaemic response (eg, Jenkins *et al.*, 1983) but has been found in longer term studies to improve glucose tolerance (Brodribb and Humphreys, 1976; Beck and Villaume, 1987).

Other diets rich in complex carbohydrate have been shown to result in lower fasting glucose levels, lower postprandial hyperglycaemia and lower insulin concentrations in diabetic subjects (Anderson and Ward, 1979). The mechanism of action is not known, but could involve hormonal effects or adaptive changes in gut mucosa.

A long-term study of high versus low glycaemic index diets has been reported by Brand *et al.* (1990). Sixteen well-controlled Type 2 diabetic subjects, were fed for successive 12 week periods either a bread/potato-based diet of relatively high GI (=91) or a pasta/beans diet of relatively low GI (=77). The diets were otherwise equivalent in terms of energy, carbohydrate, fat, protein and fibre content. The low GI diet caused a significant reduction in glycosylated haemoglobin, indicating differences in average levels of blood glucose. However, there were no statistical differences in fasting blood glucose, total cholesterol or fasting triacylglycerols. There was a small improvement (10%) in glucose tolerance at the end of the low GI period as assessed by responses to standard meals over 8hr. The authors suggested that a moderate reduction in the GI of the diet had a favourable effect on carbohydrate metabolism in well-controlled Type 2 individuals. It is doubtful whether effects of this size will prove a sufficient incentive to diabetic subjects or their advisors to instigate a switch from high to low GI carbohydrates.

In conclusion, then, there is some evidence that choosing low GI foods can help to reduce blood glucose levels. Whether the long term benefits of adopting this type of regime will outweigh any long term disadvantages remains to be seen.

CHAPTER 11
CLINICAL IMPLICATIONS OF COMPLEX CARBOHYDRATES FOR DIABETES

11.1 INTRODUCTION

Diabetes mellitus is characterised by a raised concentration of glucose in the blood due to an absolute or relative lack of the hormone insulin. In Type 1, or insulin dependent diabetes mellitus (IDDM) there is an absolute deficiency of insulin and the patient requires regular injections of insulin to maintain glycaemic control. Type 2 or non-insulin dependent diabetes mellitus (NIDDM) is a condition in which the cells become resistant to the action of insulin and the clinical condition is precipitated by a fall in insulin secretion. The peak incidence of Type 1 diabetes is between 10 and 12 years of age but it can occur at any age; the majority of Type 2 diabetics develop the condition in middle age or later. Type 2 diabetes can usually be controlled by diet and oral hypoglycaemic drugs.

11.2 THE ROLE OF COMPLEX CARBOHYDRATES IN THE DEVELOPMENT OF DIABETES

There has been much interest in the role of diet in the aetiology of diabetes, particularly of NIDDM. Analysis of the diabetic mortality rates in the UK during the 1940s and 1950s suggested an inverse association with the consumption of high extraction, high 'fibre' National flour. (Trowell, 1974). The immediacy of the association however raises doubts that the relationship between diabetes and 'fibre' consumption is a causal one. Cross cultural comparisons also showed an inverse relationship between the percentage of energy from all carbohydrates and the prevalence of diabetes in selected countries (West, 1972).

A prospective trial of 10000 Israeli men followed for 10 years, however failed to show a relationship between any dietary variable and the subsequent risk of diabetes (Medalie et al., 1975). In this study obesity was a more important risk factor than diet. Two prospective studies have shown that the risk of diabetes increases steeply at 25–35% overweight (Medalie et al., 1975; Westlund and Nicolaysen, 1972). Reaven's current hypothesis (Foster, 1989) states that diabetes is just one of a group of underlying conditions which becomes manifest in the obese state. In particular, the acquisition of excessive amounts of intraabdominal fat is associated with the diabetic state (Björntorp, 1988), a hypothesis originally put forward by Vague in 1956. The direct transport of free fatty acids via the portal vein to the liver is thought to be important in determining insulin resistance, but proof is still lacking.

11.3 THE ROLE OF COMPLEX CARBOHYDRATES IN THE TREATMENT OF NIDDM

11.3.1 History of the dietary management of diabetes

Although the role of diet, particularly complex carbohydrates, in the development of NIDDM remains uncertain, the importance of diet in the treatment of diabetics has long been recognised. The idea that total dietary energy restriction was beneficial probably first occurred at least three hundred years ago (Willis, 1684), but proper documentation only began to appear in the second half of the nineteenth century when, for example, Bouchardat noted that his diabetic patients were clinically improved by the scarcity of food during the Siege of Paris in 1871 (Wood and

Bierman, 1972). Subsequently he, and other physicians, varied the levels of dietary energy derived from fat, carbohydrates and protein, and concluded that very strict restriction of all carbohydrates seemed beneficial.

The position on carbohydrate restriction hardened with the accumulation of good experimental evidence in the early years of the twentieth century. By the 1920s, while there were many variations in the details of the day-to-day dietary regimens, total carbohydrate energy could be as low as 10%. The idea that carbohydrate energy was detrimental to glucose metabolism persisted through the 1930s until the work of Himsworth and others demonstrated that carbohydrate tolerance was improved by increasing the proportion of carbohydrate in the diet, and underlined the overriding importance of control of total dietary energy (Himsworth, 1935).

Since the 1930s there has been an evolution towards diets higher in total carbohydrate and lower in fat, to the high complex carbohydrate diets advocated today. The evolutionary process is still occurring; recognition that the old dogma on near complete avoidance of sugar may not be entirely correct has resulted in revised guidelines from the British Diabetic Association (1982). There is no evidence however, to allow free use of sugars, as has been mistakenly suggested.

11.3.2 Aims of dietary management of diabetes

The risk of coronary heart disease is 2–3 times greater in diabetics than non-diabetics and microvascular complications such as diabetic nephropathy and retinopathy are also a problem. In addition, most individuals with NIDDM are overweight, which exacerbates many of the metabolic risk factors for coronary heart disease.

Dietary management of NIDDM therefore has two interrelated aims:

(i) to maintain blood glucose and lipid levels at as near normal levels as possible and so reduce the risk of both microvascular and macrovascular complications.
(ii) to achieve and maintain ideal weight.

11.3.3 The effects of high complex carbohydrate diets

Diets rich in complex carbohydrates could theoretically have beneficial effects on blood glucose and blood lipid control and on weight management, and therefore reduce the risks of macrovascular disease and the microvascular complications.

11.3.3.1 Effects on blood glucose levels

Research by Jenkins et al. on the glycaemic index (GI) of different foods (see Chapter 10) led to the understanding that the rate of digestion of carbohydrate and absorption of glucose was important in maintaining glycaemic and insulinaemic control. Diets containing low GI foods produce smoother blood glucose and insulin profiles and reduce the mean blood glucose and insulin levels when compared with diets of the same carbohydrate content but containing high GI foods. Smoother blood glucose levels reduce the risk of both hyperglycaemia and hypoglycaemia.

A similar approach has been followed by studies which have looked at the effects of diets containing large amounts of non-starch polysaccharides and a high proportion of energy from carbohydrate. The initial studies carried out in metabolic wards gave encouraging results but their applicability to more general use was weakened by the extremely high levels of non-starch polysaccharide used, (65–95g 'fibre'/day) (Kiehm et al., 1976; Simpson et al., 1981b; Monnier et al., 1981). More recent studies using realistic levels of non-starch polysaccharides (35–45g 'fibre'/day) have shown small but significant improvements in both mean blood glucose levels and in 24 hr blood glucose profiles (Karlstrom et al., 1984, 1987). There is some suggestion that diets rich in non-starch polysaccharides from cereal sources (generally insoluble) have a greater effect on fasting blood glucose levels (Karlstrom et al., 1988) while

Table 11.1   Trials of the effects of different diets on glucose variables in diabetics

Patient types	Experimental design	Diets used	Glucose variables*	Reference
6 IDDM 8 NIDDM	3 10-day periods	low CHO 42% / low 'fibre' 20g high CHO 53% / low 'fibre' 16g high CHO 53% / high 'fibre' 54g	Baseline unchanged reduced	Riccardi *et al.* (1984)
4 IDDM 4 NIDDM	3 10-day periods	low CHO 42% / low 'fibre' 20g high CHO 53% / low 'fibre' 16g high CHO 53% / high 'fibre' 54g	Baseline unchanged reduced	Rivelesse *et al.* (1980)

IDDM = Type I Insulin dependent diabetes mellitus; NIDDM = Type 2 Non-insulin dependent diabetes mellitus; * glucose variables = 2 h postprandial glucose and 24 hour profile.

those rich in soluble non-starch polysaccharides from beans and legumes have more effect on post-prandial blood glucose levels (Fuessl *et al.*, 1987).

Studies have also been undertaken to try to separate the effect of high carbohydrate levels from the high non-starch polysaccharide content of the diets. Several metabolic studies have been reported (Rivellese *et al.*, 1980; Riccardi *et al.*, 1984) which show that improvement occurs only in the high carbohydrate, high 'fibre' treatment groups (see Table 11.1).

Studies using supplements of purified water soluble non-starch polysaccharides such as guar and pectin and foods fortified with these polysaccharides, such as guar-enriched bread have also shown beneficial effects on blood glucose levels (Jenkins *et al.*, 1976, 1978b).

In addition to the effects on hyperglycaemia, a smoother blood glucose profile would suggest the possibility that hypoglycaemic episodes may be reduced, or that patients would have greater warning of impending hypoglycaemia and be able to take preventive action. Kinmonth *et al.* (1982) however, suggested that episodes of mild hypoglycaemia may be more frequent due to the overall reduction in blood glucose levels. A study in non-diabetic gastrectomy patients who are also prone to hypoglycaemia, showed that glucomannan (a soluble polysaccharide similar to guar) was effective in preventing post-prandial hypoglycaemia in these patients (Hopman *et al.*, 1988).

Whether tighter control of blood glucose levels will reduce the risk of microvascular complications such as diabetic retinopathy and nephropathy is uncertain. It has been suggested that a general reduction in hyperglycaemia, assessed by serial measurements of glycosylated haemoglobin may be associated with decreased retinopathy (McCance *et al.*, 1989) but the evidence for a causal association is equivocal, and other factors (such as age and sex) would also seem to be important (Finotti and Piccoli, 1990).

11.3.3.2 Effects on blood lipid levels
The major long-term health risk for diabetic patients is accelerated coronary heart disease. Control of blood lipids is therefore of major importance in the dietary management of diabetes. The effects of complex carbohydrates on blood lipids are covered in greater detail elsewhere in this Report (Chapter 14) and only brief consideration of their effects will be given here.

Soluble non-starch polysaccharides have been shown to lower plasma cholesterol in diabetic patients (Jenkins *et al.*, 1980) as in some normal subjects and hyper-lipidaemic subjects. The effects of complex carbohydrates on plasma triacylglycerols or VLDL are less certain. Riccardi *et al.* (1984) showed that increasing the percentage energy from carbohydrate led to elevated plasma VLDL in NIDDM patients but that this effect could be opposed by leguminous non-starch polysaccharides.

11.3.3.3 Dietary recommendation for diabetes

As a result of the accumulating evidence, Diabetic Associations revised their dietary recommendations in the early 1980's. The British Diabetic Association (1982) guidelines recommend that at least 50% of dietary energy should be obtained from low glycaemic index foods, rich in complex carbohydrates. High glycaemic index foods (that is foods containing rapidly absorbed carbohydrate) should only be taken in small quantities as part of a non-starch polysaccharide-rich meal. In addition fat intake should be reduced to 35% of energy, primarily by a reduction in saturated fat. There are no specific recommendations for 'fibre' or non-starch polysaccharide intake apart from consumption as 'fibre'-rich foods. The use of purified supplements of soluble non-starch polysaccharides is of limited practicable value.

Warnings of the deleterious effects of high carbohydrate diets on plasma triacylglycerols (Reaven, 1980) and the difficulty of achieving intakes of even 40g 'fibre'/day by many diabetic patients (Thomas, 1981) has led to suggestions that a more 'Mediterranean' style diet, with greater emphasis on monounsaturated fats and fatty fish may be a more suitable way of achieving the same goals.

11.4 POSSIBLE MECHANISMS OF ACTION

The beneficial effects on blood glucose, insulin and lipid levels of a diet rich in complex carbohydrates are probably due to a number of different mechanisms which might include:

i)   the effects of complex carbohydrates on glycaemic response (Chapter 10) result in less marked rises of blood glucose and insulin after meals. This, and the secondary metabolic consequences (changes in insulin sensitivity) presumably account for the improvement in glycaemic control.

ii) the effects of diets high in complex carbohydrate (especially non-starch polysaccharide) on limiting energy intake are important to many overweight and obese diabetics (see Chapter 12). Energy restriction leads to a decrease in blood glucose levels even before any weight loss has occurred. Weight loss also reduces cardiovascular risk factors and extends the life-expectancy of NIDDM patients.

iii) fermentation of resistant starch and fermentable non-starch polysaccharides leads to the production of short chain fatty acids (acetate, propionate and butyrate). Propionate may lead to reduced cholesterol synthesis via its inhibition of HMG-CoA reductase, the rate limiting step in cholesterol synthesis.

iv) the production of acetate, may have an insulin-sparing effect by providing an insulin independent energy substrate. Butyrate and propionate are removed by the liver on the first pass but acetate appears in the peripheral circulation after meals and provides an alternative energy source to glucose.

CHAPTER 12
CLINICAL IMPLICATIONS OF COMPLEX CARBOHYDRATES FOR OBESITY

The aetiology of obesity is complex. In some people, genetic and psychological factors may be as important as dietary ones. Nevertheless it is easier to eat to excess with some foods than others. The role of complex carbohydrates in the diet will be considered in two sections: short term effects on satiety and long-term effects on food intake.

12.1 SHORT TERM EFFECTS ON SATIETY

There are many uncertainties with studies of satiation. Nevertheless, after reviewing all the evidence, Blundell and Burley (1987) concluded that '"fibre' does exert effects on the short-term control of food consumption". It is not clear that 'fibre' does this independently of its effects on food form. Some of the most compelling pieces of evidence can be summarised thus:

12.1.1 'Whole' foods

'Whole' foods (ie containing intact cellular architecture) tend to be solid and firm-textured. Such foods have a number of properties and effects which, it has been suggested, would limit energy intake and absorption (Heaton, 1973; van Itallie, 1978; Krotkiewski and Smith, 1985). These are as follows:

- 'Whole' foods require chewing. Chewing makes ingestion slower and more laborious.
- 'Whole' food is swallowed as partly chewed lumps. These are retained in the stomach until reduced to 1–2 mm by antral churning. This slowing down of gastric emptying might be accompanied by slower return of appetite and hunger. Experimentally, slower gastric emptying is associated with increased feelings of satiety (Di Lorenzo et al., 1988).
- Intact cells and clumps of cells entering the small intestine are likely to release their stored carbohydrate and other nutrients more slowly than when cell walls are absent or disrupted. Consequently, less insulin is secreted which means that post-prandial hypoglycaemia is less likely with its accompanying feelings of hunger.

These ideas have been supported by test-meal studies which showed that whole fruits (apples, oranges, grapes) were more satisfying than their respective juices and, in the case of apples, their respective pureé. Post-prandial hypoglycaemia occurred with apple and orange juice but not with the whole fruits. Comparisons of whole cereal grains (wheat, rice, maize) with their milled counterparts have shown that milling increases digestibility and hence the insulin response (Heaton et al., 1988). Effects on hunger and satiety have not been reported, perhaps because the milled products were still solid.

12.1.2 Wheat bran

McCance and Widdowson (McCance et al., 1953) gave normal volunteers a meal based on wholemeal bread and showed it took longer to eat than one based on white bread and distended the stomach more.

Two recent studies have found wholemeal bread to be more satiating but one has not. (Blundell & Burley, 1987)

12.1.3 Mixed non-starch polysaccharides

When healthy women ate a 608kcal breakfast containing branflakes and guar bread they were more satiated than after a 697kcal breakfast of cornflakes and white bread with a quarter of the 'fibre' content (Burley et al., 1987).

When 20 healthy young people swallowed seven tablets containing mixed 'fibre' (80% insoluble) before each meal for four weeks, they were significantly less hungry than when they took placebo tablets (Rigaud et al., 1987)

12.1.4 Viscous polysaccharides

When concentrates of viscosity-conferring polysaccharides such as guar gum and pectin were added to test meals in sufficient amounts they slowed down gastric emptying and increased feelings of satiety (Krotkiewski, 1984; Di Lorenzo et al., 1988).

12.1.5 The role of the small intestine

The small intestine probably contributes to feelings of hunger and satiety. The water-holding properties of non-starch polysaccharides have the potential to distend the small intestine and so increase satiety (see Chapter 5).

When fatty plant foods like nuts are eaten histologically intact, it is likely that the absorption of the fat is delayed and more reaches the lower small intestine. This could activate the 'ileal brake', ie. slowing of gastric emptying, which might increase satiety and reduce food intake.

12.2 EFFECTS OF COMPLEX CARBO-HYDRATES ON LONG-TERM ENERGY INTAKE

Short-term control of food consumption is not, of course, synonymous with long-term control of body weight. Nevertheless it is a hypothesis worth testing that, when a diet is eaten which provides more satiety for the same number of calories, fewer calories will be eaten.

It is difficult to design a study of the effect of non-starch polysaccharide on spontaneous energy intake which is at the same time realistic and properly controlled, and it is well nigh impossible to blind people to a change in non-starch polysaccharide intake. All published studies can be criticised on one or more of these grounds.

12.2.1 Experimental evidence

The most recent and best-designed study (Stevens et al., 1988) measured the ad libitum, but closely monitored food intake of 12 overweight young women during four 2-week periods during which each of the three daily meals began with the ingestion of 12 biscuits. During one 2-week period the biscuits were low in non-starch polysaccharides, being made from a wheat-based batter. In the other three periods, the biscuits were rich in wheat bran, in psyllium gum (ispaghula) and in a bran-gum mixture respectively. The biscuits and their accompanying spreads and drinks provided 37–42% of total energy intake so there was scope for variation only in the remaining 58–63% of food intake. Nevertheless, when the gum-rich biscuits, were eaten there was a significant fall in total energy intake, which represented an 11% fall in freely chosen food energy. With the bran biscuits, there was no change and the combination biscuits gave an intermediate result. These data suggest that enriching the diet with a concentrate of soluble non-starch polysaccharide reduces

Table 12.1 Controlled trials of dietary 'fibre' supplements and 'fibre'-rich foods on weight loss

Non-starch polysaccharides or source	Daily dose	Double blind	Duration (weeks)	Number of subjects	Background diet	Weight change (kg)	Reference
Methylcellulose tablets	4.5g	Yes	8	21	energy-reduced	NS	Duncan et al. (1960)
Cellulose-enriched bread	12 slices	No	8	6	energy-reduced	F: −8.8 C: −6.3	Mickelsen et al. (1979)
Bran-enriched bread	625g	No	5	17	usual	NS	Henry et al. (1978)
Guar gum	15g	Yes	18	11	usual	F: −2.5 C: −0.4	Tuomilehto et al. (1980)
Guar gum	20g	No	5	9	usual	F: −4.7 C: −3.2	Krotkiewski (1984)
Glucomannan	3g	Yes	8	10	usual	F: −2.5 C: +0.7	Walsh et al. (1984)
Oat bran, wheat bran, guar	40g DF	Yes	12	60	formula and low calorie	NS	Russ and Atkinson (1986)
55% sterculia, 5% guar gum granules	12g DF	No	6	26	energy-reduced	F: −3.6 C: −1.8	Valle-Jones (1980)
Cereal (80%) and citrus (20%) 'fibre' tablets	4g DF	Yes	8	30	energy-reduced	F: −2.8 C: −1.5	Solum (1983)
Cereal and citrus fibre tablets	10g DF	Yes	11	45*	energy-reduced	F: −6.3 C: −4.2	Ryttig et al. (1984)
Cereal and citrus fibre tablets	6g DF	Yes	12	30	energy-reduced	F: −8.5 C: −6.4	Solum et al. (1987)
Grain and citrus fibre tablets	5g DF	Yes	8	30	energy-reduced	F: −7.0 C: −6.0	Rössner et al. (1987)
Grain and citrus fibre tablets	7g DF	Yes	12	28	energy-reduced	F: −6.2 C: −4.1	Rössner et al. (1987)
Grain and citrus fibre tablets	6.5g DF	Yes	10	31	energy-reduced	NS	Rössner et al. (1988)

C = control treatment; F = 'fibre' treatment; DF = dietary 'fibre'; * 6 dropped out, vs 11 of 45 on placebo tablets ($p = 0.05$)

the intake of food energy over a 2-week period, but the findings cannot safely be extrapolated to enriching the diet with naturally 'fibre'-rich foods over a period of years.

Other workers have reported decreased food intake in volunteers when they took methyl cellulose, oat bran or guar gum before meals (Evans and Miller, 1975).

However, short-term experiments in which large amounts of a concentrated 'fibre' preparation are given before meals are highly artificial. Many experiments have been done in which 'fibre' supplements of all kinds have been taken *with* meals which is the physiological way to take 'fibre' and weight loss is rarely, if ever, reported. Energy intake did not change when bran supplements were given, (Kahaner et al., 1976). Nor did it fall when actual 'fibre'-rich foods were used to increase fibre intake in obese people (Russ and Atkinson, 1985) and in diabetics (Stevens et al., 1985). Weight loss does not occur when people who habitually eat substantial amounts of white bread switch to wholemeal bread (Heaton et al., 1976).

12.2.2 Epidemiological evidence

There are no ecological studies, international, inter-regional or migrant, which have specifically examined the relationship between complex carbohydrate intake and obesity. Such studies would be hard to interpret because diets naturally rich in complex carbohydrate are likely to be low in fat and sugars. Kay et al. (1980) obtained 24h dietary recall data on 200 men and found a positive correlation between 'fibre' intake and energy intake. Less predictably, there was a weak but statistically significant *negative* correlation between 'fibre' intake and relative body weight. Dietary 'fibre' intake may simply have been an index of health consciousness since, in this population, it also correlated negatively with smoking. Similarly, the tendency of vegetarians to be slim could be due to their greater health consciousness rather than to their high dietary 'fibre' intake (or any other dietary factor).

12.3 DIETARY 'FIBRE' AND 'FIBRE'-RICH FOODS AS AIDS TO WEIGHT-REDUCING DIETS

The lay public and some health professionals have enthusiastically embraced the idea that dietary 'fibre' is an aid to slimming diets.

This is probably true in one very restricted sense, namely, the taking of concentrates of viscous polysaccharides such as guar gum, glucomannan and citrus pectin, before meals. Table 12.1 summarises the controlled trials which have been published. Most show that such treatment is an aid to weight reduction, though the extra weight lost is modest (1–3kg over 8–12 weeks). The mode of action of the viscous polysaccharides is uncertain. When hunger ratings have been measured they have generally been lowered. This should aid compliance with the diet and may occur because of slower gastric emptying or greater distension of the gut.

Despite the popularity of slimming regimens based on whole foods rich in cell wall material there are no controlled trials to indicate that they are more effective than other regimens.

Weight control is a life-long problem for many people and the real question is whether a successful regimen can be continued or its effects maintained by ordinary dieting over a period of years. There are no data to indicate the answer with respect to foods naturally rich in complex carbohydrate. One controlled trial has shown that a polysaccharide supplement helps weight *maintenance* over a prolonged period after successful slimming (Ryttig et al., 1989). More long term trials are needed to verify this finding.

CHAPTER 13
CLINICAL IMPLICATIONS OF COMPLEX CARBOHYDRATES FOR GALLSTONES

13.1 THE NATURE OF GALLSTONE DISEASE

Stones form in the gallbladder when three conditions are fulfilled:

(i) gallbladder bile becomes supersaturated with one or more of the components of gallstones. This is usually cholesterol, but is often calcium carbonate or phosphate, and less often calcium palmitate, calcium bilirubinate and bilirubin polymers;
(ii) nucleating agents (such as glycoproteins) are present, or the balance of pro- and anti-nucleating factors favours the former; and
(iii) gallbladder emptying is impaired, allowing time for crystals to form, grow and agglomerate.

Population surveys show that most gallstones are not associated with pain. It is only in the 20–30% of cases where a gallstone tries to migrate and gets stuck in the neck of the gallbladder, the cystic duct or at the lower end of the common bile duct that symptoms arise. These are most likely to be biliary 'colic', acute cholecystitis, jaundice, cholangitis or pancreatitis.

13.2 EPIDEMIOLOGY

13.2.1 Prevalence

National incidence figures for gallstones are not available. Prevalence data can be obtained relatively easily by ultrasound scanning of a random sample of the population and are available for Copenhagen (Jörgensen 1987), Sirmione in N. Italy (Barbara et al., 1987), and for women over 40 years of age in Oxford (Pixley et al., 1985). These studies show that gallstones are twice as prevalent in women as in men, that they increase in prevalence (but not necessarily incidence) with age and that they are commoner in obese people and in multiparous women.

Gallstone risk is strongly associated with a raised fasting plasma triacylglycerol concentration. It is also associated, perhaps less strongly, with raised fasting plasma insulin levels, low plasma levels of high density lipoprotein cholesterol and high biliary levels of the secondary bile salt deoxycholate (Heaton, 1988). All of these risk indicators are also associated with increased saturation of gallbladder bile with cholesterol, probably due to increased secretion of cholesterol by the liver into the bile.

13.3 ROLE OF NON-STARCH POLY-SACCHARIDES IN THE DIET

The role of the diet has been studied in three main ways: by case-control studies of dietary intake, by dietary intervention studies with analysis of bile composition, and by animal experiments. All three lines of enquiry have suggested a protective role for non-starch polysaccharides but not consistently or conclusively.

13.3.1 Case-control studies

Once people know they have gallstones, they are very likely to alter their diet (a low fat diet is standard treatment, and many patients awaiting removal of gallstones are

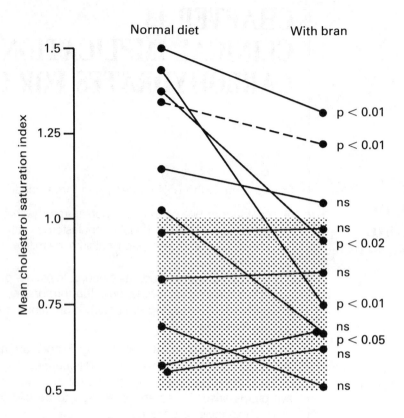

Figure 13.1   Effect of bran on cholesterol saturation index of gallbladder bile. Mean values in 11 groups of subjects. The shaded area represents bile which is unsaturated with cholesterol and from which cholesterol cannot precipitate. (From Heaton, 1987)

advised to lose weight). Only two studies have been carried out pre-diagnosis with a detailed dietary analysis including 'fibre'. In Adelaide, Scragg et al. (1984a) found no difference in estimated 'fibre' intake between patients with gallstones and community-based controls but, after multiple regression analysis controlling for other risk factors, there was a protective effect of 'fibre'. In Oxford there was no difference in estimated 'fibre' intakes between cases and controls (Pixley and Mann, 1988), despite a lower prevalence of gallstones in vegetarians.

In two population-based studies in Rome, there was an inverse relationship between the frequency of vegetable consumption and the risk of gallstones (Attili *et al.*, 1984; Attili *et al.*, 1987) but this did not reach statistical significance, possibly because of rather small sample sizes.

Thus, case-control studies are inconclusive but suggest that a high intake of vegetables (and fruit) may be protective. Possible reasons for negative results from case-control studies include inaccurate recall of past eating habits and a restricted range of intakes in the study population.

13.3.2 Dietary intervention studies

Several groups have studied the effect of adding wheat bran to the diet on the lipid composition of bile (Heaton, 1987). Figure 13.1 shows that when the bile is initially supersaturated with cholesterol, ie the saturation index is above 1.0, bran usually lowers the saturation index. This should lower the risk of gallstone formation. However, it does not necessarily reduce the index to a point at which precipitation

Table 13.1 Diets which cause cholesterol-rich gallstones in experimental animals

Animal	Special features of diet	Carbohydrate in diet	Reference
Hamster	Best if fat free	72% glucose or sucrose	Dam (1971) Hikasa *et al.* (1969)
Mouse	31% fat Added cholesterol and cholic acid	51% glucose	Tepperman *et al.* (1967)
Prairie dog	41% fat Added cholesterol 2.6% cellulose	34% sucrose 14% corn starch	Brenneman *et al.* (1972)
Rabbit	15% olive oil 15% cellulose	7% sucrose 6.5% glucose 6.5% corn starch	Borgman and Haselden (1968)
Squirrel monkey	25% butter Added cholesterol	44% sucrose	Osuga and Portman (1971)

of cholesterol cannot occur. This may explain why, when bran was added to the diet of patients whose gallstones had been dissolved by medical treatment, the recurrence of gallstones was not prevented (Hood *et al.*, 1988).

13.3.3 Animal experiments

Gallstones have been induced in several mammalian species by feeding semi-synthetic diets, rich in sugars or refined starch and devoid of plant cell wall material (Table 13.1). Animals given a chow diet, based on whole ground cereals, form gallstones only if they are fed excessive amounts of cholesterol. The possibility that semi-synthetic diets cause gallstones because they are depleted of plant cell-wall material is supported by two observations:

(i) The diet loses some, or all, of its stone-forming effect in hamsters if it is supplemented with lignin (especially if lactulose is added) (Rotstein *et al.*, 1981) or with bulking agents, or even if the animals are allowed to eat the straw laid on the floor of their cage (Hikasa *et al.*, 1969).
(ii) Stones dissolve rapidly if rabbits are fed ordinary chow (Borgman and Haselden, 1968).

13.3.4 How do non-starch polysaccharides affect gallstone formation?

13.3.4.1 Reduction of deoxycholate content?

The beneficial effect of bran on the cholesterol saturation of bile is possibly due to the fact that it reduces the deoxycholate content of bile. All measures which lower bile deoxycholate also lower the cholesterol saturation index (Marcus and Heaton, 1988).

Experiments by Thornton *et al.* (1983) do not, however, agree with this idea. They gave a diet naturally rich in plant cell wall material to women with asymptomatic gallstones. After six weeks the mean cholesterol saturation index was 1.2, whereas after six weeks on a diet low in plant cell wall material, the index was 1.5. The beneficial effect of the diet on bile could not be explained. It was not thought to be due to a 'bran effect' since it was accompanied by only a small reduction in bile deoxycholate.

13.3.4.2 Non-specific laxative effect?

The effects of bran on bile may be quite non-specific, ie simply due to its laxative action since they can be reproduced by giving a chemical laxative, standardised senna (Marcus and Heaton, 1986). Absorption of deoxycholate from the colon is a slow, inefficient process depending on passive diffusion, and transit time through the colon may well be a rate-limiting factor.

13.3.4.3 Fermentation effect?

The effects of bran are also mimicked by those of the unabsorbed sugar, lactulose, even when this is given in sub-laxative doses. Lactulose is efficient in reducing the deoxycholate in bile and it is believed to do this by lowering the acidity in the caecum to below pH6 (via its fermentation products, the short chain fatty acids). This inactivates the bacterial enzyme responsible for converting cholate to deoxycholate. An acidic pH also encourages precipitation of deoxycholate and its binding to solid matter. Since bran is partly fermented to short chain fatty acids it may act, in part, like lactulose. It is quite likely that bran has more than one mode of action.

13.3.4.4 Other non-starch polysaccharides

The effects of other 'fibre' concentrates on bile are scantily documented. Cellulose seems to reduce deoxycholate but, paradoxically, pectin raises it. The effects of cellulose and pectin on the cholesterol saturation of bile in people with supersaturated bile are not known.

13.4 ROLE OF STARCH IN THE DIET

13.4.1 Evidence that starch may protect against gallstones

Very little work has been done on the role of starch in the aetiology of gallstones. Gallstones are less common in South India where starch is eaten mainly as whole grains (rice) than in North India where starch is eaten mainly as flour (Malhotra 1968; – this is relevant because the digestibility of starch in rice and wheat is increased by milling the grains into flour – O'Dea *et al.*, 1981, Heaton *et al.* 1988). Furthermore, when hamsters eating a sugar-rich, fat-free diet start eating a diet rich in raw starch diet, they stop forming gallstones (Hikasa *et al.*, 1969).

13.4.2 How might starch affect gallstone formation?

If resistant starch has the same effects as bran (and lactulose) on bile acid metabolism, then one would expect a high intake of starch or resistant starch to be protective against gallstones. Conversely readily digestible starch could contribute to gallstone formation via the greater secretion of insulin which is induced by such starch compared with resistant starch. A raised plasma insulin level is associated epidemiologically with an increased risk of gallstones (Scragg *et al.* 1984b) and insulin stimulates the synthesis of cholesterol (Neprokoeff *et al.*, 1974). There is clearly a need for more experimental and epidemiological studies on the role of starch in gallstone formation.

CHAPTER 14
CLINICAL IMPLICATIONS OF COMPLEX CARBOHYDRATES FOR CORONARY HEART DISEASE

14.1 CORONARY HEART DISEASE

Coronary heart disease (CHD) is a multifactorial disease and any discussion of the role of complex carbohydrates in the aetiology or the treatment of CHD must be considered within the wider framework of other components of the diet and the non-dietary risk factors. The disease process is complex and is influenced by hereditary factors as well as environmental factors. Factors such as smoking, lack of exercise and the proportion of energy intake from fat are considered to be all 'modifiable' risk factors whereas age, being male and having a genetic predisposition to hyper-cholesterolaemia are obviously not.

14.1.1 Cholesterol synthesis and circulation

Dietary cholesterol and dietary triacylglycerol are incorporated into chylomicrons originating in the small intestine – these are metabolised by lipoprotein lipase in peripheral capillaries, triacylglycerol being taken up by peripheral cells leaving chylomicron remnants which are taken up by the liver via chylomicron remnant receptors. Dietary cholesterol is thus transferred to the liver via this route which is sometimes referred to as the exogenous pathway (Figure 14.1).

Cholesterol is secreted from the liver in very low density lipoprotein (VLDL) particles which are also hydrolysed in the peripheral capillaries by lipoprotein lipase. Triacylglycerol is taken up by the tissues and the remaining particle is the intermediate density lipoprotein (IDL), some of which is taken up again by the liver, some converted to low density lipoprotein (LDL) in the liver or peripheral tissues. High density lipoprotein, (HDL) synthesised in the liver or small intestine, carries cholesterol from peripheral tissues back to the liver directly or by transferring cholesterol esters to other lipoprotein particles. The role of HDL in transferring cholesterol from the periphery to the liver is thought to be related to the association between high HDL levels and low CHD risk.

14.1.2 Pathogenesis of CHD

Coronary heart disease develops from concurrent disturbances in the structure of the arterial walls (atherosclerosis) and in the tendency of the blood to form clots (thrombosis). This can cause a blockage of one of the coronary arteries and result in myocardial infarction. Serum lipids, particularly the low density lipoprotein (LDL) cholesterol but also triacylglycerol are associated with the development of calcified fatty deposits (atheromatous plaques) in the walls of coronary arteries. It has been postulated that free radical damage which oxidises the polyunsaturated fatty acids in LDL cholesterol causes cholesterol to be taken up by the scavenger receptor system of monocytes. These are then converted to macrophages and become embedded in the arterial wall. Further oxidised LDL cholesterol is taken up, which stimulates a proliferation of smooth muscle cells, damages the endothelial cells, and results in the formation of atheromatous plaques.

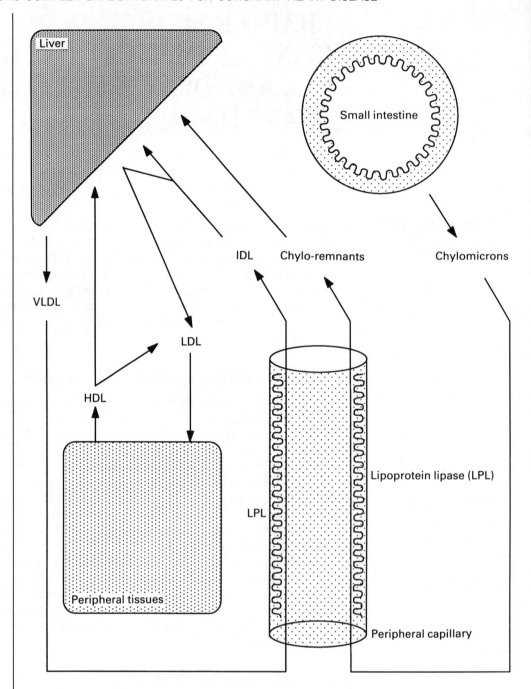

Figure 14.1   Diagram to illustrate lipid circulation and metabolism.

14.1.3 Dietary risk factors

Various dietary factors can ameliorate the disease process. The proportion of energy from fat, and in particular some saturated fatty acids, is positively associated with serum LDL cholesterol levels. The antioxidant vitamins and minerals protect against damage from free radical attack. The long-chain polyunsaturated fatty acids of the n–3 series deriving from α-linolenic acid can reduce the blood-clotting tendency of blood. Complex carbohydrates appear to influence CHD via their effects on serum cholesterol levels.

Table 14.1 Summary of studies investigating the relationship between complex carbohydrate intake and coronary heart disease

Location	Design	Type of complex carbohydrate	Result	Reference
London	Prospective n = 377, 7-day weighed food intake, 20-year follow-up	Total dietary 'fibre' Cereal 'fibre' 'Fibre' from fruit, veg, pulses, nuts	Intakes lower in CHD cases* Intakes lower in CHD cases* Intakes not significantly different in CHD cases	Morris *et al.* (1977)
Honolulu	Prospective n = 7705, 24 hr dietary recall, 6 year follow-up	Starch Complex carbohydrates	Intakes lower in CHD deaths and MI cases** Intakes lower in CHD deaths and MI cases**	Yano *et al.* (1978)
Puerto Rico	Prospective n = 8281, 24 hr dietary recall, 6 year follow-up	Starch	Intakes lower in CHD deaths and MI cases* for urban men aged 45–64	Garcia-Palmieri *et al.* (1980)
Zutphen	Prospective n = 871, cross-check dietary history, 10 year follow-up	'Dietary fibre' Polysaccharides	Intakes lower CHD deaths (ns) (RR = 0.25) Intakes lower in CHD deaths*	Kromhout *et al.* (1982)
Ireland – Boston	Prospective cohort n = 1001, food frequency questionnaire 20-year follow-up	'Fibre' intake: within population analysis Vegetable foods Starch	Intakes lower in CHD deaths* (RR = 0.57) Intakes lower in CHD deaths* Intakes not significantly different	Kushi *et al.* (1985)

* $p < 0.05$; ** $p < 0.01$, ns not significant; MI myocardial infarction

14.2 EPIDEMIO-LOGICAL STUDIES

The epidemiological evidence for a relationship between coronary heart disease and complex carbohydrates is weak and inconsistent. Historical trends of complex carbohydrate consumption and mortality rates from CHD in the United States from 1909 to 1968 show an inverse relationship (Friend *et al.*, 1979): however many other changes in lifestyle occurred during this period.

14.2.1 Prospective studies

A number of prospective studies have shown an inverse association between intake of starch or complex carbohydrates with the risk of death from CHD (Table 14.1).

Morris *et al.* (1977) studied middle aged men in London and found that their consumption of cereal 'fibre' but not the consumption of 'fibre' from vegetables, fruits, legumes or nuts was inversely correlated with the number of CHD cases.

The 20 year mortality from CHD data in the Ireland–Boston Diet–Heart study showed no difference in mortality between brothers born in Ireland who had emigrated to Boston and those who were still living in Ireland (Kushi *et al.*, 1985). Within population analysis however, showed that 'fibre' and vegetable intake were significantly lower among those who died from CHD than among those who survived. This difference was not significant after adjustment for other risk factors. No significant difference in starch intake was found between those who survived and those who died of CHD.

The Zutphen study (Kromhout *et al.*, 1982) showed that mortality from CHD over a 10 year period was four times higher in middle aged men with the lowest intake of 'fibre' than for those with the highest. This inverse relationship disappeared after multivariate analyses. There was, however, no significant difference in the average 'fibre' consumption of those who died from CHD and those who survived. The study did show a significant difference in the polysaccharide consumption; those who survived consumed more polysaccharide than those who died from CHD.

The Honolulu Heart study (Yano *et al.*, 1978) showed that the consumption of starch and complex carbohydrates was significantly lower in those who died from CHD or survived myocardial infarction than in non-cases.

Garcia-Palmieri *et al.* (1980) in the Puerto Rico Heart Health Programme found the intake of starch was significantly lower in those urban men aged between 45–64 who died of CHD or survived myocardial infarction than in non-cases.

14.2.2 Intervention trials

One of the tests to see whether these observed associations reflect a true causal relationship is to show that changing the intake of certain nutrients alters the CHD mortality rate. The Diet and Reinfarction Trial (DART) (Burr *et al.*, 1989) was a secondary intervention trial on 2033 Welsh men who either were or were not given advice on fat, fish and cereal 'fibre'. After two years there was no significant change in mortality from CHD in the group given advice to increase their intake of cereal 'fibre'. However, this was a secondary prevention trial in patients with well-established coronary arterial disease and does not give any information about how non-starch polysaccharides might influence the development of atherosclerosis: a primary prevention trial is needed.

14.3 THE EFFECTS OF STARCHES ON BLOOD LIPIDS

The main effect of starches on serum lipid levels is on triacylglycerol levels. Serum triacylglycerol levels rise after a meal containing fat and gradually fall to fasting levels as triacylglycerols are removed from the blood. Dietary carbohydrates are converted into triacylglycerol once the body's glycogen stores have been replenished.

Serum triacylglycerol levels are positively associated with coronary heart disease although there is still some debate about whether or not they are an independent risk factor. It is possible that triacylglycerol plays a role in the generation of coronary risk, particularly in those with low HDL cholesterol levels (Castelli, 1986). However, high triacylglycerol levels may simply be an indicator of the presence of other lipoprotein abnormalities more directly associated with coronary arterial disease (NRC, 1989).

The effects of starches on serum triacylglycerol levels can be divided into their short-term and long-term effects.

14.3.1 Short-term effects

Fasting triacylglycerol levels rise, in the short-term, in subjects on high-carbohydrate diets, whereas postprandial levels may be lower (Schlierf & Dorow 1973).

14.3.2 Longer-term effects

Triacylglycerol levels may be lowered or at least may not rise after long-term feeding of high-carbohydrate diets to subjects with initially raised levels. The effect may however, depend on the degree of insulin resistance. In those with appreciable insulin resistance, where regulation of free fatty acid metabolism may be lost and triacylglycerol synthesis thus increased, high-carbohydrate diets may increase insulin resistance and exaggerate the raised levels of triacylglycerol (Reaven 1988).

14.4 THE EFFECTS OF NON-STARCH POLY-SACCHARIDES ON SERUM CHOLESTEROL LEVELS

14.4.1 Non-soluble NSP

Most studies, whether in free-living individuals or in metabolic wards, have failed to demonstrate that wheat bran or cellulose lower serum LDL or total cholesterol (Kay and Truswell, 1977; Kritchevsky, 1974).

14.4.2 Soluble NSP

14.4.2.1 Guar gum

Since the original observation by Jenkins *et al.* (1975) on the hypocholesterolaemic effects of guar gum, (a water soluble non-cellulosic polysaccharide) many similar reports have been published. They consistently show reductions in total cholesterol and LDL-cholesterol in normal subjects (Khan *et al.*, 1981, Smith and Holm, 1982; Penagini, 1986) in hyperlipidaemic subjects (Jenkins 1979, 1980; Simons, 1982; Wirth, 1982; Tuomilehto, 1983; Aro, 1984; Gatti, 1984) and in diabetic patients (Botha, 1981; Jenkins, 1980). However, most of the studies, with the exception of Simons (1982), have been of less than 3 months duration and there is some doubt that the reduced plasma cholesterol levels can be sustained in the long term (Aro, 1984; Gatti, 1984). Locust bean gum, a compound similar to guar gum and gum arabic, have also been shown to lower plasma cholesterol in the short-term in hyper-cholesterolaemic patients (Zavoral, 1983) and in normal men (McLean Ross, 1983).

14.4.2.2 Oats and oat bran

Oats, rye, barley and legume seeds contain relatively high quantities of soluble non-cellulosic polysaccharides. The soluble NSP β-glucan is found in oat gum, particularly in the bran. De Groot *et al.* (1963) first demonstrated a non-significant hypocholester-olaemic effect of large doses of rolled oats which has been confirmed in more recent studies (Table 14.2). Significant reductions in serum cholesterol have been reported using smaller quantities of oat bran, a more concentrated source of β-glucan.

These studies have all been of short-term duration only (six weeks or less) and only one study (Anderson, 1984a) has shown that the improvements in cholesterol status can be maintained over a longer term (99 weeks) once the subjects left the metabolic ward and continued the diet at home. The studies suggest that oat products selectively lower serum LDL cholesterol, leading to more favourable LDL:HDL ratios. The high quantities of oat products needed to produce significant effects should be noted. Studies using beans, which also contain large amounts of water-soluble non-starch polysaccharides have also shown similar results (Anderson, 1984a; Anderson, 1984b). A meta-analysis of published data (Lund *et al.*, 1990) showed that the cholesterol-lowering effect of oat bran diminished with decreasing initial plasma cholesterol concentration.

14.4.3 Possible mechanisms

There are several hypotheses regarding the mechanism of the hypocholesterolaemic effect of the water-soluble non-starch polysaccharides. It may be that different non-starch polysaccharides exert their effects through different mechanisms.

14.4.3.1 Effects on bile acid excretion

Some NSP may alter bile acid absorption and metabolism causing a drain on the body's pool of cholesterol. Oat bran has been shown to increase faecal bile acid excretion, although not significantly, whereas beans showed a significant reduction in faecal bile acid excretion. (Anderson,1984a). Oat bran derived NSP may bind bile acids and cholesterol thus decreasing their absorption. Bile acid binding resins, used to lower cholesterol in hypercholesterolaemic individuals, cause decreased enterohepatic circulation of bile acids and depression of 7 alpha-hydroxylase thus increasing conversion of cholesterol to bile acids. Hepatic LDL receptor activity is

Table 14.2   Effect of oat products on lipids and lipoproteins in humans (% change)

	Gram/day	Cholesterol	LDL	HDL	LDL/HDL
Oat bran					
Kirby *et al.* (1981)	100	−13.0**	−13.6**	−2.0	−12.0
Anderson *et al.* (1984a)	100	−19.3**	−21.6**	−5.6	−17.0
Anderson *et al.* (1984b)	50	−23.4**	−23*	−20*	−
Van Horn *et al.* (1988)	60	−5.4	−8.3	+1.7	−9.6
Oat meal					
Judd and. Truswell (1981)	125	−8.0	−13.3	+4.7	−17.3
Van Horn *et al.* (1988)	60	−6.5	−8.7	+2.4	−10.3
Turnbull and Leeds (1987)	150	−5.0*	−13.9**	+16.6	−26.3
Van Horn (1988)	56	−3.1	−10.6	−	−

* p < 0.05, ** p < 0.01, − not given.

enhanced and fractional catabolism of LDL increased. Guar gum (a purified non-starch polysaccharide) has been clearly shown to increase the fractional catabolism of LDL, suggesting a similarity in mechanism between guar gum and anion-exchange resins (Turner *et al.*, 1990).

14.4.3.2 Effects of short chain fatty acids
Fermentation of non-starch polysaccharides and resistant starch leads to the formation of the short chain fatty acids (SCFA) acetate, propionate and butyrate. These SCFA appear to inhibit cholesterol synthesis in the liver and in peripheral tissues resulting in decreased LDL synthesis and an increase in LDL clearance (Chen and Anderson, 1986).

14.4.3.3 Effects on insulin status
Intake of soluble NSP such as guar, pectin and β-glucan in a test meal produce lower post-prandial glycaemic and insulinaemic responses (see Chapter 10). Elevated plasma insulin levels have been found in prospective studies to predict the development of CHD, although the association is non linear (Pyorala *et al.*, 1985; Welborn and Wearne, 1979; Cambien *et al.*, 1986; Pyorala, 1979). Hyperinsulinaemia may lead to the development of CHD through increased triacylglycerol levels and decreased HDL-cholesterol levels.

14.4.3.4 Substitution for hypercholesterolaemic foods
An alternative suggestion has been that oat-bran products may lower serum cholesterol levels indirectly by replacing foods in the diet which contain saturated fat rather than by the direct action of the soluble non-starch polysaccharides. Swain *et*

al. (1990) showed that there was no significant difference in the hypocholesterolaemic properties of a high oat-bran diet and a low 'fibre', refined wheat diet and concluded that this was because they both replaced dietary saturated fats. However, other studies, have shown that the reduction in serum cholesterol is additional to that achieved by low/modified fat diets (Van Horn, 1986; Turnbull and Leeds, 1987).

14.4.3.5 Effects on reducing total energy intake

Another suggestion is that oat gum might exert some of its effects on cholesterol levels indirectly via its effect on reducing total energy intake (Lund *et al.*, 1990).

CHAPTER 15
CLINICAL IMPLICATIONS OF COMPLEX CARBOHYDRATES FOR IRRITABLE BOWEL SYNDROME AND CONSTIPATION

15.1 CHARACTER-ISTICS OF IRRITABLE BOWEL SYNDROME

Irritable Bowel Syndrome (IBS) is characterised by an alteration in bowel habit which may either be diarrhoea or constipation and abdominal distension discomfort or pain. Since routine clinical investigations fail to identify a cause, IBS is often a diagnosis of exclusion. Manning *et al.* (1978) have attempted to identify the positive discriminative symptoms for IBS, but many of these features are shared by patients with other bowel diseases (Thompson, 1984) and may only identify a subset of the disease.

There is no general agreement about the pathogenesis of IBS or how it should be categorised. Some insights may be gained from a careful history. Since patients' perceptions of both diarrhoea and constipation vary considerably, it is important to ask more detailed questions about bowel habit.

(i) A large proportion of patients complain of symptoms such as a frequent desire to defaecate, feelings of incomplete evacuation, abdominal pain relieved by defaecation and urgency. Their bowel habit may be either constipation or diarrhoea. These symptoms are suggestive of rectal irritability and are shared by patients with inflammatory bowel disease (Thompson, 1984; Rao *et al.*, 1988) and solitary rectal ulcer syndrome (Sun *et al.*, 1989). They are often associated with upper gut symptoms such as feelings of early satiety, nausea, and bloating after meals (Whorwell *et al.*, 1986). This subset of IBS may represent the common end result of a number of pathophysiological processes, some of which affect just the lower bowel, and some the whole gastrointestinal tract. Emotional tension is commonly considered to be the most important of these but other possible pathogenic factors include bile acid malabsorption, impaired gut permeability with activation of immunoreactive cells, and gastrointestinal inflammation.

(ii) Patients who present with constipation and abdominal bloating and pain often do not have features of rectal irritability and should perhaps be categorised in a different subset. The most severely affected patients in this subset have a disturbance in the function of the enteric nervous system and a mild form of chronic intestinal pseudo-obstruction.

(iii) Another major subset appears to be those patients who suffer with diarrhoea, wind and bloating after meals. These patients may include those who have inadequate absorption of, or are intolerant to, complex carbohydrates (see Chapter 18).

For the purpose of therapeutic trials, patients with widely different presenting features (the only common factor being the failure of the physician to find a cause for the symptoms) are lumped together and the effect of treatment is often gauged only on the basis of global symptomatic responses. It is not surprising that no effective treatment for this condition has emerged, though some would claim that psychotherapy helps most patients.

Table 15.1 Summary of studies treating IBS patients with complex carbohydrates

Number of patients, controls	Age of patients (mean or median plus range)	Source of 'fibre' and daily dose	Duration of treatment	Effect of 'fibre' vs control	Comments	Reference
29,23	40 (18-73)	Fine bran 30g in biscuits	6 wk	No difference in overall assessment nor in days with pain	Diverticular disease patients included; no laxative effect of bran apparent; placebo biscuits had marked effect	Soltoft et al. (1976)
13,11	20-60	Fine bran 20g or equivalent wholemeal bread	6 wk	Pain less severe and less frequent; bowel habit improved; less mucus passed	Colonic motor activity reduced by bran; placebo (dummy diet sheet) had little effect	Manning et al. (1977)
38,28	32 (19-61)	Coarse bran 20 g	1 m	No difference in any symptoms except constipation	Placebo tablets had marked effect, but bran always given first	Cann et al. (1984)
12,12	38 (16-69)	Ispaghula (Fybogel) 7 g	3 m	Overall improvement only on active agent (in 5 out of 12 patients)	Placebo powder had no effect	Ritchie and Truelove (1979)
26,34	38	Psyllium (Metamucil) 10.8 g	2 m	No difference in pain improvement or overall improvement	Diverticular disease patients included; placebo powder had marked effect and also relieved constipation	Longstreth et al. (1981)
80	28	Ispaghula	1 m	No effect on overall improvement compared with placebo	Patients already on a high 'fibre' diet	Arthurs and Fielding (1983)
28 (crossover)	-	Bran biscuits (13 g fibre)	6 m	No difference despite an increase in stool weight on bran		Lucey et al. (1987)
14,10	-	Ispaghula 30 g	-	Significant improvement in symptoms including diarrhoea, increased stool weight; no change in transit time	Only Asian patients; no placebo study	Kumar et al. (1987)
80	18-63	Ispaghula 11 g	12 wk	Global assessment better on ispaghula than placebo. Improvement in constipation; no change in diarrhoea		Prior and Whorwell (1987)

15.2 TREATMENT OF IRRITABLE BOWEL SYNDROME

Table 15.1 gives a summary of results from various trials which have used complex carbohydrates to treat IBS and demonstrates how inconclusive the results have been.

15.2.1 Wheat bran

The popularity of wheat bran, a non-cellulosic polysaccharide, as a natural way to manage IBS has made it the first line of treatment for this condition for over 10 years. But is it an *effective* treatment? Manning et al. (1977) showed that the addition of 7g of wheat bran for 6 weeks to the diet of IBS patients resulted in significant improvement in symptoms.

The problem is that in many other trials, the condition shows a marked response to placebos (Cann *et al.*, 1984). Placebo controlled trials of bran in IBS have failed to show any convincing effect of bran on overall symptom patterns (Soltoft *et al.*, 1976; Arffman *et al.*, 1985). Lucey *et al.* (1987) compared the effect of supplementing the daily diet of 44 IBS patients with either 12 bran biscuits (12.8g 'fibre') or 12 placebo biscuits (2.5g 'fibre') in a 6 month double-blind crossover trial. Both placebo and bran groups experienced similar improvements in overall symptom scores. Moreover, the beneficial effects of bran were independent of any change in stool weight. The paucity of constipated patients may have influenced the conclusions from this study.

Cann *et al.* (1984) compared the independent responses of a number of typical IBS symptoms to bran with the responses to placebo tablets in 38 patients. When the characteristics of the patients who said they had improved on bran (47% of total) were compared with those who said that their symptoms had not changed (19% of total) or become worse (24% of total), the bran responders had been most constipated at the start of the trial. Constipation was the only symptom that showed a significantly greater response to bran than placebo; other symptoms responded to bran and placebo equally. Wheat bran tended to accelerate intestinal transit time in everybody and exacerbated the symptoms of diarrhoea, in contrast to previous reports (Harvey *et al.*, 1973; Paylor *et al.*, 1975).

In conclusion, it seems that some IBS patients, particularly those who are constipated, undoubtedly obtain symptomatic relief from taking bran in their diet and should continue to do so. Others find that bran induces or exacerbates symptoms of distension, flatulence, diarrhoea and abdominal pain and should not take extra bran. For the remainder, bran is a less toxic 'placebo' than many drugs (Anon, 1986). It is better than placebo for the constipation associated with IBS.

15.2.2 Viscous polysaccharides

Are other types of complex polysaccharide more effective? Ritchie and Truelove (1979) showed that ispaghula was better than wheat bran when both were given in combination with a psychotropic agent and an antispasmodic. In a large double-blind study, Prior and Whorwell (1987) reported overall symptomatic improvement in 82% patients, who had been taking ispaghula compared with 53% patients who had been taking placebo. Ispaghula accelerated transit time and increased stool weight in patients with constipation. There was no evidence that ispaghula improved the symptom of diarrhoea.

Kumar *et al.* (1987) investigated the optimum dose of ispaghula for IBS and the correlation between the relief in patients' symptoms and colonic function. Ispaghula caused a significant improvement in patients' symptoms, accompanied by an increase in stool weight but no significant change in transit time. Surprisingly, patients reported improvement in diarrhoea, even though stool weight increased.

15.3 CONSTIPATION

15.3.1 Characteristics of constipation

The word constipation means different things to different people (Moore-Gillon, 1984). People who complain of constipation do not necessarily pass less faeces than others (Meyer and Le Quintrec, 1981), but they may strain excessively to pass abnormally hard or bulky stools, or they may pass stools infrequently. Investigators have attempted to define constipation as a stool output of less than 35g/day or a mean transit time of greater than 72 hours.

Many constipated people also have features of the irritable bowel syndrome (see

enhanced and fractional catabolism of LDL increased. Guar gum (a purified non-starch polysaccharide) has been clearly shown to increase the fractional catabolism constipation include physical inactivity, travel, lack of toilet facilities, pregnancy and drugs, besides a host of diseases (Devroede, 1983).

In most patients, severe constipation occurs as a result of disturbance of colonic motility and/or a disorder of defaecation.

15.3.2 Is constipation a disorder of 'fibre' deficiency?

The observation that groups taking a high 'fibre' diet had a larger 24h faecal output and more rapid intestinal transit than groups taking a low 'fibre' diet (Burkitt et al., 1972) popularised the view that constipation in the British population is mainly caused by 'fibre' deficiency. More recently, studies within Britain and USA have shown that variation in 'fibre' intake is indeed a determinant of stool output but not necessarily the most important one. If vegans and vegetarians are included in the population sample, then there is a very strong correlation between 'fibre' intake and stool output (r = 0.96 in 51 subjects studied) (Davies et al., 1986). In a more normal population sample, the correlation between 'fibre' intake and 7 day stool weight was quite weak (r = 0.41) (Eastwood et al., 1984).

Psychological factors can account for as much variance in stool output as can dietary 'fibre' intake – American extroverts having bigger stools than introverts (Tucker et al., 1981). This may explain why, when normal people are given the same strictly controlled intake of 'fibre', their 24h stool weight varies over a range of at least three fold (Cummings et al., 1978; Stephen et al., 1986).

The 'fibre' intake of constipated people may be less, the same, or even more than that of controls, especially as some of them will have already tried to help themselves by eating more 'fibre' rich foods (Johnson et al., 1980; Preston and Lennard-Jones, 1986).

There is, therefore, little evidence to support the contention that constipation in all patients is wholly caused by 'fibre' deficiency and constipated patients should not be blamed for non-compliance if dietary advice fails. Constipation should probably be regarded as a disorder of colonic or anorectoral motility that may respond to the mild laxative action of complex carbohydrate, rather than simply the result of a 'fibre' deficient diet (Cummings, 1984).

15.4 ROLE OF COMPLEX CARBO-HYDRATES IN CONSTIPATION

Wheat bran and other bulk laxatives containing non-starch polysaccharides are not digested in the small intestine, but act on the colon to increase stool weight and frequency, to make the stool softer and bulkier and to reduce whole gut transit time (Manning & Heaton, 1976; Burkitt et al., 1972). They are often very effective means of relieving the symptoms associated with patients with mild or moderate constipation but are ineffective in patients with severe constipation, who often have serious neuromuscular incoordination.

Preston and Lennard Jones (1986) observed that only 9 out of 58 women with severe slow transit constipation improved on adding wheat bran to their diets; most patients were already ingesting a large amount of dietary 'fibre' and said that bran had no effect or made their symptoms worse.

Meta analysis of the data from 20 studies (Muller-Lissner, 1988) showed that:

(i) stool output and transit time responded less to 'fibre' supplementation in constipated patients than in normal subjects and

(ii) treatment of constipated patients with 'fibre' often failed to return transit time and stool output to normal.

15.5 HOW DO COMPLEX CARBO-HYDRATES WORK IN THE COLON?

The mechanism of the laxative action of bran and other types of 'fibre' on the colon is not established.

15.5.1 Bulking hypothesis

Wheat bran and bulk laxatives containing complex carbohydrates that are not digested in the small intestine make the stool softer and bulkier. How does this occur? Bannister et al. (1987) recently showed that small spheres mimicking faecal pellets are much more difficult to expel from the rectum than larger spheres. Plant cell walls may resist breakdown by bacteria; the associated polysaccharides adsorb and retain water. Complex carbohydrates also stimulate microbial cell growth, resulting in a greater faecal bacterial cell mass (see Chapter 8). Fermentation of polysaccharides releases gases which may be trapped in colonic contents, contributing to their bulk and plasticity. The increased colonic bulk promotes colonic propulsion, which leads to reduced water absorption by the colon and the easier passage of bulkier and softer stools.

In a recent study comparing the action of a number of polysaccharides with their fermentation characteristics, Tomlin and Read (1988a) suggested that polysaccharides that resisted breakdown increased stool weight, while those that were fermented, accelerated colonic transit. The best bulk laxatives appeared to be those, like bran and ispaghula, that retained their structure but were also fermented. An increase in the volume of colonic contents will distend the colon, stimulating colonic propulsion and secretion (Chauve et al., 1976).

15.5.2 Irritation hypothesis

There may, however, be other mechanisms of action. It is possible, for example, that the lignified particles of bran irritate the colonic epithelium, activating nervous reflexes that cause colonic secretion and propulsion. This may explain why coarse bran is a more potent laxative than the same amount of finely milled bran (Brodribb and Groves, 1978).

In support of this idea, Tomlin and Read (1988b) have recently observed that the addition of 15g/day of small segments of polyvinyl tubing to the diet increases stool mass and frequency, improves stool consistency and accelerates whole gut transit to the same extent as the addition of an equivalent weight of coarse wheat bran.

15.5.3 Colonic distension hypothesis

An interesting study from Italy (Marzio et al., 1985) showed that treatment of severe painless constipation with bran restored the reduced anal relaxation in response to rectal distension, but not the blunted rectal sensitivity. The mechanism of this novel finding is fascinating. Do the products of fermentation, or the particular nature of the bran, modulate responses to colonic distension? Or does the ready expulsion of the faeces allow the stretch receptors to re-adapt to lower rectal volumes?

CHAPTER 16
CLINICAL IMPLICATIONS OF COMPLEX CARBOHYDRATES FOR COLONIC DIVERTICULOSIS

16.1 WHAT IS COLONIC DIVERTICULOSIS?

This is a common condition in Western populations and it most frequently affects the left side of the colon, especially the sigmoid colon. Diverticulosis of the right colon is uncommon except in the Eastern populations. Colonic diverticula are of a pulsion type, ie a pouch of mucus membrane projecting through the intestinal muscular layer into the surrounding fat. These occur on the underside of the colon usually at the point of penetration of the main blood vessels (Morson and Dawson, 1972).

Colonic diverticulosis may be subdivided into 3 groups:

i) asymptomatic diverticulosis. This is present in a proportion of the population who never seek medical care, and is generally a normal consequence of ageing.
ii) symptomatic diverticulosis. These patients experience pain which is relieved by the passing of small ribbony stools. It is associated with increased intracolonic pressure,
iii) complicated diverticulosis. This includes fistula, haemorrhage and perforation.

16.2 POSSIBLE CAUSES OF COLONIC DIVERTICULOSIS

The development of colonic diverticular disease may progress in a number of ways. There may be changes in the colonic wall which are a feature of the ageing process (Watters *et al.*, 1985). On the other hand, prolonged increased intraluminal pressure in the sigmoid colon may lead to pulsion diverticula developing there (Painter, 1975).

16.2.1 Age

Colonic diverticulosis is a benign condition associated with an elderly population and should be regarded as a frequent concomitant of the ageing process. The condition is rare before the age of 30 years, but a third of the population have diverticulosis by the 6th decade and 50 per cent by the 9th decade (Painter, 1975). It is therefore possible that the increased incidence of colonic diverticulosis with age is secondary to a decline in the mechanical integrity of the colonic wall. There is a thickening of the circular and longitudinal muscle coats along with a progressive increase in the amount of collagen, elastin and reticular tissue of the colon wall (Whyteway and Morson, 1985).

Mechanical properties of the colon depend on the strength, stiffness and toughness of the individual elements, on their juxtaposition and their interaction. These viscoelastic properties give the colon expansibility, strength, low dissipation and maintenance of shape. The colonic tissue will stretch up to breaking point, but will resume its original length when stretched within discrete limits (Watters *et al.*, 1985). It has also been shown that the collagen fibrils in diverticulosis are similar to those of older individuals without diverticulosis (Thomson *et al.*, 1987). This suggests that the diverticulosis may be due to an enhanced ageing process in the colonic mucosa.

16.2.2 Increased colonic pressure

Painter (1975) and Arfwidsson (1954) both showed that the segmenting contractions which mix the colonic contents of the sigmoid colon were greater in patients with diverticular disease than in control subjects. Increased contractions are probably the source of pain felt by subjects.

However, in individuals with diverticula but who are symptom free, the segmenting pressures are normal. Weinreich *et al.* (1977) found no relationship between increased colonic segmenting patterns in the colon outlined by barium enema examination and high pressure activity in the colon. Weinreich and Andersen (1976) showed that there was no correlation between the presence of the diverticula and high pressure activity. This suggests that diverticulosis is complicated by high pressure and indicates that high pressure is not one of the causes of the condition.

16.2.3 Deficiency of dietary 'fibre'

Painter (1975) first suggested that colonic diverticulosis is due to a deficiency primarily of dietary 'fibre'. The colonic muscles need to contract strongly in order to transmit and expel the small stool associated with a 'fibre' deficient diet. The increased pressure within the segmented section of bowel may result in herniation at the vulnerable point where blood vessels enter the colonic wall.

16.2.3.1 Ecological comparisons

Accurate prevalence data are not available for sufficient populations to enable comparisons to be made between prevalence of diverticular disease and 'fibre' intakes. However, there are undoubtedly differences in prevalence of colonic diverticulosis between England, Wales and Scotland and between regions of Scotland. These are, to an extent, paralleled by differences in fruit and vegetable intake (Eastwood *et al.*, 1975; Eastwood *et al.*, 1977). In England, the disease is substantially less common in vegetarians (Gear *et al.*, 1979) and some vegetarians may eat twice as much dietary 'fibre' as the general population; they also pass substantially bulkier and softer stools (Davies *et al.*, 1985; Davies *et al.*, 1986). Diverticulosis is rare in black Africans but common in black Americans (Painter, 1985).

In Japan, 'fibre' intake has fallen steadily since the Second World War and autopsy surveys suggest that the prevalence of colonic diverticulosis has risen (Ohi, 1983).

16.2.3.2 Case-control studies

Case-control studies in Japan showed that people with colonic diverticulosis had been in the habit of eating less 'fibre' than matched healthy controls (Ohta *et al.*, 1985; Nagahashi *et al.*, 1985). The same is true of Greece where Manousos and co-workers (1985) reported a significant reduction in the relative risk of colonic diverticulosis associated with doubled consumption of four 'fibre'-rich items (brown bread, spinach, lettuce, cucumber).

16.2.3.3 Animal studies

Other evidence for the hypothesis comes from lifespan studies of rats eating different amounts of cereal 'fibre' who were monitored for development of colonic diverticulosis (Fisher *et al.*, 1985). There was a progressive increase in colon circumference in rats fed the 'low' fibre diet compared with rats fed the high 'fibre' stock diet. Although rats in all diet groups had diverticula, they were much smaller in the high 'fibre' group and were observed much later in the trial than those in the rats fed on the low 'fibre' diets. There was an inverse relationship with the incidence of diverticula in the rat and the dietary 'fibre' content of the diets.

16.3 COMPLEX CARBO-HYDRATES IN THE TREATMENT OF COLONIC DIVERTICULOSIS

Colonic diverticulosis has a special place in the annals of 'fibre' as it was the first disease in which a high 'fibre' intake was claimed to have a therapeutic role (Painter *et al.*, 1972). 'Fibre' treatment seemed logical because the leading theory for the pathogenesis of diverticulosis was that the colon 'ruptured itself' in its struggle to propel abnormally small, hard stools (Painter *et al.*, 1965; Painter and Burkitt, 1971). This theory has been tested in several ways and has survived (albeit with some reservations).

16.3.1 Effect of insoluble non-starch polysaccharides

If wheat bran is given to individuals with increased colonic pressure then the result is an increase in stool weight and a decrease in intracolonic pressure (Findlay *et al.*, 1974). In general, wheat bran increases stool weight by an average of 2.5g wet weight per gram 'fibre', whereas in diverticulosis the increase is of the order of of 0.9g wet weight faeces per gram 'fibre' (Muller Lissner, 1988).

Giving unprocessed wheat bran (16–20g) caused the stool weight to increase by 60g per day in normal controls, and by 17.5g in patients with colonic diverticulosis. The effect on the motility index in the diverticulosis patients was to decrease basal and food stimulated pressure (Findlay *et al.*, 1974).

The physical nature of the wheat bran is also important; coarse bran being more effective than fine bran (Kirwan *et al.*, 1974; Brodribb and Groves, 1978). The effectiveness of wheat bran in the treatment of symptomatic diverticulosis is not affected by the origin of the bran, whether it be Canadian Red Spring wheat which is used for bread making, or soft French wheat which is used for cakes (Smith *et al.*, 1981). Cooking may, however, decrease the potency of wheat bran on the colon (Wyman *et al.* 1976).

16.3.2 Effect of soluble non-starch polysaccharides

In contrast to wheat bran, ispaghula appeared to be better at increasing stool weight, but at the same time, it increased the basal motility index and had no effect on the food stimulated pressures (Eastwood *et al.*, 1978).

16.3.3 Effect of starches

The effect of starches in the treatment of colonic diverticulosis is an unexplored area. It will be interesting to see whether an increased intake of resistant starches can mimic any of the effects of the insoluble non-starch polysaccharides.

CHAPTER 17
CLINICAL IMPLICATIONS OF COMPLEX CARBOHYDRATES FOR COLORECTAL CANCER

17.1 BACKGROUND

The epidemiology of colorectal cancer has been reviewed in detail elsewhere (see Correa & Haenszel, 1978; Hill, 1980; Willett, 1989). The following represents a brief summary of the background epidemiology and the detailed justification of the statements made can be found in the literature cited above.

The prevalence of colorectal cancer is high in North America, North and West Europe, Australasia and the River Plate region of South America and is relatively low in Africa, Asia and the Andean countries of South and Central America (Table 17.1). Within Europe, the prevalence of the disease is higher in the west and north than in the south and the east (Table 17.1). Within the British Isles, the prevalence is much higher in Scotland and in Ireland than in the south and east of England.

Studies of groups migrating between and within countries and of cultural and religious groups living within the same geographical region (Table 17.1) have led to the general conclusion that:

(i) genetic factors are not major determinants of the risk of colorectal cancer in a population (although they may be very important determinants of risk in an individual);

(ii) the most important risk factors in a population are therefore environmental;

(iii) the cultural (or chosen) environment is more important than the physical (or shared) environment. The physical environment includes such factors as geography, climate, air pollution etc, all factors that are, of necessity, shared with all others in the same community. The cultural environment includes diet, personal hygiene, smoking and other use of drugs etc – those aspects of the environment that are chosen and which are not necessarily shared with anyone else in the local community.

The aspect of the culture that has been associated with the risk of colorectal carcinogenesis by most epidemiologists is diet, but there is little agreement on the aspect of diet most strongly incriminated.

17.2 ECOLOGICAL COMPARISONS

17.2.1 Early studies

Much of the early work on the relation between diet and colorectal cancer involved correlation of the incidence of mortality of colorectal cancer with nutritional data from the same populations. For example Drasar and Irving (1973) compared the statistics from 37 countries, Armstrong and Doll (1975) compared 32 countries whilst Gregor et al. (1969) studied 28 countries. In these and other such correlations the cancer statistics used were those compiled by the IARC (see Doll et al., 1970) or by Segi and Kurihara (1972). The information on nutritional intake was taken from the statistics assembled by the Food and Agriculture Organisation (1969). These are based on food sold in shops and take no account of other food sources (eg home produced food) or of food wastage. Furthermore the populations used to compile the food

Table 17.1 Colorectal cancer in various countries

Area	Incidence		Area	Incidence	
	Colon	**Rectum**		**Colon**	**Rectum**
Europe			**Africa**		
(West)					
France	19.9	21.0	Nigeria	0.4	0.4
Switzerland	22.9	16.2	Zimbabwe	1.9	0.8
West Germany	16.5	12.9	Senegal	0.6	1.5
United Kingdom			South Africa		
Birmingham	16.3	16.7	White	13.1	4.2
E. Scotland	23.1	14.6	Black	3.8	0.5
			Coloured	2.2	1.7
(East)					
Hungary	9.7	16.1	**North America**		
East Germany	10.7	13.3			
Poland					
Warsaw	11.6	9.4	Canada (BC)	21.5	14.9
Rural	5.2	5.6	USA (California)		
Czechoslovakia	8.5	13.1	White	25.6	14.6
			Japanese	26.7	15.3
(North)			New Mexico		
Denmark	19.0	17.0	Hispanic	10.9	6.0
Sweden	16.3	10.9	Amerindian	5.6	5.2
Finland	8.3	8.7			
(South)			**S and Central America**		
Spain	6.6	6.2			
Yugoslavia	7.7	11.2	Colombia	4.5	3.4
Romania	5.5	6.8	Jamaica	8.7	3.7
Italy	19.9	15.7	Cuba	7.1	4.4
			Puerto Rico	7.6	6.2
Asia			Antilles	7.4	4.1
Japan	8.3	9.2	**Australasia**		
India (Bombay)	3.5	4.5			
China (Shanghai)	6.7	9.0	Australia (NSW)	21.5	12.8
Israel					
Jews	13.9	13.1	New Zealand		
non-Jews	3.3	3.1	Maori	9.0	9.8
Singapore			Non-Maori	25.5	16.1
Chinese	14.9	14.2			
Malay	4.7	6.6			
Indian	8.6	6.6			

(data are per 100 000 males per annum, age standardised to the world population)

intake statistics in a given country usually differ from those used by the Cancer Registry whose tables will have been used by IARC or by Segi and Kurihara (1972).

Drasar and Irving (1973) correlated the intake of foods rich in complex carbohydrates with the mortality from colorectal cancer. They observed a weak inverse correlation with cereal intake and saw a compensating positive correlation for potatoes and starchy root foods, nuts, and green leafy vegetables. Armstrong and Doll (1975) attempted to estimate the amount of dietary 'fibre' in the diets of populations and observed no correlation with either colon or rectal cancer incidence or mortality. There have been many more such studies using statistical methods of increasing sophistication. However these studies have failed to produce convincing evidence, one way or another, that complex carbohydrates are important aetiological agents in this disease.

Two major weaknesses in ecological studies have already been identified, namely the inherent 'softness' of the data being correlated and the fact that the two sets of data being correlated are usually based on different samples within the population. A further major limitation is that, when carrying out the simple correlation between diet and colorectal cancer risk, it is assumed that all the other ways in which the populations differ are unimportant. This has still to be demonstrated, but can be controlled for in part by comparing populations within a country. Such a study was carried out in Hong Kong (Hill *et al.*, 1979). In three socio-economic groups there was a positive correlation between the risk of colorectal cancer and the intake of all food classes (starchy foods, cereals, rice, meat, fats, vegetables etc). Unfortunately, non-dietary variables were not controlled within the different groups.

17.2.2 More recent studies

The early ecological studies, which tended to show a strong correlation with dietary fat or meat and only weak correlations with complex carbohydrates, were heavily criticised because of the lack of good food tables outside of Europe and North America. This made the attempted quantitation of the intake of complex carbohydrates even less precise than the other nutritional information. As a consequence, there were renewed attempts to develop new analytical tools and to apply them to the analysis of the diets of populations.

One of the first such studies was the IARC study of four populations in Scandinavia, two each in Finland and Denmark (IARC Working Party, 1982). The study showed little relation between the incidence of colorectal cancer and the intake of total non-starch polysaccharide but showed a highly significant inverse correlation with the pentosan fraction. This study has been widely quoted but nevertheless, it must be recognised that the populations investigated were small (only 30 people in each), the number of fractions of non-starch polysaccharides was large (making it likely that 'significant' differences might arise by chance) and the differences between the populations seen were small.

The same group of workers also compared the 15 hospital regions in England and Wales using the same methods (Bingham *et al.*, 1979) and again observed a highly significant inverse correlation with the pentosan fraction. Again, the differences in intake between the various regions were small, but at this stage the level of significance seen in two successive studies was generally regarded as convincing. However following a re-evaluation of the assay methods, these results were later retracted (Bingham *et al.*, 1985); this presumably also calls into question the conclusions from the earlier IARC Scandinavian study.

Further evidence from populations has cast doubt on the inverse correlation between complex carbohydrate intake and colorectal cancer. It has been shown that the intake of non-starch polysaccharide by Indian and Japanese populations (both with a low risk of colorectal cancer) is lower than that of either the British or the Americans (Bingham *et al.*, 1985). In a study of four populations in South Africa (white, black, coloured and Indian), there was a positive correlation between the risk of colorectal cancer and the intake of foods rich in non-starch polysaccharide (Bingham *et al.*, 1985). This was also reported in the study of Hong Kong populations (Hill *et al.*, 1979). In both of these investigations, it was noted that the populations with the highest income (and with the highest colorectal cancer risk) simply consumed more of all types of food than did the low income group.

17.2.3 Interrelationships with other components of diets

A rationalisation of the results of the early ecological studies that was widely accepted in the earlier part of the decade was that a high risk of the disease was associated with the consumption of fat and meat. In populations with a high consumption of fat/meat (the 'at-risk' population) there was an inverse relation between cancer risk and the intake of complex carbohydrates; in populations with a low intake of fat/meat (the low risk populations) there was no relation between risk and complex carbohydrate intake.

In recent years, the possible contribution of resistant starch to the complex carbohydrate entering the colon has been reassessed. It has been realised that, under certain conditions (Englyst *et al.*, 1987a), resistant starch may contribute 90% or more of the total complex carbohydrate reaching the colon. All estimates of the latter are probably low, often by more than an order of magnitude. Under these circumstances, it is difficult to see how a protective role for complex carbohydrates can be verified from ecological studies.

17.3 RETROSPECTIVE ANALYTICAL STUDIES

17.3.1 Limitations of case-control studies

In general, the data from case-control studies on the relation between colorectal cancer risk and the intake of complex carbohydrates is even more confused than is that from the ecological studies and is almost certainly less reliable. The supposed strength of the case-control approach is that, in theory at least, all of the possible confounding factors can be controlled and the investigation is then confined to the two variables to be compared.

In the case of colorectal cancer and diet this can be extremely difficult. Colorectal cancer is normally diagnosed on the basis of its major symptoms, namely diarrhoea, constipation and abdominal pain and blood in the stools. All of these are common in non-malignant disease and are experienced by most people at least for short periods during their lifetime. Because of their familiarity, these symptoms rarely cause alarm initially and in consequence there is a long lag period between the onset of symptoms and the diagnosis of disease. During this lag period, patients may attempt to make themselves more comfortable by changing their diet, often subconsciously and in a way that they would find difficult to document.

Immediately before hospitalisation, there may be either a period of fear or relief during which eating habits could change in any direction. In consequence, the diet of the patient is in part determined by the disease rather than the converse. It is necessary, then, to determine the presymptoms diet by recall techniques that are notoriously inaccurate. Ideally, more studies should be planned on patients without symptoms who are picked out by population screening.

17.3.2 Results from case-control studies

It is hardly surprising that with the inbuilt inaccuracies outlined above, almost all dietary items have been correlated with the disease. In particular, foods rich in complex carbohydrate have been correlated both positively and inversely (Table 17.2) although most studies showed no relation with colorectal cancer. These have been reviewed recently by Riboli (1987). A solution to the problem of the effect of

Table 17.2   Case-control studies relating colorectal cancer risk to intake of complex carbohydrates

Source of complex carbohydrates	Positive correlation	Inverse correlation	No relation
Cereal 'fibre'	1	0	1
Vegetable 'fibre'	0	0	3
All 'fibre'	2	2	4
Vegetables	1	4	0
Starches	2	0	1

(From Riboli, 1987)

symptoms is to choose asymptomatic patients and this has been done by Bristol *et al.* (1985). They observed a weak protective effect of complex carbohydrates, a weak positive correlation with fat and a stronger positive correlation with refined sugar and with starches.

In general, the conclusion to be drawn from the case-control studies is that very little has been learned about the relation between any component of the diet and colorectal cancer by this approach. In the case of complex carbohydrates the situation has been further confused by the recent realisation of the importance of resistant starch (see Chapter 4).

17.4 PROSPECTIVE ANALYTICAL STUDIES

All of the problems associated with the case-control approach can be avoided by the prospective study of cohorts. A large population of healthy persons is assembled, the parameters of interest measured and the cohort followed for sufficient time to yield the number of cases required for statistical analysis. In the United Kingdom, a population of 8,000 persons aged 50–70 years at recruitment would be expected to yield 50–80 cases of colorectal cancer if followed for 10 years. Clearly cohort studies are lengthy, extremely expensive and involve heavy analytical loads.

The only study of this type currently in progress relating diet to cancer risk is being conducted in Japan, a low-incidence country and involves a cohort of more than 250,000 persons (Hirayama, 1985). Yellow-green leafy vegetables have been found to be highly protective against colorectal cancer, but there has been no indication yet of the contribution of their complex carbohydrates to this protection.

17.5 ANIMAL STUDIES

The advantage of a good animal model is that it permits experimental studies of carcinogenesis to be made under strictly controlled conditions in genetically homogenous strains of animals fed standardised diets and using strictly applied protocols. Highly invasive techniques can be used that would be totally unacceptable to patients and, for example, endoscopy can be carried out at a frequency that permits close monitoring of the formation, growth and development of precancerous lesions and their progression to malignancy. Animal model studies would have been expected, therefore, to have made an impressive contribution to our understanding of the role of diet in colorectal carcinogenesis. However, although good models of colorectal carcinogenesis are available and have proved to be of great value to those studying the cell biology, the histopathenogenesis, the cell kinetics, the immunology and the chemotherapeutic treatment of colorectal cancer, they have provided no clear answers to the questions concerning the causation of the human disease.

The animal models used for colorectal cancer have been well reviewed by Nigro

Table 17.3 The effect of source of complex carbohydrates, initiating carcinogen and sex of the rats on experimental colon carcinogenesis

Type of non-starch polysaccharide	Carcinogen	Rat model Route	Sex	Effect
Cellulose (20% or 40%)	AOM	Sc	M	None
Cellulose	DMH	Sc	M	Protects
Cellulose (15%)	DMH	Oral	M	None
Hemicellulose	DMH	Sc	M	None
Hemicellulose	DMH	Oral	M	Protects
Bran (20%)	DMH	Oral	M	Protects
Bran (20%)	DMH	Sc	M	None
Bran	DMH	Sc		Promotes
Bran (20%)	DMH	Oral	F	None
Carrot (20%)	DMH	Sc	M	Promotes
Pectin (15%)	DMU	IR	F	None
Pectin (15%)	AOM	Sc	F	Protects
Pectin	DMH	Sc	M	Promotes

Sc = subcutaneously; IR = Intra-rectal
(Updated from review by Kritchevsky, 1986)

(1985). A wide range of carcinogens is available to induce colorectal cancer in rodents including aflatoxin, cycasin, dimethylhydrazine (DMH), azoxymethane (AOM), N-methyl nitrosourea (NMU), N-methyl-N-nitro-N-nitrosoguanidine (MNNG) and dimethylaminobiphenyl (DMAB). NMU and MNNG are direct-acting carcinogens and so are usually administered by direct injection into the rectum; cycasin and DMAB are usually given orally and DMH and AOM are usually given subcutaneously. Most of the work has been carried out using rats. Guinea pigs are much more resistant than rats, mice or hamsters to the carcinogenic action of AOM or DMH, and there is a wide range in sensitivity to DMH amongst strains of rats (eg Sprague-Dawley rats are much more sensitive than are Wistar rats). The most commonly used model is the rat treated with DMH or AOM.

Table 17.3 illustrates the confused state of the literature. Clearly almost any hypothesis regarding the role of any class of complex carbohydrate or any food source of carbohydrate, whether postulating promotion or protection against tumorigenesis, can be supported or refuted by a judicious selection from the evidence. At present, therefore, the animal models contribute little that is constructive to the debate on the aetiology of colorectal cancer.

17.6 STUDIES OF PRECANCEROUS LESIONS

Colorectal cancer is a multistage process (Hill *et al.*, 1978). The first stage is the formation of a small benign adenoma, followed by adenoma growth, then the development of increasingly severe epithelial dysplasia and finally progression to malignancy. Since the epidemiology of the precursor benign adenoma differs from that of the final carcinoma, it is likely that the role of dietary factors in the formation of adenomas differs from that in the stages of progression to carcinoma. There have been few studies of the relation between complex carbohydrate intake and adenoma formation. In a study carried out in Marseilles (Macquart-Moulin *et al.*, 1986) there was an inverse relation to complex carbohydrate intake (and a positive relation to sugar intake); similar results were reported from a study in Oslo (Hoff *et al.*, 1986). Currently, there is a large ongoing study of the relation between diet and both the presence and the size of colorectal adenomas organised by the European Research Group for Cancer Prevention (ECP) and described by Faivre *et al.* (1985). In addition there is a similar study in progress in Nottingham (Little, personal communication). These studies of the individual stages of colorectal carcinogenesis are potentially likely to yield clearer insights into the role of diet than are the case-control or population studies of the overall process of carcinogenesis, and provide the best opportunity for resolving the question of the relation between intake of complex carbohydrate and the risk of colorectal cancer.

17.7 MECHANISMS BY WHICH COMPLEX CARBO-HYDRATES COULD PROTECT AGAINST CANCER

If complex carbohydrates protect against colon carcinogenesis Burkitt (1969) has proposed a number of mechanisms by which this might occur. These include dilution of colonic contents, more rapid rate of transit giving less time for carcinogen action and less substrate for bacterial production of carcinogen. Since then, additional hypotheses have been proposed including the role of butyrate in maintaining mucosal health, and the role of short chain fatty acids (SCFAs) in stimulating bacterial growth and utilisation of colonic ammonia.

These postulated mechanisms have been discussed critically elsewhere (Hill and Fernandez, 1990; Hill, 1987). There is good evidence that stool bulking results in a dilution of the colonic contents and this should decrease the risk associated with luminal carcinogens or tumour promoters. The butyrate theory is initially attractive but there is no evidence in its favour; further, the *decreased* risk of colorectal cancer in germ-free rodents treated with a range of initiators and in whom there is no colonic butyrate is crushing evidence against a key role for this SCFA in protection against tumorigenesis. Similarly, the evidence is against the involvement of the other proposed mechanisms in protecting against colorectal cancer.

CHAPTER 18
CLINICAL IMPLICATIONS OF COMPLEX CARBOHYDRATES FOR FOOD INTOLERANCE

18.1 INTRODUCTION

During the present decade there has been growing interest and controversy about the role of food intolerance in the pathogenesis of several separate clinical conditions ranging from migraine to functional diarrhoea. Many different types of food have been implicated and several mechanisms for the intolerance suggested. Complex carbohydrates have been implicated in several of the conditions but their role in the pathogenesis of the conditions remains to be determined and it is possible that, in many cases, other constituents of the food are responsible for the symptoms produced. There is some evidence to suggest that some patients with irritable bowel syndrome may react to certain complex carbohydrates by changes in their colonic bacterial metabolism.

18.2 CLINICAL CONDITIONS THAT ARE OR MIGHT BE DUE TO FOOD INTOLERANCE

18.2.1 Coeliac disease

The link between gluten and coeliac disease is well accepted and requires no further elucidation. Wheat starch is not considered to be toxic and low gluten foods may be manufactured by removing the gluten from wheat and replacing it by other proteins.

18.2.2 Irritable bowel syndrome

The irritable bowel syndrome (IBS) is a collection of poorly understood clinical conditions which produce gastrointestinal symptoms but in which no pathological abnormality is apparent (see Chapter 15). There is now considerable evidence that one factor involved in IBS is food intolerance, particularly to complex carbohydrates (see Table 18.1). (Alun Jones et al., 1982; Hunter, 1985; Nanda et al., 1989).

18.2.3 Crohn's disease

The link between Crohn's disease and carbohydrate intolerance is more controversial. It is now generally accepted that this condition improves after treatment with total parenteral nutrition, and elemental or polymeric diets (Hunter, 1985). Although many patients have achieved remission after such feeding, considerable doubt exists as to the best way of maintaining this improvement. Many clinicians continue with corticosteroids and other medications, but some have claimed that remission may be prolonged by reintroducing foods one by one and subsequently avoiding any which provoke symptoms (Alun Jones et al., 1985). This procedure is difficult and time consuming but remission rates of over 60% after 2 years have been claimed and are superior to the results of other medical treatments. Direct comparison in controlled trials with corticosteroids is awaited. Lutz (1985) has similarly reported prolongation of remission in patients on a low carbohydrate diet.

18.2.4 Migraine

Although migraine has long been linked to the ingestion of certain foods, particularly those containing tyramine such as cheese, red wine and chocolate, recent studies (eg, Egger et al., 1983) have shown that foods rich in complex carbohydrates are also important.

18.2.5 Hyperactivity in children

This is another controversial subject. Initial dietary studies in the United States implicated food additives as a possible cause of hyperactivity, but work at Great Ormond Street Hospital suggested that wheat and other cereals might be equally important (Egger et al., 1985).

18.3 POSSIBLE MECHANISMS OF FOOD INTOLERANCE

18.3.1 Immunological effects

Although reactions to food are widely referred to as 'food allergy', it is clear that most patients with these conditions do not have any immunological abnormality. Thus normal concentrations of IgE have been reported by several workers (Lessof et al., 1980, Alun Jones et al., 1982, Smith et al., 1985). Skin prick or RAST tests are of little or no value in establishing whether food intolerance is really present and the incidence of atopic disease in this group is no greater than that of the general population (10%) (Hunter et al., 1985). Furthermore, the time course of the food reaction is slower than classical type I reactions (Egger et al., 1983) and there is no increase in immune complexes, eosinophil count or plasma histamine after food challenge (Alun Jones et al., 1982).

There are undoubtedly patients who develop symptoms as a result of a classical IgE mediated reaction (Amlot et al., 1987). Bentley et al. (1983) found that all their patients with IBS who had food intolerances were atopic. However, other groups have found that patients such as these are unusual (Hunter et al., 1985). Gerrard (1979) has drawn attention to the phenomenon of 'Delayed Food Allergy' in which symptoms develop slowly after administration of large amounts of the food in question, IgE concentrations are not raised and the incidence of atopic disorders is not greater than in the general population. Although it is still possible that there may be some unsuspected local immunological abnormality in the gut, it seems likely that the investigation of other recognised mechanisms of food intolerance may prove more rewarding.

18.3.2 Chemical effects

Examples of chemicals which are commonly contained in food and which may produce idiosyncratic reactions are monosodium glutamate, tyramine and histamine (both in cheese), phenylthylamine (chocolate), octopamine (citrus fruits) and food additives (eg annatto, tartrazine).

18.3.3 Effects on enzyme systems

Many dietary and environmental chemicals which are potentially toxic are metabolised by important enzyme systems eg,

(i)   monoamine oxidase (MAO) deactivates excess tyramine; foods such as yeast, cheese and red wine which are high in tyramine can cause problems if MAO levels are low.

(ii) the administration of acarbose, an inhibitor of glucosidase which leads to delayed degradation of starch in the small intestine, has been shown to produce increased flatulence and diarrhoea in normal human volunteers (Scheppach et al., 1988).

18.3.4 Microbiological effects

One of the best known examples of food intolerance in clinical practice is seen in patients with hepatic cirrhosis who develop encephalopathy associated with the ingestion of protein. Intestinal bacteria metabolise the protein and produce compounds which enter the systemic circulation through numerous collateral vessels developing as a result of portal hypertension. Treatment with antibiotics such as neomycin is highly effective and it is clear that the role of the bacteria in breaking down dietary protein to toxic amino-compounds is of great importance.

18.4 THE MICRO-BIOLOGICAL HYPOTHESIS FOR INTOLERANCE TO COMPLEX CARBO-HYDRATES

18.4.1 Background to the hypothesis

The suggestion that toxic products might be derived by bacterial fermentation of foods, including carbohydrates as well as protein, in the colon was first proposed by Metchnikoff (1907). He suggested that constipation led to disease because of auto-intoxication by chemicals which were not eliminated sufficiently quickly. This theory is no longer accepted but a modern refinement of Metchnikoff's theory has been proposed, viz: residues from specific foods, particularly complex carbohydrates may be metabolised in the colon to form toxic compounds if changes occur to the healthy microflora (Hunter, 1990).

18.4.2 Evidence for the hypothesis

18.4.2.1 Complex carbohydrates can pass into the colon
It is now appreciated that as much as 40 g starch, 4 g fat, 14 g protein and 20 g non-starch polysaccharides enter the colon each day in normal individuals (Stephen, 1985). This provides a rich substrate for fermentation by the bacterial flora and it is known that short chain fatty acids and ammonia may be produced along with soluble waste products and hydrogen (see Chapter 8).

Since hydrogen can be measured in expired air, this has provided a simple means of indicating that a number of compounds contained in food may reach the colon in both normal subjects and patients with functional gut disorders. These include sugars, such as sucrose (Bond *et al.*, 1981), fructose (Ravich *et al.*, 1983) and sorbitol (Hyams, 1983). Levitt *et al.* (1986) have demonstrated considerable increases in hydrogen excretion from the ingestion of oats, wholewheat, potatoes, corn and baked beans but rice had only a minimal effect. Some foods which result in a large increase in hydrogen are those which have been found to be associated with food intolerance in many IBS patients but there is not a clear-cut relationship (Table 18.1).

18.4.2.2 Symptoms of food intolerance can be provoked by complex carbohydrates and then disappear on their withdrawal from the diet
References in American literature earlier this century (Duke, 1921; Duke, 1923; Rowe, 1928) have been confirmed in recent years by several groups of workers, (Lessof *et al.*, 1980; Alun Jones *et al.*, 1982; Bentley *et al.*, 1983; Farah *et al.*, 1985; Smith *et al.*, 1985; Nanda *et al.*, 1989). Some patients with IBS found that their symptoms disappeared completely when they avoided the foods which upset them and this effect could be confirmed by double-blind challenges using disguised foods administered by naso-gastric tube. No specific diagnostic criteria are available for the detection of food intolerance and the choice of patients to undergo dietary studies remains subjective. Patients responding to dietary exclusions of this sort are more prone to suffer from abdominal pain and diarrhoea rather than from constipation. Differences in the selection of patients seem the likely reason for wide variations in the reported frequency of food intolerance in this group, ranging from 6 to over 60%.

Table 18.1 Percentage of patients with Irritable Bowel Syndrome who are intolerant to particular foods

Cereals	(%)	Banana	11	Sprouts	18
Wheat	60	Rhubarb	12	Peas	17
Corn	44			Carrots	15
Oats	34	Fish		Lettuce	15
Rye	30	White fish	10	Leeks	15
Barley	24	Shell fish	10	Broccoli	14
Rice	15			Soya beans	13
		Meat		Spinach	13
Dairy Products		Beef	16		
Milk	44	Pork	14	Miscellaneous	
Cheese	39	Chicken	13	Coffee	33
Butter	25	Lamb	11	Eggs	26
Yoghurt	24			Tea	25
		Vegetables		Chocolate	22
Fruit		Onions	22	Nuts	22
Citrus	24	Potatoes	20	Preservatives	20
Apples	12	Cabbage	19		

(From Levitt et al., 1986)

18.4.2.3 Abnormalities of the colonic microflora are present in patients with symptoms of intolerance to complex carbohydrates

Sufficient substrate may enter the colon from the small intestine to provide a basis for both bacterial fermentation and for the possible provocation of symptoms in susceptible individuals. It may be that there are either differences in the colonic bacteria or differences in the relative input of substrate in patients exhibiting food intolerance. The composition of bacteria in the colon is complex (see Chapter 8); each gram of faeces may contain 10^{12} anaerobes and 10^6 aerobes and the assessment of changes in the faecal flora thus presents an enormous task. A number of observations have suggested that the colonic bacteria may be important in food intolerance. Large quantities of food are required to produce reactions and the symptoms may develop slowly (Gerrard, 1979). This time scale is fully consistent with the hypothesis that food residue must be metabolised by colonic bacteria in order to produce toxic compounds. Furthermore, it is known that diarrhoea may follow attacks of gastroenteritis or the administration of antibiotics (Alun Jones et al., 1984). Both these events are known to be capable of inducing changes in the colonic bacteria (Van Der Waaij, 1983).

Recent studies have suggested that the bacteria of the colon may be abnormal in patients with IBS. Bayliss et al. (1984) confirmed an earlier report by Balsari et al. (1982) of high counts of facultative anaerobes in these patients and further showed that the counts increased after double blind challenge with the foods to which the patients were intolerant. It seems unlikely that the facultative anaerobe count itself is the crucial abnormality in the faecal bacteria of food intolerant IBS as a larger scale study failed to demonstrate any significant difference between the two groups. However, in a prospective study of patients developing bowel symptoms after hysterectomy there was a correlation between symptom score and the facultative anaerobe count in the stools (Bayliss et al., 1986). Further studies on the colonic bacteria of patients with IBS and food intolerance are required.

18.4.3 Limitations of the hypothesis

At present, the hypothesis that foods rich in complex carbohydrates can cause symptoms of food intolerance by their effects on the colonic bacteria must be regarded as speculative. The hypothesis would be strengthened if experiments could demonstrate:

(i)   which particular components of these foods are responsible
(ii) whether the changes in colonic bacteria are primary in nature or result from differences in the input of substrate
(iii) whether the symptoms of intolerance result from the changes in the bacteria themselves or from changes in their products of fermentation
(iv) whether the effects of complex carbohydrates reflect their chemical structures or their physical or mechanical properties
(v)   whether the observed changes in colonic bacteria are related directly to the effects of diarrhoea.

It is also important to demonstrate that the intolerance is not caused as a secondary effect of malabsorption of certain foods higher up the gastrointestinal tract. Further evidence for the hypothesis would be provided if bacterial metabolites were identified from patients after ingestion of foods which provoke symptoms but were not produced by normal people eating the same diet.

CHAPTER 19
CLINICAL IMPLICATIONS OF COMPLEX CARBOHYDRATES FOR DENTAL CARIES

19.1 INTRODUCTION

Dental caries is predominantly a disease of childhood; in 1983 49% of children aged 5 had one or more decayed teeth, which rose to 93% of 15 year old children. The average number of decayed permanent teeth is 5.9 per child. The recent decrease in caries prevalence seen over the last 15 to 20 years appears to have slowed or halted in children (Rugg-Grunn *et al.*, 1988) despite increased use of fluorides. Adults between 35 and 44 years have, on average, 19 decayed, missing or filled (DMF) teeth (Todd *et al.*, 1982).

19.2 METABOLISM OF COMPLEX CARBO-HYDRATES BY PLAQUE BACTERIA

Dental caries results from demineralisation of the tooth enamel by acid. Acid is produced as a result of the fermentation of sugars by plaque bacteria. Most dietary sugars are easily metabolised by the plaque bacteria and are thus potentially cariogenic. In addition, some forms of dietary starch can be broken down in the mouth by salivary amylase to sugars which can then be fermented by the plaque bacteria to form acid. A demineralised tooth is, however, capable of being remineralised if the duration, severity and frequency of demineralisation are not overwhelming. The acidogenic potential of a food is not therefore equivalent to its cariogenic potential.

Various methods are used to assess the cariogenicity of different foods. These include human epidemiological and observational studies, human intervention studies, animal experiments, *in vivo* measurements of plaque acidity, *in vivo* enamel slab experiments and *in vitro* incubation experiments. The evidence relating complex carbohydrates, and in particular starch, with dental caries will be reviewed according to the experimental evidence in Sections 19.3 to 19.5. The non-starch polysaccharides, not being digestible by salivary amylase are non-cariogenic but their physical structure may affect the availability of other fermentable carbohydrates, and in some circumstances, they can have a protective effect. Other protective factors associated with foods rich in complex carbohydrates, although not due to the complex carbohydrates themselves, will be mentioned, in Section 19.6.

19.3 HUMAN EPIDEMIO-LOGICAL STUDIES

Human observational studies are generally complicated by the reciprocal relationship between the consumption of simple sugars and complex carbohydrates. Epidemiological evidence on the intake of complex carbohydrates alone and dental caries is scarce, and it is often difficult to distinguish the effect of a high proportion of complex carbohydrates in the diet from that of a low proportion of simple carbohydrates.

19.3.1 Cross-cultural comparisons

A study comparing cereal availability and dental caries in 47 nations using data on cereal supplies, obtained from the Food and Agriculture Organisation and data on dental caries in 12-year old children from the World Health Organisation's Oral Epidemiology Bank, suggested an inverse association between total cereal consumption (wheat, rice, maize and others), expressed as a proportion of total energy intake, and caries score. In contrast, individual cereals related quite differently. The caries index increased with the supply of wheat, and decreased with the supply of maize and the availability of rice had no significant effect (Screebny, 1983).

Clearly these results could reflect something other than the consumption of cereals. The author himself suggested that one factor might be the different market economies of the various nations but the same pattern of association persisted in the more homogeneous group of developed nations in the study. It would be unwise to conclude that there is a direct causal relationship between low dietary intake of cereal and high dental caries prevalence until the variability is explained.

19.3.2 Studies of changing food patterns over a period of time

Populations who have changed from a traditionally high complex carbohydrate diet to one rich in refined sugar and flour provide an opportunity to study dental caries incidence against changing food habits.

In addition to the striking association observed between the consumption of sugar and the incidence of caries, a low caries prevalence is seen in groups whose diets contain a high intake of starch foods and a correspondingly low intake of sugar (Hardwick, 1960).

Several developing communities have also been studied over a period of time. Initial caries incidence, when the diets are high in starchy foods but low in sugars, has generally been slight. As diets have changed to include a higher proportion of refined sugar, the incidence of dental disease has increased quite dramatically (Fisher, 1968; Osborne and Noriskin, 1937).

Studies in Papua New Guinea, however, demonstrate that the consumption of a high starch diet (sago), low in sugars, does not guarantee an absence of caries. In this case the local habits, such as betel-chewing and micronutrient deficiencies have been considered more important in determining caries distribution (Schamschula *et al.*, 1978).

19.3.3 Within population comparisons

Studies within special population groups have tended to show that communities who habitually eat a diet low in simple sugars and high in complex carbohydrates have low caries scores. Obviously a number of factors could be involved and one, the frequency of intake, has not been taken into consideration in many studies (British Nutrition Foundation, 1987).

19.3.3.1 Hereditary Fructose Intolerance

Patients with Hereditary Fructose Intolerance form a population which habitually consumes a low-sugar, high-starch diet. Due to the absence of a liver enzyme (fructose 1–phosphate aldolase enzyme) these patients are unable to utilise fructose and, therefore, cannot tolerate sucrose. Starch and starchy foods such as bread and potatoes are well tolerated however since they are complex polymers of glucose. Although only limited evidence is available to date, it suggests that many individuals with this condition are caries-free and the majority certainly have a low caries level (Newburn *et al.*, 1980).

19.3.3.2 Diabetes

Diabetics also commonly have a low intake of simple sugars but maintain a normal intake of complex carbohydrates. Several studies have been undertaken to compare the caries and periodontal disease experience in diabetics and non-diabetics. These have shown contradictory results, but generally it would appear that the prevalence of dental caries amongst diabetics is low, while that of periodontal disease and plaque scores are moderate to high. Caries experience in children with well-monitored insulin dependent diabetes (IDDM) and a family history of diabetes is significantly lower than that of children with IDDM and no such family history (Galea *et al.*, 1986). This may reflect a lower exposure to sugars in those who live in an environment with other diabetics. The restricted intake of sugars may have a beneficial effect which outweighs the cariogenic effect of xerostomia and the increased content of glucose in saliva and gingival crevicular exudate seen in diabetics (Galea *et al.*, 1986).

19.3.4 Prospective studies

Prospective studies have an advantage in that the incidence of dental caries can be measured over the same time period as the dietary record. A prospective study by Rugg-Grunn *et al.* (1984) found no significant difference in the number of new DMF's between children on a high sugar/low starch diet and those on a low sugar/high starch diet.

19.4 HUMAN INTERVENTION STUDIES

The control groups of two important clinical studies consumed a high starch diet which was almost sugar-free. Subjects in the Vipeholm study developed virtually no new caries on the high starch diet (Gustaffson *et al.*, 1954) and the xylitol group of the Turku clinical trial who consumed significant amounts of starch, developed minimal new decay during the study period (Scheinin and Makinen, 1975) though there is the possibility that xylitol had a cariostatic effect. Frequency of intake was strictly controlled in these studies, itself an important factor.

19.5 EXPERIMENTAL STUDIES

19.5.1 Plaque acidity experiments

In vitro and *in vivo* experiments to examine the ability of a test food to be metabolised by plaque bacteria measure the acidogenic potential of a food rather than its cariogenic potential. The techniques can be modified to measure the amount of mineral which is dissolved by the acid. It is, however, impossible to reproduce exactly the conditions in the mouth and 'artificial mouths' cannot give accurate values of the cariogenicity of different foods.

Numerous studies have shown that starch degradation in the mouth will lead to acid production and to a drop below the critical value of pH5 which is necessary for demineralisation to occur (Edgar *et al.*, 1975; Rugg-Grunn 1978; Jensen and Schachtele, 1983). The total quantity of acid produced is also important in determining the amount of demineralisation which occurs. Plaque pH curves for starchy foods tend to show a more shallow but more prolonged reduction than those for a glucose solution.

Experiments investigating the demineralising effects of different foods have shown that starch does lead to less demineralisation than sucrose, glucose or lactose (Huang *et al.*, 1981).

19.5.2 Enamel slab experiments

Enamel slab experiments overcome some of the drawbacks of the artificial mouth. Intra-oral appliances holding slabs of enamel are worn for 1–4 weeks. The appliance is removed several times during the day and put in a solution of a food, and then re-inserted in the mouth. The main drawback is that the food is not eaten and so the stimulatory effects on saliva are not taken into account.

Results from these experiments have shown that the cariogenicity of cooked starch is about one quarter that of sucrose (Brudevold, 1985). Raw starch, in these experiments, appears to be non-cariogenic. Experiments have shown that solutions of cooked starch are rapidly hydrolysed *in vitro* by saliva. The hydrolysis of raw starch, however, is very much slower (Brudevold *et al.*, 1985).

The demineralising ability of the cooked starch solution could be related to its rapid hydrolysis and the consequent high concentrations of maltose in saliva (but see Section 19.5.3.2). The changes in the nature of the starch granules on heating may not only facilitate enzyme hydrolysis but make the starch more adherent and prolong contact time with the teeth.

19.5.2.1 Factors affecting the enzymatic hydrolysis of starch

The end products of complete α-amylolysis of amylose and amylopectin are glucose and maltose but the α-amylase of saliva produces predominantly maltose and maltotriose. Very few studies have attempted to quantify *in vivo* amylolytic hydrolysis of dietary starch in its various forms. Mörmann and Mühlemann (1981) followed interdental plaque pH in relation to *in vivo* hydrolysis of wheat starch in 3 forms, namely a boiled starch solution, a bread and a biscuit. The results showed that the nature and form of the starch influenced the rate of starch hydrolysis. For example, solutions of boiled starch were 'almost completely' destroyed by amylase but there was much less hydrolysis of bread. *In vivo* studies in rats comparing raw and cooked starch, however, found no difference in their cariogenicities (Grenby, 1965), both being very low.

In an extensive review of the literature, Rugg-Grunn concluded that cooked starchy foods such as rice, bread and potatoes have low cariogenicity and that raw starch is non-cariogenic (Rugg-Grunn, 1986).

19.5.3 Animal experiments

The main advantage of animal experiments is that the diet can be carefully controlled but animal studies have given variable results. When the frequency of feeding is standardised, however, cooked starch or starchy foods (eg bread) have been shown to be capable of causing caries but to be less active than sucrose (Konig, 1967).

19.5.3.1 Starch/sucrose mixtures

Some animal experiments have suggested that starch/sucrose mixtures may be more cariogenic than sucrose alone. Firestone *et al.* (1982) found cooked wheat starch alone to be cariogenic but less so than sucrose. The cariogenicity of alternating sucrose and cooked wheat starch meals was as great as an equal number of sucrose meals, but a mixture of wheat starch and sucrose was more cariogenic than an equal number of sucrose meals. The synergistic effect was time-dependent and might be the result of increased retention of sucrose in a sticky starch base, though the precise mechanisms remain unclear.

19.5.3.2 Inhibitory effect of maltose on extracellular polysaccharide production

One aspect of the dental caries process is the production of extracellular polysaccharides by oral bacteria. *Streptococcus mutans* has been strongly implicated in the development of dental caries in animals and in man (Edgar, 1978) through its ability to form bacterial plaque. This is in part due to the production of extracellular polysaccharides (dextrins or glucans) which have high viscosity and adhesiveness. The production of these polysaccharides is increased in the presence of sucrose. Maltose, on the other hand, has been shown to reduce the rate of extracellular polysaccharide synthesis when added to *Streptococcus mutans* cultures containing sucrose, and to inhibit the enzyme glycosyltransferase, necessary for the production of extracellular polysaccharides (Sharma *et al.*, 1974). This is not thought to be of major significance in cariogenesis however.

19.6 FOODS RICH IN INTACT CELL WALLS

Foods rich in intact cell walls are generally considered to have a protective effect on caries formation possibly due to the physical structure of these compounds and to the presence of other protective factors associated with these foods.

19.6.1 Sequestration of sugars

The presence of intact cell walls in whole fruits and vegetables reduces the availability of the sugars to plaque bacteria.

19.6.2 Increased chewing time

Foods containing intact cell walls require more mastication (Duncan *et al.*, 1983) which could result in increased saliva production and thus greater neutralisation of acid formed.

19.6.3 Mechanical cleansing

Foods rich in intact cell walls might have a mechanical cleansing action in the mouth. An experiment conducted to test the ability of fruits to remove previously eaten foods showed an effect comparable to rinsing with water (see Bibby, 1983).

19.6.4 Factors associated with foods rich in intact cell walls

Early observations in the South African Bantu (Osborne and Noriskin, 1937), suggested that a protective factor might be present in unprocessed food which is removed by refining. It was postulated to be an organic phosphate, now identified as phytate (myoinositol hexaphosphate) which can adsorb to enamel surfaces and thus prevent acid dissolution. An experiment in rats comparing wholemeal and white bread failed to show this protective effect (Konig, 1967).

Similarly, plant lectins, known to cause bacterial clumping and to inhibit metabolism have not been shown to reduce cariogenic activity. Nevertheless it has been concluded that the cariogenicity of whole fruits is low in humans (Rugg Grunn, 1986). The 1989 COMA report on dietary sugars (Department of Health, 1989) recommended that the consumption of fresh fruit, vegetables and starchy foods should increase to replace non-milk extrinsic sugars, in order to reduce the risk of dental caries.

CHAPTER 20
BASIS OF RECOMMENDATIONS ABOUT THE DESIRABLE DAILY INTAKE OF COMPLEX CARBOHYDRATES

20.1 TOTAL COMPLEX CARBO-HYDRATES AND STARCHES

Recommendations on intakes of total complex carbohydrates are rarely addressed or quantified directly. Instead, they are often given indirectly, or secondarily to recommendations for reducing fat intake. The 1984 COMA Report of 'Diet and Cardiovascular Disease', for instance, said 'The Panel sees advantages in compensating for a reduced fat intake with increased fibre-rich carbohydrates (eg bread, cereals, fruit, vegetables) provided that this can be achieved without increasing total intake of common salt or simple sugars.'

What proportion of dietary energy intake should be accounted for by complex carbohydrates? The answer can only be arrived at by default. So, if the maximum fat intake is recommended as 35%, the maximum alcohol intake is recommended as 5% and the optimum protein intake is taken as 10–12% of total energy, this leaves 48–50% of total energy for total carbohydrates.

Within this figure for total carbohydrates, how much should be accounted for by starches? Again, no recommendations have ever been given. The desirable amount of starch in the diet as a proportion of total energy, can only be estimated by default from numerical values which are set for simple sugars. The 1984 COMA report recommended that intake of simple sugars should 'not be increased further' but did not state an optimum amount. The 1989 COMA report on 'Dietary Sugars and Human Disease' said 'The Panel recommends that consumption of non-milk extrinsic sugars by the population should be decreased. These sugars should be replaced by fresh fruit, vegetables and starchy foods'.

Overall, most authorities recommend that starches should account for the majority of the energy associated with the carbohydrate fraction of the diet.

20.2 NON-STARCH POLY-SACCHARIDES

20.2.1 Review of recommendations

For the purposes of consistency of this report, and in line with our recommendation that complex carbohydrates should be defined as starches plus non-starch polysaccharides, we have sub-divided this chapter on recommendations in the same way. However, there have been no specific recommendations for non-starch polysaccharides and so this section will, of necessity, have to review the recommendations that have been given for dietary 'fibre' instead.

A number of official or quasi-official national and international bodies have considered the optimum intake of dietary 'fibre'. All have agreed that, on average, Western populations should increase their intake (Table 20.1). However, only some have felt able to specify a figure for minimum or optimum intake. There are good reasons for and against. These reasons are summarised in the next two sections:

Table 20.1 Recent recommendations on dietary 'fibre' intake of healthy adults

Body	Recommendation
Royal College of Physicians, London: Working Party on Medical Aspects of Dietary Fibre (1980)	'Eat foods which are closer to the natural grain, vegetable or fruit . . .'
National Advisory Committee on Nutrition Education – NACNE (1983)	'It is recommended that the intakes should be increased to an average of about 30 g dietary "fibre" per day for adults' (nb A timescale was suggested of achieving an intake of 25 g by the end of the 1980s)
Committee on Medical Aspects of Food Policy (COMA) Report of the Panel on Diet in Relation to Cardiovascular Disease (1984)	'The panel sees advantages in compensating for a reduced fat intake with increased 'fibre'-rich carbohydrates (eg bread, cereals, fruit, vegetables) provided this can be achieved without increasing total intake of common salt or simple sugars'
Health and Welfare, Canada (1987): Expert Advisory Committee on Dietary Fibre	'At least double (current) intake of 5.8–8.0 g/1000 kcal' by selecting a variety of 'fibre'-rich foods'
Health and Welfare, Canada (1988) Health Protection Branch	'Not in a position to recommend a specific level . . . those who consume a diet low in 'fibre' (should) increase 'fibre'-containing foods in wide variety'
Federation of American Societies for Experimental Biology, USA (1987)	'10–13 g/1000 kcal', by means of naturally 'fibre'-rich foods in wide variety; minority dissented
International Life Sciences Institute Working Party at meeting in Portugal (1987)	'Not yet in a position to make a general recommendation for a minimum level of intake'
Nordic Dietary Guidelines (1988)	3g/MJ ($\simeq$ 12g/1000 kcal)
US Department of Health and Human Services. The Surgeon General's Report on Nutrition and Health (1988)	'Increase consumption of whole grain foods and cereal products, vegetables (including dried beans and peas) and fruits'
National Research Council Report Diet and Health (1989)	Every day, eat five or more servings of a combination of vegetables and citrus fruits; also increase intake of starches and other complex carbohydrates by eating six or more daily servings of a combination of breads, cereals and legumes; increase total carbohydrate to 55% of energy intake primarily by increasing complex carbohydrates

20.2.2 The case against making numerical recommendations

- The heterogeneity of the structure and physical state of non-starch polysaccharides in the diet means that a single figure for total non-starch polysaccharide intake may hide a wide diversity of biological effects (as would a single figure for the intake of vitamins and minerals).

- Though certain non-starch polysaccharide components have well documented effects (e.g. soluble non-starch polysaccharide lowers serum cholesterol in some circumstances, wheat bran raises 24 hour faecal weight), paucity of dose-response studies and also biological variability (sex, age) rule out valid recommendations on the intakes of these non-starch polysaccharide components.

- Individuals vary greatly in their response to standardised increments of dietary non-starch polysaccharide. People who have most to gain from an effect of 'fibre' may be the ones who are least responsive to it. For example, constipated people may have a reduced laxative response to wheat bran.

- A given amount of non-starch polysaccharide can have different effects depending upon its physical state such as particle size, the presence of intact cell walls and the effects brought about by cooking (see Chapter 5).

- The biological functions and measurements which are sensitive to non-starch polysaccharide are also affected in important ways by other aspects of the diet and by psychological factors which may be very important in some individuals.

- With respect to non-starch polysaccharide supplements, as opposed to foods rich in non-starch polysaccharides, a major problem is the lack of long term studies. Thus, long-term effects on health cannot be predicted.

20.2.3 The case for making numerical recommendations

- Those in favour of giving numerical recommendations for non-starch polysaccharide intake invariably argue on the basis of the effects of non-starch polysaccharide on colonic function where the best data is available for a dose-response effect (Cummings, personal communication). Most would argue, however, that our knowledge of dose-response effects in other areas is far from complete and certainly does not allow quantitative values to be set.

- The heterogeneity of non-starch polysaccharide in the diet should not argue against the setting of a numerical value. A figure or range can be suggested as long as additional advice is given to ensure that the non-starch polysaccharide is derived from a variety of sources. (This type of advice would be in accordance with that given for proteins and fats).

- Variation in individual response can be demonstrated for most nutrients but has not prevented the setting of numerical values. Mean values are set as targets for the population as a whole and it is always assumed that there will be a normal distribution about this target value.

- The argument that the effects of non-starch polysaccharide relate to their physical state as well as to the chemically measured amount in the diet should not prevent numerical recommendations from being made. Again, it seems to justify the couching of the recommendations in more general terms as far as dietary sources are concerned.

- An argument in favour of giving a numerical value for NSP intake is that it aids consumer awareness; it acts as a yardstick against which individual intakes can be compared. It is also difficult to explain to the consumer why no numerical value is given for one of the few favoured dietary components when numerical values for fats and sugar limits are available. Hence scientific credibility is lost.

CHAPTER 21
LABELLING CONSIDERATIONS FOR COMPLEX CARBOHYDRATES

21.1 BACKGROUND

Because consumers perceive 'fibre' to be a good thing, they want to know how much there is in different foods. As a result, the labels of many foods show the amounts of 'fibre' which they are considered to contain. Such labelling has been most common for foods which are naturally rich in non-starch polysaccharides or to which ingredients rich in them have been added.

It has been explained elsewhere in this report that because 'fibre' is not a precisely defined term, the amount that appears to be present in a food is very dependent upon the method used to measure it. This can clearly be seen from the results of a collaborative study of five different methods for determining the amount in a particular brand of cornflakes (Cummings et al., 1985). (see Table 21.1)

Table 21.1 Apparent 'fibre' content of cornflakes, as determined by five different methods

Method	g/100g
Method 1	0.71
Method 2	1.44
Method 3	4.31
Method 4	4.39
Method 5	19.62

(From Cummings et al., 1985)

It is thus necessary to standardise the definition of 'fibre', for labelling purposes. To be useful, the analytical method used should not only give values that are as consistent as possible, but should also be able to rank a wide variety of,'fibre'-containing cereal, vegetable and fruit products correctly according to their physiological effects.

There are essentially three approaches to the definition of fibre, each of which has methodological implications. The first is in chemical terms – for example, as all non-starch polysaccharides – and any method, such as the Englyst method, (Englyst et al., 1982), which measures these would be suitable. The second is in terms of the method of analysis itself – for example, as the weight of whatever is in the residue after the food has been treated with a number of specified reagents to remove fat, starch and sugars. This has been the approach in countries which have adopted one of the gravimetric Association of Analytical Chemists (AOAC) methods.

However, this must be a dead-end approach unless it can be demonstrated to give accurate, absolute and relative values for each and every food or 'fibre'-rich ingredient – for no other method could ever duplicate its results exactly. And the third approach is in physiological terms, such as in the early Trowell definition used in the first half of the Codex Alimentarius Commission of the United Nations whose Guidelines, issued in 1985, defined it as the 'edible plant and animal material not hydrolyzed by the endogenous enzymes of the human digestive tract. . . as determined by the agreed upon method' (FAO, 1985).

21.2 THE PRESENT POSITION

21.2.1 The UK position

In 1987, the UK Government issued Guidelines on Nutrition Labelling in which 'fibre' was defined as non-starch polysaccharides as determined by the Englyst procedure (MAFF, 1987). The Guidelines were revised slightly in 1988 in recognition of the fact that some foods had been declaring higher values which had included some of the starch in the food, and acknowledged that this could continue. This starch was, like some other starch fractions, resistant to digestion, and might thus have had some of the physiological properties of non-starch polysaccharides. The Government also recommended that food labels should show the amount of starch as a subdivision of the total carbohydrate in the food, as well as its sugars, protein, fat, saturates and sodium. Further recommendations for controlling *claims* for 'fibre' were made by the UK Food Advisory Committee in 1989 (MAFF, 1989). They recommended that before a claim could be made about the amount of fibre in food, each 100g or a reasonable daily intake should contain at least 3g of non-starch polysaccharide. If the food claimed to be high or rich in 'fibre', the same amount should contain at least 6g.

21.2.2 The European Community

The European Community are now about to issue a Directive on Nutrition Labelling which will control the format of nutrition of labelling throughout the Community (Commission of the European Community, 1990). Although a definition of 'fibre' has yet to be agreed for this purpose, it is probable that one of the gravimetric AOAC methods which are already in use in some countries will be adopted. If however, 'fibre' is defined in the Directive in terms of non-starch polysaccharides, the Englyst method may be included too.

21.3 PROBLEMS FOR THE FUTURE

21.3.1 'Fibre' is not a single entity

The approach to nutrition labelling so far has been to think of 'fibre' as a single entity. In practice, this is not the case, any more than it is for 'ash' or the 'water-soluble vitamin B' of the early 1920s. Each of these is in fact a mixture of a number of materials with quite different physiological properties. Just as it is meaningless to add together the weights of iron and sodium, or of nicotinic acid and vitamin B12, to describe the mineral or vitamin activity of foods, it will come to be recognised that there are different fractions of 'fibre' which have quite different activities. Consumers are already beginning to appreciate that even within these components there are different materials which may need to be defined and measured for food labelling purposes.

21.3.2 Potential to mislead consumers

A further complication may arise with ingredients which may be added to foods and claimed as 'fibre', such as modified starches, polydextrose, inulin, gum arabic and other gums, and chitin. All of these are non-starch polysaccharides which may show up to different degrees in the various analytical procedures, but each of them has quite different physiological properties. A simple chemical definition which includes all of these may thus be misleading to the consumer. But there could also be difficulties for physiological definitions because some of these ingredients, such as gum arabic are completely degraded in the human intestine and might have little or no physiological effect. Does this mean that they are not 'fibre'? Finally, gravimetric methods such as those of the AOAC are no more helpful because there is little relationship between the physiological properties of these polysaccharides and their insolubility in the reagents used, and thus in their apparent 'fibre' content.

21.3.3 Problems with health claims

Might we look forward to a time when consumers demand to have on their labels an indication of the possible health benefits of their foods, such as its faecal bulking activity, whether it comes from cellulose or lignin or even mineral oil? Or of the food's cholesterol lowering activity, whether this is derived from its hemicelluloses or its level and type of fat? Or will the need to demonstrate both the efficacy and the safety of each such material prevent such apparently medicinal claims from being made?

CHAPTER 22
CONCLUSIONS AND SUGGESTIONS FOR FURTHER RESEARCH

CHAPTER 1 INTRODUCTION

- This Task Force was set up to provide an in-depth study of complex carbohydrates, defined as starches and non-starch polysaccharides.
- It is published ten years after the last comprehensive review on dietary 'fibre' and at a time when there is much interest in the possible overlap of function between some of the starches which resist digestion in the small intestine and the non-starch polysaccharides.

CHAPTER 2 CHEMISTRY OF COMPLEX CARBOHYDRATES AND THEIR ORGANISATION IN FOODS

Conclusions

- The complex carbohydrates in foods exhibit a wide range of chemical structures and physical properties and do not form a homogeneous group. For the purposes of the present report, complex carbohydrates are defined as all polysaccharides which contain 20 or more monosaccharide residues. This definition is appropriate for distinguishing them from simple carbohydrates such as the sugars and corresponds with the development of tertiary structures.
- The complex carbohydrates can be classified chemically, or according to their role in plant foods as follows: The naturally occurring polysaccharides can be regarded as, a) storage (eg starches, mannans and fructans) or, b) structural, ie the components of the plant cell wall, which can be further divided into cellulosic and non-cellulosic polysaccharides, the latter including pectic substances and hemicelluloses.
- The structural polysaccharides are organised into complex physical structures in the plant cell wall and starch is present as granules in raw foods. This physical organisation confers additional physiological properties on the polysaccharides.
- Isolated polysaccharides are widely used as food additives and small amounts are derived from animal foods in the diet.
- The heterogeneity of the complex carbohydrates results in very complex analytical problems; fractionation and measurement of the individual species is the only satisfactory approach but, because of the complexity of the operations required, it is rarely carried out.
- Useful nutritional information can be obtained by measuring the starch and non-starch polysaccharides (NSP) separately. Starch is separated from the NSP by enzymatic hydrolysis and the NSP measured as the constituent monosaccharides and uronic acids, which provides some characterisation of the polysaccharides present. The measurement of NSP provides a satisfactory index of plant cell wall material and dietary 'fibre' in foods.

Suggestions for Further Research

● Studies are required to establish the relation between the chemical and physical properties and physiological effects of polysaccharides both individually or when organised in cell wall or granular structures.
● Analytical methodology should be studied alongside physiological studies to ensure that nutritionally relevant analytical techniques are developed.
● Nutritional labelling requires simple rapid procedures for the major classes of complex carbohydrates and collaborative studies are required to establish a range of suitable, comparable, methods.

CHAPTER 3 DIETARY SOURCES AND INTAKE OF COMPLEX CARBOHYDRATES

Conclusions

● There is worldwide variation in complex carbohydrate intake. The data for complex carbohydrates, let alone that for starch or non-starch polysaccharides, are not easy to quantify from food supply statistics. As a proportion of total energy intake, Third World countries have higher intakes than the Western World, although the actual supplies may not be that different and range between 150 and 300 g/person/day.
● Intake of starch has steadily declined in the UK during this century. Intake of non-starch polysaccharide has fluctuated; it was highest during the 1940s and then decreased during the next two decades. It began to rise again during the 1980s.
● The major sources of complex carbohydrates in the UK diet are cereals and vegetables (including potatoes and pulses). Cereal products are the major contributors to starch and to intakes of insoluble non-starch polysaccharides, excluding cellulose. The cell walls of vegetables and cereal products are the major contributors to soluble non-starch polysaccharide intake and cellulose. The cell walls of fruits and seeds also contribute.

Suggestions for Further Research

● How do the intakes of the different fractions of starch vary in different population groups, worldwide and in the UK?
● What is the intake of different classes of non-starch polysaccharides in different population groups?
● How can intakes of both starch and non-starch polysaccharides best be increased in the population at large?

CHAPTER 4 HOW DO THE FORM AND PHYSICAL PROPERTIES OF STARCHES INFLUENCE THEIR BIOLOGICAL EFFECTS?

Conclusions

● The digestibility of starches is affected by intrinsic factors such as physical accessibility, crystalline structure and the effects of heating on the starch granule, and extrinsic factors such as chewing and transit time.
● The biological effects of starch therefore depend on the proportions of rapidly digestible starch, slowly digestible starch and resistant starch contained in the food.
● Rapidly digestible starch is formed when starch granules are disrupted by moist heat causing the starch to become amorphous and dispersed. This is digested

and is absorbed as quickly as glucose, and leads to similar post-prandial glycaemic levels.

- Slowly digestible starches are mainly the starches in the crystalline forms A and C. These are digested and absorbed more slowly than glucose but are completely digested in the small intestine. They generally lead to lower postprandial glycaemic levels.
- Starches can be resistant to digestion if they are inaccessible to digestive enzymes, if they possess a particular crystalline structure, or if the amylose has been retrograded by heating and cooling. These pass into the large intestine where they may be fermented.

Suggested Areas for Further Research

- Is there an effect of resistant starch on absorption of nutrients in the small intestine?
- What is the energy value of the various starch factors?
- What are the effects of cooking and other forms of food processing on the proportions and functions of the different starch fractions?
- What are the effects of resistant starch in the large intestine? What determines fermentability? What are the effects of their products of fermentation?

CHAPTER 5 HOW DO THE FORM AND PHYSICAL PROPERTIES OF NON-STARCH POLYSACCHARIDES INFLUENCE THEIR BIOLOGICAL EFFECTS?

Conclusions

- The physical properties of non-starch polysaccharides are just as important as their chemical structure in determining biological potency. They can affect many events occurring along the gastrointestinal tract including nutrient absorption, sterol metabolism, fermentation, stool weight and cation conservation.
- The nature of the association between non-starch polysaccharides and water determines their effects on intestinal function, metabolism and fermentation. This can affect both viscosity and water holding capacity.
- The nature of the association of non-starch polysaccharides with the plant cell wall itself can have a profound influence on function. Particle size and susceptibility to bacterial fermentation can also affect their physical properties, and, therefore, their function.
- Processing and cooking may modify all the physical and biological effects of non-starch polysaccharides.
- Greatest effects in the small intestine are generally seen with substances of high viscosity, high water holding capacity and small particle size. The effects in the large intestine are related to water holding capacity, large particle size, and fermentability.

Suggestions for Further Research

- How do chemical structure, physical properties and biological effects relate to each other? If this were known, the effects of existing and new substances could be predicted.
- How do the physical properties of different non-starch polysaccharides affect absorption and fermentation in different regions of the gastrointestinal tract?
- What are the effects of new methods of cooking and food processing on the properties and actions of different fractions of non-starch polysaccharides?

CHAPTER 6 EFFECTS OF COMPLEX CARBOHYDRATES ON THE DIGESTION AND ABSORPTION OF MACRONUTRIENTS

Conclusions

- Non-starch polysaccharides are not digested or absorbed in the small intestine but can affect the digestion and absorption of other macronutrients. Starches do not seem to produce this effect, probably because of the tendency of their viscous solutions to lose viscosity quickly on digestion.
- Viscous polysaccharides inhibit movement in the gut, delay the delivery of liquids from the stomach, slow the mixing of substrate with digestive juice and impair the access of products of digestion to the epithileum. This may result in reduced absorption in the upper part of the gut and increased delivery to the lower small intestine. It may explain the relative cellular hypertrophy at that site.

Suggestions for Further Research

- How do complex carbohydrates affect the physical properties of intestinal contents and the absorption of nutrients? A systematic study of degradation of different plant foods and purified carbohydrates at different stages of the digestive process is needed to understand the physiological effects.
- Does resistant starch have the same effects as non-starch polysaccharides on digestion and absorption of macronutrients in the small intestine?
- How similar are the effects of complex carbohydrates when they are consumed as isolates compared with when they are present as components of a mixed diet?

CHAPTER 7 EFFECTS OF COMPLEX CARBOHYDRATES ON THE DIGESTION AND ABSORPTION OF MICRONUTRIENTS

Conclusions

- The bioavailability of many minerals is reduced in the presence of foods high in non-starch polysaccharides, due to binding to the carbohydrate structures and closely associated substances such as phytate, tannins and oxalate. Wheat bran is one of the most potent dietary inhibitors of calcium, iron and zinc absorption, primarily due to its high level of phytate. Fruits and vegetables contain tannins which reduce iron bioavailability, but the inhibitory effect is modified in the presence of absorption enhancers such as ascorbic acid.
- Limited research indicates that high intakes of non-starch polysaccharides may impair vitamin D absorption and vitamin B12 status.
- Non-starch polysaccharides in mixed adult, or even vegetarian, diets do not appear to compromise micronutrient status in the long term. However, new vegetarians and children may be at risk with respect to iron and possibly other micronutrients. The risk might reflect the limitation of total energy intake just as much as the high content of complex carbohydrates in the diet.
- The demonstrable *in vitro* effects of non-starch polysaccharides on micronutrients have not been confirmed by *in vivo* studies and do not justify the warnings which are often issued against the increased consumption of non-starch polysaccharides.

Suggestions for Further Research

- What are the mechanisms by which non-starch polysaccharides can reduce the bioavailability of minerals and vitamins?

- What is the effect of diets rich in non-starch polysaccharides on mineral absorption, nutritional status and health of vulnerable groups of the population (infants, children, adolescents, pregnant women, and the elderly) in the short and long term?
- Can people adapt over time to diets high in complex carbohydrates and, if so, what is the mechanism? Does the efficiency of absorption of minerals increase? How long does this adaptive period take? The answers to these questions are particularly important for people who eat large quantities of unprocessed wheat bran.
- What is the individual role of non-starch polysaccharides and inhibitory substances, such as phytate and tannins, on mineral bioavailability?
- Can the methodology be improved for studying the interactions between non-starch polysaccharides and micronutrients? Developments in stable isotope techniques, sensitive measures of micronutrient status and analytical methods for phytate and tannins are essential.
- Does resistant starch have the same effects as non-starch polysaccharides on digestion and absorption of micronutrients in the small intestine?

CHAPTER 8 INTERACTIONS BETWEEN COMPLEX CARBOHYDRATES AND BACTERIA

Conclusions

- More than 500 species of bacteria are present in the human large intestine. The total bacterial count is about 10^{11} to 10^{12} per gram wet weight of contents.
- There is a two way interaction in the gut between complex carbohydrates and bacteria:

  First, they can act as substrates for bacterial fermentation. The subsequent effects are due to the end products of fermentation ie short chain fatty acids and gases.

  Secondly, they have the ability to alter the composition and metabolic activity of the intestinal bacteria and to change their ecology.
- The major positive effects on the health of the host may be due either to changes in stool bulk and consistency or to the end products of fermentation. Such effects may result in improvement in colonocyte welfare, or in colonisation by bacteria which resist invading pathogens. Nitrogen balance might also be improved.

Suggestions for Further Research

- Can we increase our knowledge of the effects of complex carbohydrates on the bacteria of the proximal colon? This could be achieved by studying, for example, the effect of diet on the bacterial composition of ileostomy or colostomy effluent.
- How are changes in caecal bacterial ecology brought about? Which types of complex carbohydrate are most effective in inducing changes? New techniques to study caecal bacterial metabolites of complex carbohydrates will help to advance knowledge.
- How do individuals differ in the composition of their intestinal bacteria and their potential to interact with fermentable complex carbohydrates? Does the extent of this interaction show any correlation with protection against any of the colonic disorders which are thought to be influenced by the interaction?

CHAPTER 9 ENERGY VALUES OF COMPLEX CARBOHYDRATES

Conclusions

- The general energy conversion factors (energy values) are not exact and are based on a number of assumptions. They are conventional because they are useful for the calculation of energy values of whole diets. Their limitations must be recognised.
- The digestible energy value for starch depends on whether it is absorbed in the small intestine or whether it is fermented in the colon. In the former case, the digestible energy value is 3.75 kcal/g monosaccharide; in the latter case, the digestible energy value may vary, but is probably about 3 kcal/g.
- If it is necessary to assign a single, average, figure for the apparent digestible energy value of those complex carbohydrates reaching the large intestine from mixed diets, a value of about 2 kcal/g can be used. The figure can be derived from three independent methods. This average energy value is inappropriate if the apparent digestibility (fermentability) differs markedly from about 70%.
- The digestible energy value of isolates, ingredients and additives varies widely, but is again related to apparent digestibility (fermentability). If needed, specific energy values would apply for these enriched sources and would range between 0 and 3 kcal/g.
- The contribution of complex carbohydrates to the Net Energy for the Maintenance (NEm) of man is less than the estimated digestible energy because of energy losses as heat of fermentation and gas, and because the metabolism of short chain fatty acids is not as efficient as that of glucose in terms of ATP production. For mixed diets, an average NEm for the complex carbohydrates reaching the large intestine is about 1.5 kcal/g, corresponding to an apparent digestibility of about 70%. More specific values for subfractions, isolates, ingredients and additives would apply as these can vary widely.

Suggestions for Further Research

- How much starch, from various food sources, reaches the large intestine *in vivo*? *In vitro* analytical methods that truly reflect this quantity need to be developed, so that more appropriate energy values can be allocated.
- Are there any fractions of resistant starch where the digestible energy value differs appreciably from 3 kcal/g?
- Why are the energy losses to the faeces higher than expected with certain diets containing appreciable amounts of whole grain, broken grain, or flours of large particle size? Can the effects of the cell wall matrix be established?
- Will further measurements of digestible energy values of complex carbohydrates reaching the large intestine, support the use of the average value of 2 kcal/g in mixed diets?
- Can estimates of the NEm for complex carbohydrates be obtained directly or indirectly from further studies of the energy losses due to metabolism in man? Dose-response relationships and interactions between dissimilar isolates, ingredients and additives also need to be considered.

CHAPTER 10 EFFECTS OF COMPLEX CARBOHYDRATES ON THE GLYCAEMIC RESPONSE

Conclusions

- Glycaemic indices (GI) of complex carbohydrates are influenced by many factors, some of which relate to the chemical and physical properties of the food and others to physiological factors of the host. GI values can only be useful when they are obtained from reliably standardised techniques. Measurements of insulin and glucose concentrations made simultaneously can be more useful.

- Some foods rich in complex carbohydrates have lower GI values than those rich in simple carbohydrates. There is an overlap between the two, reflecting the fact that sucrose has a low glycaemic index. However, GI measures only one aspect of postprandial physiology ie the rise and subsequent fall in levels of blood glucose.

- There is some evidence that choosing a diet rich in complex carbohydrates, ie containing generally low GI foods, may help to control the blood glucose levels of diabetic patients. Long term advantages, if any, of such regimens are still to be assessed.

Suggestions for Further Research

- What is the effect on the glycaemic response of consuming foods in mixed meals? How can the GI values be well standardised and yet reflect the real life situation?

- Are there important exceptions (eg fatty foods) to the generalisation that insulin responses are broadly in line with the glucose response?

- What will be the long-term effects when normal, hyperlipidaemic and diabetic subjects eat diets of complex carbohydrates varying in both chemical composition and physical characteristics?

CHAPTER 11 CLINICAL IMPLICATIONS OF COMPLEX CARBOHYDRATES FOR DIABETES

Conclusions

- Evidence has now accumulated showing that diets rich in complex carbohydrates can improve control in diabetic patients.

- Most experimental studies have only examined metabolic variables in the short-term. Starches seem to exert greater effects on fasting blood glucose levels, and non-starch polysaccharides on post-prandial glucose levels.

Suggestions for Further Research

- Can longer term studies confirm the beneficial effects on metabolic variables that are seen in short-term studies?

- What are the ideal proportions of non-starch polysaccharides and starches in the diet used for control in diabetic patients?

- How much simple carbohydrate can be added to a diet rich in complex carbohydrates without impairing metabolic control or having serious long-term consequences?

- Is the associated risk of cardiovascular disease in diabetic patients reduced by diets rich in complex carbohydrates? Will such studies demonstrate a reduced rate of microvascular complications?

- Can controlled trials still be planned to determine the efficacy of these diets in spite of their widespread use?

CHAPTER 12 CLINICAL IMPLICATIONS OF COMPLEX CARBOHYDRATES FOR OBESITY

Conclusion

- Foods rich in non-starch polysaccharides are useful for slimmers in the context of a low energy diet. They can make a diet more satiating, and might lessen constipation.
- Tablets containing non-starch polysaccharide isolates can swell in the stomach and may promote satiety. This may aid compliance with a calorie-reduced diet.
- Diets rich in complex carbohydrates are *pari passu* low in fat and, therefore, less energy-dense. Excess starch intake could, of course, contribute to excess energy intake.

Suggestions for Further Research

- What are the short-term effects of food form and texture on appetite and satiety? What is the effect of mastication?
- What are the effects of reduced digestibility of food on the energy balance equation? What is the relationship between starch-digesting efficiency and the tendency to gain weight?
- What are the long-term effects of diets rich in plant cell-wall material, or the effects of isolates, on weight control and on compliance with weight reducing regimes?

CHAPTER 13 CLINICAL IMPLICATIONS OF COMPLEX CARBOHYDRATES FOR GALLSTONES

Conclusions

- The epidemiological evidence that complex carbohydrates are protective against gallstones is scanty, but suggestive. A better relationship might be found if starches were considered as well as non-starch polysaccharides.
- Wheat bran reduces the relative amount of cholesterol in bile; probably because it interferes with the formation or absorption of the secondary bile acid, deoxycholate. This may be a simple laxative effect or due to acidification of the colon.
- If complex carbohydrates have a role in either the causation or prevention of gallstones, it is probably less than that of total energy, but it might still be important.

Suggestions for Future Research

- Complex carbohydrates have the potential to reduce two risk factors for gallstones – plasma insulin levels and biliary deoxycholate levels. Can evidence for this effect be shown in practice?
- What is the mechanism of action of the different fractions of non-starch polysaccharides in the prevention of gallstones?
- What is the role of starch, and especially of resistant starch, in the prevention of gallstones?

CHAPTER 14 CLINICAL IMPLICATIONS OF COMPLEX CARBOHYDRATES FOR CORONARY HEART DISEASE

Conclusions

- There is some epidemiological evidence showing a relationship between the intake of complex carbohydrates and indices of coronary heart disease

(CHD). However, on an isocaloric basis, low fat diets are usually high in complex carbohydrate, so the direct relationship between fat intake and CHD is an indirect relationship between complex carbohydrate and CHD.

- Soluble non-starch polysaccharides such as those found in oats, rye, barley and legume seeds may, in some circumstances reduce total and LDL cholesterol. The long term sustainability of the effects is unknown. Isolates such as guar gum, locust bean gum and gum arabic may have similar effects.
- Resistant starch and non-starch polysaccharides may improve blood glucose control and improve insulin sensitivity via their effects in the small intestine, thus decreasing one of the possible coronary risk factors.

Suggestions for Further Research

- Are the lipid-lowering effects of soluble non-starch polysaccharides sustainable over the long-term and demonstrable in realistic quantities?
- How do soluble non-starch polysaccharides exert their lipid lowering effects? How much of the effect is due to alteration in other variables, e.g. lower total fat, lower total energy?
- How important is the initial lipid level on the size of the effect?
- What is the role of complex carbohydrates in the primary prevention of CHD?
- How important are blood insulin levels in the development of atherosclerosis? Do variations in starch digestibility influence them significantly?

CHAPTER 15 CLINICAL IMPLICATIONS OF COMPLEX CARBOHYDRATES FOR IRRITABLE BOWEL SYNDROME AND CONSTIPATION

Conclusions

- It seems likely that there are different varieties of the irritable bowel syndrome, each responding in different ways to different treatments.
- Not all patients with the irritable bowel syndrome respond to treatment with non-starch polysaccharides; some may actually get worse.
- Of the symptoms associated with the irritable bowel syndrome, constipation (particularly in elderly people) responds best to treatment with non-starch polysaccharides. Those substances which are only partially fermented appear to have the best laxative properties eg wheat bran and ispaghula. Patients with severe slow transit constipation are unlikely to obtain benefit from such treatment.
- Constipation is not simply a disorder of 'fibre' deficiency, but is rather a disturbance of colonic motility. Non-starch polysaccharides can be useful because of their mild laxative properties.

Suggestions for Further Research

- Which physiological measurements can be used to identify subsets of patients with the irritable bowel syndrome and constipation so that treatment can be focused on discrete pathophysiological entities?
- How can the fermentation of non-starch polysaccharides in the large intestine be related to their physiological action?

CHAPTER 16 CLINICAL IMPLICATIONS OF COMPLEX CARBOHYDRATES FOR COLONIC DIVERTICULOSIS

Conclusions

- It is not yet clear whether colonic diverticulosis is a consequence of the ageing process or a long term deficiency of non-starch polysaccharides in the diet.
- Epidemiological, and other studies, provide some evidence for the deficiency hypothesis. They are limited because diverticulosis can only be identified by a barium enema. There is the problem of determining incidence and prevalence in asymptomatic and symptomatic populations.
- Symptomatic colonic diverticulosis can be treated with a diet rich in non-starch polysaccharides which should, at least, relieve the symptoms.
- Wheat bran only lowers pressure in the sub-set of patients with a high intracolonic pressure. Ispaghula has no effect on the pressure but is better at increasing stool weight.

Suggestions for Further Research

- Can the epidemiological observations be extended to provide more conclusive evidence that diets low in non-starch polysaccharides can cause colonic diverticulosis independent of the effects of ageing? Which types of non-starch polysaccharides are most protective?
- Can sub-sets of 'symptomatic' patients, who will respond best to treatment with non-starch polysaccharides be identified? Which type of non-starch polysaccharide will provide the most effective treatment for which sub-set of patients?
- Can long-term studies elucidate the relationship between increased colonic pressure and the ageing process?

CHAPTER 17 CLINICAL IMPLICATIONS OF COMPLEX CARBOHYDRATES FOR COLORECTAL CANCER

Conclusions

- There is little firm evidence from either ecological comparisons or analytical studies to support the original hypothesis that the development of colorectal cancer can be linked to a deficiency of non-starch polysaccharides in the diet. The limited evidence can only suggest that non-starch polysaccharides, particularly from vegetables, have a protective effect. The evidence from experimentally-induced tumours in animals is also inconclusive.
- The most promising lines of evidence that some non-starch polysaccharides can be protective against colorectal cancer are emerging from prospective studies and studies of precancerous lesions.

Suggestions for Further Research

- Would the study of the individual stages of colorectal cancer, (eg adenoma formation, adenoma growth etc), give more reproducible correlations with intakes of non-starch polysaccharides?
- Will better definition of non-starch polysaccharides clarify the situation? Can the contribution of different amounts of resistant starch in different diets help to explain the contradictory results?
- Will further studies of the possible mechanisms of action of complex carbohydrates clarify the situation?

CHAPTER 18 CLINICAL IMPLICATIONS OF COMPLEX CARBOHYDRATES FOR FOOD INTOLERANCE

Conclusions

- Intolerance to foods rich in non-starch polysaccharides, especially cereals, has been suggested in several clinical conditions (eg Crohn's disease & migraine) but conclusive evidence is lacking for most disorders.
- It is possible that some cases of irritable bowel syndrome are due to changes in the bacterial metabolism caused by non-starch polysaccharides. This hypothesis is based mainly on the correlation observed between fermentable gas release from the non-starch polysaccharides which provoke most symptoms, and clinical evidence showing that symptoms can occur and then disappear with the appropriate double-blind challenges. At present, the hypothesis has severe limitations.

Suggestions for Further Research

- Which particular components of foods, rich in non-starch polysaccharides, are responsible for which symptoms?
- Are changes in gut bacteria a cause or effect of ingesting non-starch polysaccharides which provoke the symptoms?
- Do the symptoms of intolerance result from changes in the bacteria themselves, or changes in their products of fermentation?
- Could the symptoms of intolerance be a secondary result of malabsorption of certain foods in the small intestine?

CHAPTER 19 CLINICAL IMPLICATIONS OF COMPLEX CARBOHYDRATES FOR DENTAL CARIES

Conclusions

- Epidemiological evidence suggests that populations with a high intake of complex carbohydrates and relatively low sugar consumption have a low incidence of dental caries.
- Foods rich in intact cell walls require longer chewing which leads to increased production of saliva and greater acid neutralisation. They also sequester the simple sugars and reduce their access to bacterial enzymes. Factors associated with foods high in complex carbohydrates, for example lectins and phytate, may also have a protective effect on cariogenesis.
- The cariogenicity of starch depends on its form: uncooked starch has a very low cariogenicity, finely ground and cooked starch can cause caries but their cariogenicity is less than sugars. Starch in conjunction with sucrose can be as cariogenic, or more so, than sucrose alone.

Suggestions for Further Research

- What factors affect starch digestibility by salivary amylase? How much starch fermentation actually occurs in the mouth?
- Does maltose inhibit extracellular polysaccharide synthesis by *Streptococcus mutens* in man as it does in the rat?
- What are the mechanisms of the synergistic starch/sucrose effects on cariogenicity?

CHAPTER 20 BASIS OF RECOMMENDATIONS ABOUT THE DESIRABLE DAILY INTAKE OF COMPLEX CARBOHYDRATES

Conclusions

- All the official bodies who have addressed the question of desirable levels of intake of complex carbohydrates have recommended an increase in the amount in Western Diets. Even committees who have not directly looked at the issue of complex carbohydrates have suggested an increase indirectly, by advising that fat intakes should provide a certain proportion of the energy intake and that complex carbohydrates should make up the shortfall in energy.
- Within the general guidelines to increase complex carbohydrates, numerical values have occasionally been set for intake of 'fibre'. These values have been somewhere between 12–30 g for 'fibre' (roughly equivalent to 10–18 g non-starch polysaccharides)
- There are good reasons for and against the setting of numerical values for recommendations for non-starch polysaccharides. If numerical values are deemed to be appropriate in the future, then there must be universal agreement about the analytical procedures on which they are based, together with general guidance to the consumer about how they are to be interpreted.

Suggestions for Further Research

- Can the differences in analytical techniques be resolved so that numerical recommendations are expressed in a consistent manner in different countries?
- Can certain sub-sets of the population be identified for whom recommendations to increase complex carbohydrates are particularly appropriate (or inappropriate)?
- Should the general guidance to increase intake of starch and non-starch polysaccharides be made more specific as our knowledge about the effects of their sub-fractions increases?

CHAPTER 21 LABELLING CONSIDERATIONS FOR COMPLEX CARBOHYDRATES

Conclusions

- Current UK guidelines and the 1990 European Commission Directive on Nutrition Labelling allow food labels to show a single value for starch and for 'fibre'.
- In this situation, such 'fibre' should have a chemical definition (eg non-starch polysaccharides) rather than be defined by a method of analysis.
- Since different non-starch polysaccharides can have different physiological properties the declaration of a single value for 'fibre' is potentially misleading. Consideration should be given to distinguishing non-starch polysaccharides by their physiological properties.

Suggestions for Further Research

- How can consumers be made aware that high 'fibre' values on labels might not always reflect high biological effects? Some less active non-starch polysaccharides can quite legitimately be added to foods and labelled as 'fibre'.
- How can the inclusion of values for starch and 'fibre' on food labels be brought to the attention of consumers and how can nutrition education explain what these values mean?
- As more evidence accrues that both starches and 'fibre' are not single entities as regards their biological effects, will more precise definitions need to be put on food labels?

CHAPTER 23
GENERAL CONCLUSIONS AND RECOMMENDATIONS

1) *Complex carbohydrates consist of starches and non-starch polysaccharides*. This Task Force recommends that, in future, scientists should define the functions and origins of complex carbohydrates more specifically so that their biological effects can be correlated with both their chemical structure and the physical state of their specific sub-fractions.

   Studies on dietary 'fibre' in food and its effects in man have been hampered by the use of the word 'fibre'. This implies that 'fibre' exists as a single entity and this is too imprecise for scientific purposes. *This Task Force recommends that the word 'fibre' should become obsolete*, at least in the scientific literature.

2) There is a variety of foods which are rich in complex carbohydrates (such as cereals, vegetables, pulses, nuts and fruit) and they display great diversity in their physical and biological properties. This is, at least in part, due to the complex carbohydrates which they contain. It is difficult to make generalisations about either the physical, chemical or biological properties of complex carbohydrates. Therefore, it is *virtually impossible to draw general conclusions* about the effects of either the starches as a group, or of the non-starch polysaccharides as a group. This important point should be borne in mind throughout the remainder of this section.

3) There is more *overlap* between the behaviour and properties of the starches and the non-starch polysaccharides than was previously thought. This overlap may have obscured some important relationships between dietary components and disease and should not be ignored in the future.

   Starches are mainly digested and absorbed in the small intestine. Starches which escape digestion (resistant starches) and non-starch polysaccharides primarily exert their biological effects through their mechanical and physico-chemical actions in the lumen of both the small and large intestines, and through fermentation in the large intestine.

4) Starches which are digested in the small intestine contribute an *energy value* of 3.75 kcal/g monosaccharides. Resistant starches and non-starch polysaccharides contribute variable amounts of energy depending, amongst other things, on the proportion of each which is fermented prior to excretion. Digestible energy values could therefore lie anywhere between 0 and 3 kcal/g.

5) Hypotheses that many *Western diseases*, such as colonic diverticulosis, colorectal cancer, and irritable bowel syndrome, are caused by a deficiency of dietary 'fibre' have not been substantiated; nor have hypotheses that 'fibre' can protect against diabetes, obesity and coronary heart disease. There is, however, little or no

evidence to refute these hypotheses and more research is needed. At present, the best evidence exists for the effects of some non-starch polysaccharides on increasing stool weight and of some non-starch polysaccharides on reducing serum glucose, insulin and cholesterol concentrations in some circumstances.

6)   Non-starch polysaccharides appear to exert their functions as much through their various *physical properties*, such as solubility, viscosity, and their degree of disruption and through their intimate association with the plant cell wall, as through their innate chemical composition.

7)   All complex carbohydrates in foods exert their function as *an integral part of a mixed diet* in which they are inevitably associated with other nutrients and anti-nutrients, such as phytate. Experiments with isolated complex carbohydrates cannot ever hope to mimic all the real situations with conventional foods – a multidimensional approach is essential in the study of the effects of a diet rich in complex carbohydrates.

8)   As a natural corollary to conclusion (7), human studies investigating the effect of complex carbohydrates and their individual fractions are, by nature, *difficult to design*. Results from most experiments must therefore be interpreted with caution.

9)   For most *adults* consuming nutritionally adequate diets, an increased intake of complex carbohydrates is unlikely to lead to deficiencies in *micronutrients*.

10) The role of complex carbohydrates in the *young and elderly* is a relatively *unexplored* area. The potential advantages of consuming a diet rich in non-starch polysaccharides should never prejudice the consumption of an appropriate diet. Particular caution is necessary if the diets lead to increased intakes of phytate and tannin.

11) There is likely to be confusion in the minds of consumers, as well as scientists, if *controversies over the analysis and labelling* of complex carbohydrates cannot be resolved. Ideally, labelling should be related to the functional characteristics of both starches and non-starch polysaccharides.

12) Taking into account all the evidence, this Task Force considers it is sensible for the average person in Britain *to increase intakes* of *a variety of foods which are rich in complex carbohydrates*.

DIAGRAM OF THE GASTROINTESTINAL TRACT

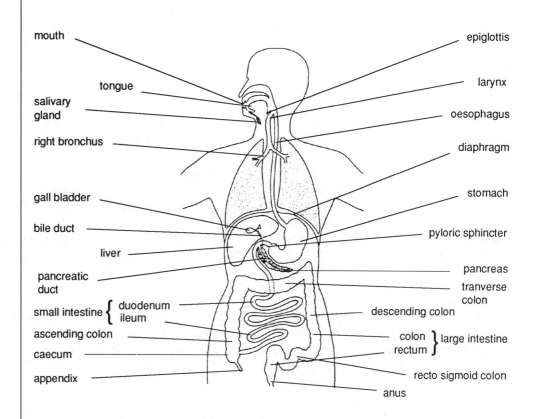

mouth

tongue

salivary gland

right bronchus

gall bladder

bile duct

liver

pancreatic duct

small intestine { duodenum ileum

ascending colon

caecum

appendix

epiglottis

larynx

oesophagus

diaphragm

stomach

pyloric sphincter

pancreas

tranverse colon

descending colon

colon } large intestine rectum }

recto sigmoid colon

anus

GLOSSARY

Acetylation the addition of an acetyl group (CH_3CO-) to a compound

Additive a compound added to, or used in, a food to serve the function of an antioxidant, artificial sweetener, colour, emulsifier, stabiliser, flavouring, preservative etc

Adenoma a benign tumour of epithelial origin that is derived from glandular tissue; it may become malignant

Aerobe any organism, particularly a microbe, that requires the presence of free oxygen for life and growth

Aerotolerant any organism which is tolerant to the presence of free oxygen

Aetiology the study or science of the causes of disease

Agglutination the clumping of microscopic antigenic particles such as red blood cells or bacteria so that they form visible clumps

Amylose the linear form of starch; the glucose units are joined by α1-4 linkages

Amylopectin the branched chain form of starch; the glucose molecules are linked by both α1-4 and α1-6 linkages

Anaerobe any organism, particularly a microbe, which is able to live and grow in the absence of free oxygen. *Facultative anaerobe* - an organism which is capable of some growth in the absence of free oxygen, but which grows best in the presence of oxygen

Anorexia loss of appetite

Antispasmodic a drug that relieves spasm of smooth muscle

Antral churning the mixing produced by contractions of the part of the stomach near the pylorus

Apoprotein a protein which transports lipids in the blood

Apparent digestibility proportion of ingested unavailable complex carbohydrate (UCC) which does not appear in the faeces, ie

$$\frac{\text{Ingested UCC} - \text{Faecal UCC}}{\text{Ingested UCC}}$$

Atherogenesis the development of atherosclerosis

Atherosclerosis a disease of the larger arteries in which fatty plaques develop on the inner walls and may eventually disrupt blood flow

Atopic disease a form of allergy in which the hypersensitivity reaction may be distant from the region of contact with the substance responsible

Bacteriophage a virus that attacks bacteria

Bile acids the organic acids present in bile, mostly in the form of their sodium salts and conjugated with an amino acid; the main bile acids are cholic acid, deoxycholic acid, chenodeoxycholic acid (glycocholic acid and taurocholic acid)

Bioavailability the proportion of a nutrient in a food or diet that can be utilised by the body for normal metabolic functions

Blood lipids the lipids carried in the blood as part of the various lipoprotein complexes, ie cholesterol, triacylglycerol, fatty acids, phospholipids

Blood rheology the study of the various factors affecting blood flow

Bran *coarse bran* - 95% passes through sieves with holes of 1.5 to 0.5 mm; *fine bran* - 95% passes through sieves with holes of less than 0.5 mm

Caecum the first part of the large intestine; it is a capacious sac in which bacterial fermentation proceeds apace

Calculus a hard pebble-like mass formed within the body

Caloric conversion factors the energy values of carbohydrate, protein and fat; the factors equal 3.75kcal/g of monosaccharide, 4kcal/g protein and 9kcal/g fat

Cannula	a hollow tube designed for insertion into a body cavity such as the bladder or a blood vessel
Catharsis	the purging or cleansing out of the bowels by the giving of a laxative
Cation	a positively charged ion
Cation exchange	the ability of a substance to exchange the positively charged ions bound to it for other positively charged ions
Carcinogenesis	the development of cancer or a carcinoma
Cariostatic	capable of inhibiting or retarding the formation of caries in teeth
Cell kinetics	the rates of the different biochemical reactions which occur in a cell
Chemotherapy	the prevention or treatment of a disease by the use of a drug
Cholangitis	inflammation of the bile ducts
Cholecystitis	inflammation of the gall bladder
Chelating agent	a chemical compound which forms complexes by binding metal ions and removing them from solution
Coacervation	the spontaneous separation of a continuous one-phase aqueous solution of a polymer into two aqueous phases, one having a relatively high polymer concentration and the other a relatively low concentration
Coeliac disease	a condition in which the small intestine is harmed by the protein gliadin found in gluten in wheat; malabsorption occurs as a result
Colectomy	the removal of the colon
Collenchyma	a supporting polygonal cellular structure with thickened cellulose walls
Colloid	a system whose properties are intermediate between a solution and a suspension
Colorimetry	a method of determining the concentration of a substance by comparing the intensity of colour with that of a solution of known concentration
Colonocyte	a cell in the lining of the colon wall
Complex carbohydrate	a polysaccharide containing 20 or more monosaccharide residues
Corticosteroids	the steroid hormones synthesised by the adrenal cortex; the two main groups are the glucocorticoids and the mineralocorticoids
Coronary thrombosis	the formation of a blood clot in one of the arteries supplying the heart; it can cause the heart to beat irregularly or stop beating completely
Cracked grains	grains which have been broken into 3 or 4 pieces
Crohn's disease	a condition in which segments of the gastrointestinal tract, mainly in the terminal ileum, become inflamed and ulcerated; this causes diarrhoea and abdominal pain
Cystic duct	the duct through which the gall bladder drains into the common bile duct and hence the duodenum
Diabetes Mellitus	a disorder of carbohydrate metabolism due to the relative or total lack of the hormone insulin; cells are unable to take up glucose to use as an energy source and are forced to obtain energy from fatty acids instead
Dialysis	a method of separating particles of different sizes in a liquid by the use of a semi-permeable membrane which acts as a sieve
Dicotyledon	a seed having 2 cotyledons – a form of modified leaf which contains food reserves
Diffusion coefficient	the quantity of solute diffusing per second across a surface area of 1.0 cm^2 when there is a concentration gradient of one
Digestible energy	the difference between the gross energy of a food and the energy lost in the faeces
Diverticulosis or diverticular disease	a condition in which sacs or pouches are formed at weak points in the walls of the intestine; if these burst and inflammation occurs at the site of the leakage, the condition is known as *diverticulitis*
Ecological study	a type of epidemiological study in which the incidence or prevalence of a disease in different countries or communities is plotted against a variable
Elemental diet	an artificial diet containing no complex carbohydrate or other polymers, which is completely absorbed in the small intestine
Endoscopy	the examination of the interior of the body by the use of a tube with light at the end, containing optical fibres which transmit the image to the examiner's eye
Enterocolitis	inflammation of the colon and the small intestine

Enterohepatic	the circulation of some compounds eg bile acids from the liver, through the bile duct
circulation	into the intestine and back via the blood stream to the liver
Epidemiology	the study of disease in relation to populations
Epithelial dysplasia	the abnormal development of the epithelium
Epithelium	the tissue that covers the external surface of the body (skin) and lines hollow structures, with the exception of blood and lymphatic vessels
Eosinophil	a type of white blood cell which ingests foreign particles and is present in large numbers in the lining or covering surfaces within the body; they are involved in the allergic response
Essential fatty acid	an unsaturated fatty acid which cannot be synthesised by the body but which must be supplied by the diet; linoleic acid and linolenic acid are the main dietary sources
Fibrinolysis	the process by which blood clots are broken down and removed from the circulation
Gel	the result of the coagulation of a sol to a more or less rigid mass, entrapping and enclosing all of the water in solution
Gelatinisation	the formation of a gel
GLC	gas-liquid chromatography – a method of separating volatile gases by passing them in an inert carrier gas over a stationary liquid phase; the more volatile gases pass through more quickly while the less volatile gases are held back
Glucose tolerance	a measure of a person's ability to restore the blood levels of glucose to normal after being given a glucose load
Gluten	the viscoelastic protein component of dough comprising the nitrogen storage proteins gliadin and glutenin
Glycaemic index	the comparison of the rise in blood glucose produced by a standard carbohydrate dose to that produced by the same amount of a test food
Glycogen	the principal form of storage carbohydrate in the body consisting of branched chains of glucose units
Glycosidic bond	the bond formed between two monosaccharide units by the elimination of a molecule of water
Haemorrhoids	'cushions' of spongy tissue lining the anal canal which become pushed down and appear at the anus
Hemicellulose	polysaccharides insoluble in water and soluble in dilute alkali
Hepatic encephalopathy	a condition secondary to liver damage in which brain function is impaired by toxic substances absorbed from the colon, which are usually detoxified by the liver
Heteropolysaccharide	a polysaccharide containing different monosaccharide residues
Histo-pathogenesis	the development of disease in a tissue
Homo-polysaccharide	a polysaccharide containing only one type of monosaccharide
HPLC	high performance liquid chromatography – a method of separating a mixture of compounds in the liquid state
Hydrophilic	the property of being attracted to water
Hydrophobic	the property of being repelled by water
Hyper-cholesterolaemia	the presence of excess cholesterol in the blood
Hyperinsulinaemia	the presence of excess insulin in the blood
Hyperlipidaemia	the presence of excess lipids in the blood, including triacylglycerols and cholesterol
Hyperglycaemia	the presence of excess glucose in the blood
Hypertension	high blood pressure
Hypertriglyceridaemia	the presence of excess triacylglycerol in the blood
Hypocholesterolaemia	a low/lower level of cholesterol in the blood
Hypoglycaemia	an abnormally low level of glucose in the blood. *Rebound hypoglycaemia* occurs after a period of hyperglycaemia due to excess insulin excretion
IDDM	Insulin Dependent Diabetes Mellitus (Type I diabetes); a form of diabetes requiring regular injections of insulin in order to maintain glucose control

IgE	one of the structurally related blood proteins that act as antibodies
Ileal receptors	receptors in the ileum
Ileostomy	a surgical operation in which the ileum is brought through the abdominal wall to create an artificial opening through which the intestinal contents may be discharged
Immunolabelling	a technique for observing the amount and distribution of an antibody or antigen in a tissue section by labelling the antibody with a fluorescent dye
Incidence	the number of new cases arising in a defined population over a particular period of time
Insulinaemia	the presence of insulin in the blood
Ischaemic heart disease	a condition in which the heart muscle is damaged due to an inadequate flow of blood and the resulting lack of oxygen
Isocaloric	having equivalent energy values
Isolate	a purified fraction of one of the components of the non-starch polysaccharides
Jaundice	a condition due to excess bilirubin (a bile pigment) in the blood; characterised by yellowing of the skin and the whites of the eyes
Laminarin	a storage polysaccharide found in algae
Lignified sclerides	elongated supporting cells with lignified walls
LDL cholesterol	low density lipoprotein cholesterol; cholesterol carried on the low density lipoproteins from the liver to the tissues
Lipaemic	the presence of an abnormally large amount of lipid in the blood
Lithogenic	the tendency to cause stone formation
Lumen	the interior of a hollow organ
Maltose	a disaccharide containing two molecules of glucose
Maltotriose	a trisaccharide containing three molecules of glucose
Micelle	sub-microscopic particles containing hydrophilic (detergent-like) and hydrophobic particles
Microflora	a bacterial population, e.g. that which inhabits the colon
Microvascular	of the capillaries and other small blood vessels
Monoglyceride	a molecule of glycerol with one fatty acid attached to it
Monosaccharide	a simple sugar having the general formula $(CH_2O)_n$ where $n = 3-9$; most monosaccharides have 6 carbon atoms
Morphological adaptation	the alteration of the structure or form of a tissue
Mucilage	a thick aqueous solution of a gum
Multiparous	having given birth to two or more offspring
Myocardial infarction	death of a segment of heart muscle following interruption of the blood supply to it, (ie a heart attack)
Myxoedema	the syndrome due to a lack of thyroxine in adult life which includes coarsening of the skin, weight gain and mental dullness
NIDDM	Non-Insulin Dependent Diabetes Mellitus (Type 2 diabetes); a form of diabetes in which the cells become resistant to the action of insulin
Newtonian flow	the flow of a liquid within a tube in which the liquid in the centre flows faster than that at the edges
Nucleating agent	a particle around which a stone can form
Oligo-	a prefix denoting 'a few'
Pancreatitis	inflammation of the pancreas
Parenchymatous	of the functional cells of the tissue
Pellicle	a thin layer of polysaccharide attaching bacteria to the teeth
Peripheral vascular disease	any disease (usually atherosclerosis) causing narrowing of the blood vessels to the limbs and so poor blood supply, especially to the lower limbs
Pentosan fraction	the polysaccharide fraction containing the pentoses; arabinose and xylose
Phospholipid	a lipid that contains a phosphate group; a constituent of biological membranes
Placebo	an ineffective substance which may nevertheless relieve a condition because of the faith the patient has in its powers
Polymeric diet	an artificial diet which contains whole protein, glucose polymers and long-chain

triacylglycerols and adequate vitamins and minerals

Polysaccharide a complex carbohydrate containing many monosaccharide residues

Post-prandial occurring after a meal

Post-prandial hypoglycaemia the fall in blood glucose to below normal levels which can occur after a meal due to the excess release of insulin

Psychotropic agent an agent which affects mood

Pylorus the lower end of the stomach which connects it with the duodenum; it is kept closed by a ring of muscle, the pyloric sphincter

Prevalence the number of cases existing either at a particular time or over a stated period, in a population

Radiotelemetry device used to measure pH in the large intestine

RAST test Radio Allergosorbent Test – a method of identifying antibodies to particular antigens, in order to determine whether an allergic reaction has been produced

Rectosigmoid colon the region of the colon around the junction of the sigmoid colon and the rectum

Resistant starch starch which is resistant to digestion by the digestive enzymes of the small intestine, either because it is physically inaccessible, or it is in a particular crystalline form or because the amylose has been retrograded

Retrogradation the process by which amylose chains form hydrogen bonds on cooling after heating and form a crystalline structure which is resistant to enzymatic hydrolysis *in vitro*

SCFA short chain fatty acids – these include lactic acid, acetic acid, propionic acid and butyric acid

Simple sugar a mono or disaccharide

Sol a colloidal system in which the water phase is continuous and the large molecules form disperse phases; its properties are intermediate between a solution and a suspension

Starch a polysaccharide consisting of glucose chains; linear chains are called amylose, the branched chains are called amylopectin

Stereochemistry the three-dimensional structure of a molecule

Stoichiometric equation an equation defining the ratio of reactant and product molecules

Subcutaneously beneath the skin

Supersaturated a solution in which more than the normal maximum amount of solute is dissolved without it having precipitated

Thixotropy the reversible transformation of a colloidal solution from a sol to a gel

Thrombosis the formation of a blood clot which may obstruct the blood flow to an organ if it occurs in an artery

Total parenteral nutrition the administration of nutrients directly into the circulation, by-passing the gastrointestinal tract completely

Triacylglycerol a glycerol molecule with 3 fatty acid molecules attached to it

Triose sugar a monosaccharide containing 3 carbon atoms

Trophic effect causing growth or development

Unavailable carbohydrate (UC) those carbohydrates which are not digested as sugars and if absorbed as carbohydrates are not metabolised by normal pathways (for example, xylose)

Unavailable complex carbohydrates (UCC) complex carbohydrates which are not digested in the small intestine but pass into the large intestine where they may be fermented; it includes both resistant starch and non-starch polysaccharides (NSP)

Urolytic bacteria bacteria which are able to metabolise urea

Viscosity the property of resisting shearing forces

Xerostomia dryness of the mouth resulting from decreased secretion of saliva

X-ray diffraction pattern the characteristic patterns produced by crystals when a beam of X-rays are scattered by the electrons surrounding each atom

REFERENCES

Allen, L.H. (1982) Calcium bioavailability and absorption: a review. *Am. J. Clin. Nutr.*, **35**, 783-808.

Alun Jones, V., McLaughlan, P., Shorthouse, M., Workman, E. and Hunter, J.O. (1982) Food Intolerance: A major factor in the pathogenesis of irritable bowel syndrome. *Lancet*, **2**, 1115-1117.

Alun Jones, V., Wilson, A.J., Hunter, J.O. and Robinson, R.E. (1984) The aetiological role of antibiotic prophylaxis with hysterectomy in irritable bowel syndrome. *J. Obs. Gyn.*, **5**, (Suppl 1), S22-S23.

Alun Jones, V., Dickinson. R.J., Workman, E., Wilson, A.J., Freeman, A.H., Hunter, J.O. (1985) Crohn's disease: maintenance of remission by diet. *Lancet*, **2**, 177-180.

Amlot, P.L., Kemeny, D.M., Zachary, C., Parkes, P. and Lessof. M.H. (1987) Oral allergy syndrome (OAS): symptoms of IgE-mediated hypersensitivity to foods. *Clin. Allergy*, **17**, 33-42.

Anderson, A. and Eastwood, M.A. (1987) Flow characteristics and the water retention properties of wheat bran. *J. Sci. Food Agric.*, **39**, 185-194.

Anderson, I.H., Levine, A.S., Levitt, M.D. (1981) Incomplete absorption of the carbohydrate in all purpose wheat flour. *N. Eng. J. Med.*, **304**, 891-892.

Anderson, J.W. (1980) In *Medical Aspects of Dietary Fiber.* (eds G.A. Spiller and R.M. Kay), Plenum Medical Book Company, New York, pp193-221.

Anderson, J.W. (1986) In *Dietary Fiber: Basic and Clinical Aspects.* (eds G.V. Vahouny and D. Kritchevsky), Plenum Press, New York, pp343-360.

Anderson, J.W. and Gustafson, N.J. (1988) Hypocholesterolaemic effects of oat and bean products. *Am. J. Clin. Nutr.*, **48**, 749-753.

Anderson, J.W. and Ward, K. (1979) High carbohydrate, high fiber diets for insulin-treated men with diabetes mellitus. *Am. J. Clin. Nutr.*, **32**, 2312-2321.

Anderson, J.W., Story, L., Sieling, B., Chen, W.J.L., Petro, M.S. and Story, J. (1984a) Hypocholesterolaemic effects of oat-bran or bean intake for hypercholesterolaemic men. *Am. J. Clin. Nutr.*, **40**, 1146-1155.

Anderson, J.W., Story, L., Sieling, B. and Chen, W.L. (1984b) Hypocholesterolaemic effects of high-fibre diets rich in water-soluble plant fibres. *J. Can. Diet. Assoc.*, **451**, 140-149.

Anon. (1986) Some antispasmodic drugs for the irritable bowel syndrome. *Drugs Ther. Bull.*, **24**, 93-95

Arffman, S., Anderson, J.R., Hegnhoj, J. *et al.* (1985) The effect of coarse wheat bran in the irritable bowel syndrome. A double-blind cross-over study. *Scand. J. Gastroenterol*, **20**, 295-298.

Arfwidsson, S. (1954) Pathogenesis of multiple diverticula of the sigmoid colon in diverticular disease. *Acta. Chir. Scan.* (Supp. 342).

Armstrong, B. and Doll, R. (1975) Environmental factors and the incidence and mortality from cancer in different countries with special reference to dietary practice. *Int. J. Cancer*, **15**, 617-631.

Aro, A., Uusitupa, M., Vouilainen, E. and Korhonen, T. (1984) Effects of guar gum in male subjects with hypercholesterolaemia. *Am. J. Clin. Nutr.*, **39**, 911-916.

Arthurs, Y., Fielding, J.F. (1983) Double blind trial of ispaghula/poloxamer in the irritable bowel syndrome. *In. Med. J.*, **76**, 253-255.

Asp, N.G., and Johansson, C.G. (1984) Dietary fibre analysis. Reviews in Clinical Nutrition. *Nut. Abs. Rev.*, **54**, 735-752.

Asp, N.G., Bjorck, I., Holm, J. *et al.* (1987) Enzyme resistant starch fractions and dietary fibre. *Scand. J. Gastro.*, **22** (129),29-32.

Attili, A.F. and the GREPCO group. (1984) Dietary habits and cholelithiasis. In *Epidemiology and prevention of gallstone disease*, (eds L. Capocaccia, G. Ricci, F. Angelico, M. Angelico and A.F. Attili), MTP Press, Lancaster, pp175-81.

Attili, A.F. and the Rome Group for the Epidemiology and prevention of Cholelithiasis (GREPCO) (1987) Diet and gallstones: result of an epidemiologic study performed in male civil servants. In *Nutrition in gastrointestinal disease*, (eds L. Barbara, G. Porro Bianchi, R. Cheli and M Lipkin), Raven Press, New York, pp225-31.

Atwater, W.O. (1910) Principles of nutrition and nutritive value of foods. *USDA Bulletin*, **142**, (2nd Review).

Atwater, W.O. and Bryant, A.P. (1900) The availability and fuel value of food materials. *12th. Annual Report (1899) of the Storrs*, C.T. Agricultural Experimental Station.

Avioli, L.V., (1972) Intestinal absorption of calcium. *Arch. Intern. Med.*, **129**, 345-50.

Balekjian, A.Y., Longton, R.W., Cole, J.S. and Guidry, M.S. (1977) The effect of disaccharides on the plaque forming potential of streptococcus mutans. *J. Dent. Res.*, **56**, 1359-63.

Balsari, A., Ceccarelli, A., Dubini, F., Fesce, E., Poli, M. (1982) The faecal microbial population in the irritable bowel syndrome. *Microbiologica*, **5**, 185-194.

Bannister, J.J., Davison, P., Timms, J.M., Gibbons, C.G., Read, N.W. (1987) Effect of the stool size and consistency of defaecation. *Gut*, **28**, 1246-1250.

Barbara, L., Sama, C., Labate, A.M.M. *et al.* (1987) A population study on the prevalence of gallstone disease. The Sirmione study. *Hepatology*, **7**, 913-7.

Bayliss, C.E., Houston, A.P., Alun Jones, V., Hishon, S., Hunter, J.O. (1984) Microbiological studies on food intolerance. *Proc. Nutr. Soc.*, **43**, 16a.

Bayliss, C.E., Bradley, H.K., Alun Jones, V. and Hunter, J.O. (1986) Some aspects of colonic microbial activity in irritable bowel syndrome associated with food intolerance. *Ann. 1st Super. Sanita 22*, N3 595-964.

Beck, B. and Villaume, C. (1987) Nutrient homeostasis: Long-term interrelations between pancreatic hormones, blood glucose and dietary wheat bran in men. *J. Nutr.*, **117**, 153-158.

Behall, K.M., Scholfield, D.J., Lee, K., Powell, B.S., Moser, P.B. (1988) Mineral balance in adult men: effect of four refined fibres. *Am. J. Clin. Nutr.*, **46**, 307-14.

Bentley, S.J., Pearson, D.J. and Rix, K.J.B. (1983) Food hypersensitivity in irritable bowel syndrome. *Lancet*, **2**, 295-297.

Berghouse, L., Hori, S., Hill, M., Hudson, M., Lennard-Jones, J. and Rogers, E. (1984) Comparison between the bacterial and oligosaccharide content of ileostomy effluent in subjects taking diets rich in refined or unrefined carbohydrate. *Gut*, **25**, 1071-77.

Berry, C.S. (1986a) Resistant starch: Formation and measurement of starch that survives exhaustive digestion with amylolytic enzymes during the determination of dietary fibre. *J. Cereal. Sc.*, **4**, 301-314.

Berry, C.S. (1986b) Production of resistant starch in food by heat-processing: the role of amylose retrogradation and its implications for dietary fibre determination. In *Nahrungsfasern dietary fibres*, (eds R. Amado and T.F. Schweizer).

Betian, H.G., Linehan, B.A., Bryant, M.P. and Holdeman, L.V. (1977) Isolation of allalolytic *Bacteroids* spp from human feces. *Appl. Env. Microbiol.*, **33**, 1009-1010.

Bibby, B.G. (1983) Fruits and vegetables and dental caries. *Clin. Prev. Dent.*, **5**, 3-11.

Bijlani, R.L., Mahaptra, S.C., Sahi, A., Sud, S., Thomas, S. and Nayer, U. (1986) Effect of Isabgol and cellulose on the digestion and absorption of sucrose by everted sacs of adult hampster intestine. *Trop. Gastroenterol.*, **6**, 162-5.

Bingham, S.A., Williams, D.R. and Cummings, J.H. (1985) Dietary fibre consumption in Britain: new estimates and their relation to large bowel cancer mortality. *Br. J. Cancer*, **52**, 399-402.

Bingham, S., Williams, D.R.R., Cole, T.J. and James, W.P.T. (1979) Dietary fibre and regional large bowel cancer mortality in Britain. *Br. J. Cancer*, **40**, 456-463.

Bjorntorp, P. (1988) Abdominal obesity and the development of NIDDM. *Diabetes Met. Res.*, **4**, 615-622.

Blackburn, N.A., Holgate, A.L.M. and Read, N.W. (1984b) Does guar gum improve postprandial hyperglycaemia in humans by reducing small intestinal contact area? *Br. J. Nutr.*, **52**, 197-204.

Blackburn, N.A., Redfern, J.S., Jarjis, M., Holgate, A.M., Hanning, I., Scarpello, J.H.B., Johnson, I.T. and Read, N.W. (1984a) The mechanism of action of guar gum in improving glucose tolerance in man. *Clin. Sci.*, 329-336.

Blackburn, N.A., Redfern, J.S., Jarjis, M. *et al.* (1984) The mechanism of action of guar gum in improving glucose tolerance in man. *Clin. Sci.*, **66**, 329-336.

Blundell, J.E., Burley, V.J. (1987) Satiation, satiety and the action of fibre on food intake. *Int. J. Obesity*, **11**, Supp 1, 9-25.

Bond, J.H., Currier, B.E., Buchwald. H. and Levitt, M.D. (1981) Colonic conservation of malabsorbed carbohydrate. *Gastroenterology*, **78**, 444-447.

Borgman, R.F. and Haselden, F.H. (1968) Cholelithiasis in rabbits: effects of diet upon formation and dissolution of gallstones. *Am. J. Vet. Res.*, **29**, 1287-92.

Bornet, F.R.J., Costagliola, D., Rizzcalla, S.W. *et al.* (1987) Insulinemic and glycemic indexes of six starch-rich foods taken alone and in a mixed meal by type 2 diabetics. *Am. J. Clin. Nutr.*, **45**, 588-595.

Botha, A.P., Steyn, A.F., Esterhuysen, A.J. and Slabbert, M. (1981) Glycosylated haemoglobin, blood glucose and serum cholesterol levels in diabetics treated with guar gum. *S. Afr. Med. J.*, **59**, 333-334.

Bown, R.L., Gibson, J.A., Sladen, G.E., Hicks, B. and Dawson, A.M. (1974) Effects of lactulose and other laxatives on ileal and colonic pH as measured by a radiotelemetry device. *Gut*, **15**, 999-1004.

Brand, J.C., Colagiuri, S., Crossman, S., Allen, A. and Truswell, A.S. (1990) Low glycaemic index carbohydrate foods improve glucose control in non-insulin dependent diabetes mellitus (NIDDM). *Proc. 14th Int. Con. Nutr.*, (ed. S. Kim) (in press).

Brenneman, D.E., Connor, W.E., Forker, E.L. and DenBesten, L. (1972) The formation of abnormal bile and cholesterol gall stones from dietary cholesterol in the prairie dog. *J. Clin. Invest.*, **51**, 1495-1503.

Brieger, L. (1878) *J. Prakt. Chem.*, **17/18**, 124.

Bristol, J.B., Emmett, P.M., Heaton, K.W. and Williamson, R.C.N. (1985) Sugar, fat and risk of colorectal cancer. *Br. Med. J.*, **291**, 409-29.

British Diabetic Association. (1982) Dietary recommendations for diabetics for the 1980's. *Hum. Nutr.: App. Nutr.*, **36A**, 378-94.

British Nutrition Foundation. (1987) Sugars and Syrups. *The Report of the British Nutrition Foundation's Task Force*, BNF, London.

British Nutrition Foundation. (1989) Calcium. *The Report of the British Nutrition Foundation's Task Force*. BNF, London.

Brodribb, A.J.M. and Groves, C. (1978) Effect of bran particle size in stool weight. *Gut*, **19**, 60-63.

Brodribb, A.J.M. and Humphreys, D.M. (1976) Diverticular disease: Three studies. *Br. Med. J.*, **2**, 424-430.

Brown, R.C. Kelleher, J. and Losowsky, M.S. (1979) The effect of pectin on the structure and function of the rat small intestine. *Br. J. Nutr.*, **42**, 357-65.

Brudevold, F., Goulet, D., Tehrani, A., Attarzakeh, F. and van Houte, J. (1985) Intraoral demineralization and maltose clearance from wheat starch. *Caries Res.*, **19**, 136-144.

Burkitt, D.P. (1969) Related disease - related cause? *Lancet*, **2**, 1229-31.

Burkitt, D.P. and Trowell, H.C. (1975) Refined carbohydrate foods and disease. *Some implications of dietary fibre*. Academic Press, London.

Burkitt, D.P., Walker, A.R.P. and Painter, N.S. (1972) Effect of dietary fibre on stools and transit times, and its role in the causation of disease. *Lancet*, **2**, 1408-1412.

Burley, V.J., Leeds, A.R. and Blundell, J.E. (1987) The effect of high and low-fibre breakfast in hunger, satiety and food intake in a subsequent meal. *Int. J. Obesity*, **11**, supp 1, 87-93.

Burr, M.L., Fehily, A.M., Gilbert, J.F., Rogers, S., Holliday, R.M., Sweetnam, P.M., Elwood, P.C. and Deadman, N.M. (1989) Effects of changes in fat, fish and fibre intakes on death and myocardial reinfarction: Diet and Reinfarction Trial (DART) *Lancet*, **2**, 757-761.

Calloway, D.H. and Kretsch, M.J. (1978) Protein and energy utilization in men given a rural Guatemalan die, and egg formulas with and without added oat bran. *Am. J. Clin. Nutr.*, **31**, 1118-1126.

Calvert, R., Schneenan, B.O., Satchitnanandam, J., Cassidy, M.N. and Vahouney, G. (1985) Dietary fibre and intestinal adaptation: effect on intestinal and pancreatic digestive enzyme activities. *Am. J. Clin. Nutr.*, **41**, 1249-1256.

Cambien, F., Jacqueson, A., Richard, J.L., Warnet, J.M., Dacimetiere, P. and Claude, J.K. (1986) Is the level of serum triglyceride a sufficient predictor of coronary death in 'normal cholesterolaemic' subjects? The Paris Prospective Study. *Am. J. Epid.*, **124**, 624-632.

Cann, P.A., Read, N.W. and Holdsworth, C.D. (1984) What is the benefit of coarse wheat bran in patients with irritable bowel syndrome? *Gut*, **24**, 168-173.

Carlson, J. and Griffiths, C.J. (1974) Fermentation products and bacterial yields in glucose-limited and nitrogen-limited cultures of streptococci. *Arch. Oral. Biol.*, **19**, 1105-1109.

Castelli, W.P. (1986) The triglyceride issue: a view from Framingham. *Am. Heart. J.*, **112**, 432-437.

Chauve, A., Devroede, G., Baston, E. (1976) Intraluminal pressure during perfusion of the human colon in situ. *Gastroenterology*, **70**, 336-344.

Chen, W.J.L. and Anderson, J.W. (1986) Hypocholesterolaemic effects of soluble fibre, In *Basic and clinical aspects of dietary fibre*, (eds G.V. Vahouny and D. Kritchevsky) Plenum, New York, pp275-86.

Chew, I., Brand, J.C., Thorburn, A.W. and Truswell, A.S. (1988) Application of glycemic index to mixed meals. *Am. J. Clin. Nutr.*, **47**, 53-56.

Cleave, T.L. (1966) *Diabetes, coronary thrombosis and the Saccharine Disease*. John Wright, Bristol.

Collier, G.R., Wolever, T.M.S., Wong, G.S. and Josse, R.G. (1986) Prediction of glycemic response to mixed meals in non insulin dependent diabetic subjects. *Am. J. Clin. Nutr.*, **44**, 349-352.

Collings, P., Williams, C. and MacDonald, I. (1981) *Effects of cooking on serum glucose and insulin responses to starch*. B.M.J., **282**, 1032.

Collison, R. (1968) In *Starch and its Derivatives*. (eds J.A. Radley) Chapman and Hall, London, pp194-202.

Commission of the European Community (1990) *Proposals for Council Directive on nutrition labelling rules for foodstuffs intended for sale to the ultimate consumer*. In preparation.

Correa, P. and Haenszel, D. (1978) The epidemiology of large bowel cancer. *Adv. Cancer Res.*, **26**, 1-141.

Coulston, A.M., Hollenbeck, C.B. and Reaven, G.M. (1984) Utility of studies measuring glucose and insulin responses to various carbohydrate-containing foods. *Am. J. Clin. Nutr.*, **39**, 163-165.

Crowther, J.S., Drason, B.S., Goddard, P., Hill, M.J. and Johnson, K. (1973) The effect of a chemically defined diet on the faecal flora and faecal steroid concentration. *Gut*, **14**, 790-793.

Cullen, R.W. and Oace, S.M. (1980) Impact on B12 status of pectin and six dietary fibres in rats. *Fed. Proc.*, **39**, 785.

Cullen, R.W., Oace, S.M. (1978) Methylmalonic acid and vitamin B12 excretion of rats consuming diets varying in cellulose and pectin. *J. Nutr.*, **108**, 640-7.

Cummings, J.H. (1982) Consequences of the metabolism of fiber in the human large intestine. In *Dietary Fiber in Health and Disease* (eds G. Vahouny and D. Kritchevsky) pp9-22, Plenum, New York.

Cummings, J.H. (1983) Fermentation in the human large intestine: Evidence and implications for health. *Lancet*, **1**, 1206-1208.

Cummings, J.H. (1984) Constipation, dietary fibre and control of large bowel function. *Postgrad. Med. J.*, **60**, 811-819.

Cummings, J.H., Hill, M.J., Bone, E.S., Branch, W.J. and Jenkins, D.J.A. (1979) The effect of meat protein with and without dietary fibre on colonic function and metabolism. II Bacterial metabolites in faeces and urine. *Am. J. Clin. Nutr.*, **32**, 2094-2101.

Cummings, J.H., Southgate, D.A.T., Branch, W., Houston, H., Jenkins, D.J.A., James, W.P.T. (1978) Colonic responses to dietary fibre from carrot, cabbage, apple, bran, and guar gum. *Lancet*, **1**, 5-9.

Cummings, J.H., Englyst, H.N. and Wood, R. (1985) Determination of dietary fibre in cereals and cereal products - collaborative trials. Part I: initial trial. *J. Assoc. Pub. Anal.*, **23**, 1-35.

Dam, H. (1971) Determinants of cholesterol cholelithiasis in man and animals. *Am. J. Med.*, **51**, 596-613.

Davies, G.J., Crowder, M., Read, B. and Dickerson, J.W.T. (1986) Bowel function measurements of individuals with different eating patterns. *Gut*, **27**, 164-9.

Davies, G.J., Crowder, M. and Dickerson, J.W.T. (1985) Dietary fibre intakes of individuals with different eating patterns. *Hum. Nutr. App. Nutr.*, **39A**, 139-48.

Davies, I.R. (1990) *The food energy values of unavailable carbohydrates assessed in the rat*. PhD Thesis submitted University of East Anglia.

Davies, I.R., Johnson, I.T. and Livesey, G. (1987) Food energy values of dietary fibre components and decreased deposition of body fat. *Int. J. Obesity*, **11**(suppl 1),101-105.

Davies, N.T. (1978) The effects of dietary fibre on mineral availability. In *Dietary Fibre. Current developments of importance to health*. (ed. K.W. Heaton), Newman Publishing, London, pp113-22.

Davies, N.T. (1982) Effects of phytic acid on mineral availability. In *Dietary Fibre Basic and Clinical Aspects*. (eds G.V. Vahouny and D. Kritchevsky), Plenum Press, New York, pp105-116.

De Groot, A.P., Luyken, R. and Pikaar, N.A. (1963) Cholesterol lowering effect of rolled oats. *Lancet*, **2**, 303-304.

Department of Health and Social Security. (1989) Dietary sugars and human disease. *Report on Health and Social Subjects 37*. HMSO, London.

Devroede, G. (1983) Constipation: mechanisms and management. In *Gastrointestinal Disease:*

Pathophysiology, Diagnosis, Management, 3rd ed. (eds M.H. Sleisenger and J.S. Fordtran) Saunders, Philadelphia, pp288-308.

DHSS Committee on Medical Aspects of Food Policy (1984) *Diet and Cardiovascular disease*. DHSS Rep. Health Soc. Subj. No 28. HMSO, London.

Di Lorenzo, C., Williams, C.M., Hajnal, F. and Valenzuela, J.E. (1988) Pectin delays gastric emptying and increases satiety in obese subjects. *Gastroenterol.*, **95**, 1211-5.

Doll, R., Muir, C.S. and Waterhouse, J. (1970) *Cancer in five continents*. Vol II, Springer, Berlin.

Drasar, B.S. and Irving, D. (1973) Environmental factors and cancer of the colon and breast. *Br. J. Cancer*, **27**, 167-172.

Duke, W.D. (1921) Food allergy as a cause of abdominal pain. *Arch. Int. Med.*, **28**, 151-165.

Duke, W.D. (1923) Food allergy as a cause of illness. *J.A.M.A.*, **81**, 886-889.

Dunaiff, G. and Scheeman, B.O. (1981) The effect of dietary fibre on human pancreatic enzyme activity in vitro. *Am. J. Clin. Nutr.*, **34**, 1034-35.

Duncan, K.H., Bacon, J.A. and Weinsier, R.L. (1983) The effects of high and low energy diets on satiety, energy intake and eating time of obese and non-obese subjects. *Am. J. Clin. Nutr.*, **37**, 763-67.

Duncan, L.J.P., Rose, K., Meiklejohn, A.P. (1960) Phenmetrazine hydrochloride and methylcellulose in the treatment of 'refractory' obesity. *Lancet*, **1**, 1262-5.

Dwyer, J. T., Diez, W.H., Andrews, E.M. and Suskind, R.M. (1982) Nutritional status of vegetarian children. *Am. J. Clin. Nutr.*, **35**, 204-216.

Eastwood, M.A., (1986) What does the measurement of dietary fibre mean? *Lancet*, **1**, 1487-8.

Eastwood, M.A., Eastwood, J. and Ward, M. (1975) *Epidemiology of Bowel Disease in Dietary Fiber*. (eds G.A. Spiller and R. Amen) Plenum Press, New York, pp. 207-239.

Eastwood, M.A. and Hamilton, D. (1970) Fatty acids in the lumen of the small intestine of man following a lipid containing meal. *Scand. J. Gastroenterol.*, **5** 225-230.

Eastwood, M.A., Sanderson, J., Pocock, S.J. *et al.* (1977) Variation in the incidence of diverticular disease within the City of Edinburgh. *Gut*, **18**, 571.

Eastwood, M.A., Smith, A.N., Brydon, W.G., *et al.* (1978) Colonic function in patients with diverticular disease. *Lancet*, **1**, 1181-1182.

Eastwood, M.A., Robertson, J.A. *et al.* (1983) Measurement of water holding properties of fibre and their faecal bulking ability in man. *Br. J. Nutr.*, **50**, 539-547.

Eastwood, M.A., Brydon, W.G., Baird, J.D. *et al.* (1984) Faecal weight and composition, serum lipids and diet among subjects aged 18-80 years not seeking health care. *Am. J. Clin. Nutr.*, **40**, 628-34.

Eastwood, M.A., Brydon, W.G. and Anderson, D.M.W. (1986) The effect of the polysaccharide composition and structure of dietary fibers on caecel fermentation and faecal excretion. *Am. J. Clin. Nutr.*, **44**, 51-55.

Eastwood, C.A., Blackburn, N.A., Craigen, L. *et al.* (1987) Viscosity of food gums determined in vitro related to their hypoglycaemic actions. *Am. J. Clin. Nutr.*, **46**, 72-77.

Edgar, W.M., Bibby, B.G., Mundorft, S. and Rowley, J. (1975) Acid production in plaques after eating snacks; modifying factors in foods. *J. Am. Dent. Ass.*, **90**, 418-425.

Edgar, W.M., Geddes, D.A.M., Jenkins, G.N. and Rugg-Grunn, A.J. (1978) Effects of calcium glycerophosphate and sodium fluoride on the induction 'in vivo' of caries like changes in human dental enamel. *Archs. Oral Biol.*, **23**, 655-661.

Edwards, C.A., Blackburn, N.A., Craigen, L., Davison, P., Tomlin, J., Sugden, K., Johnson, I.T. and Read, N.W. (1987) Viscosity of food gums determined in vitro related to their hypoglycaemic actions. *Am. J. Clin. Nutr.*, **46**, 672-7.

Edwards, C.A., Johnson, I.T. and Read, N.W. (1988) Do viscous polysaccharides reduce absorption by inhibiting diffusion or convection? *Eur. J. Clin. Nutr.*, **42**, 307-312.

Edwards, C.A., Johnson, I.T. and Read, N.W. (1990) Do viscous polysaccharides slow absorption by inhibiting diffusion or conversion? *Eur. J. Clin. Nutr.* (in press).

Egger, J., Carter, C.M., Wilson, J., Turner, M.W. and Soothill, J.F. (1983) Is migraine food allergy? A double blind controlled trial of oligoantigenic diet treatment. *Lancet*, **2**, 865-869.

Egger, J., Carter, C.M., Graham, P.J., Gurnley, D. and Soothill, J.F. (1985) Controlled trial of oligoantigenic therapy in the hyperkinetic syndrome. *Lancet*, **1**, 540-545.

Englyst, H.N. (1985) *Dietary polysaccharide breakdown in the gut of man*. Ph.D. Thesis. University of Cambridge, UK.

Englyst, H.N. and Cummings, J.H. (1985) Digestion of the polysaccharides of some cereal foods in the human small intestine. *Am. J. Clin. Nutr.*, **42**, 778-787.

Englyst, H.N. and Cummings, J.H. (1987a) Resistant starch, a 'new' food component: a classification of starch for nutritional purposes. In *Cereals in a European Context* (Ed. I.D. Morton) Ellis Horwood Limited: Chichester, pp221-233.

Englyst, H.N. and Cummings, J.H. (1987b) Digestion of polysaccharides of potato in the small intestine of man. *Am. J. Clin. Nutr.*, **45**, 423-431.

Englyst, H.N. and Kingman, S.M. (1990) Dietary fiber and resistant starch. A nutritional classification of plant polysaccharides. In *Dietary Fiber*, (ed. G. Vahouny) (in press).

Englyst, H.N. and Macfarlane, G.T. (1988) Breakdown of resistant and readily digestible starch by human gut bacteria. *J. Sci. Food Agric.*, **37**, 699-706.

Englyst, H., Wiggins, H.S. and Cummings, J.H. (1982) Determination of the non-starch polysaccharides in plant foods by gas-liquid chromatography of constituent sugars as alditol acetates. *Analyst*, **107**, 307-318.

Englyst, H.N., Trowell, H.W., Southgate, D.A.T., Cummings, J.H. (1987a) Dietary fibre and resistant starch. *Am. J. Clin. Nutr.*, **46**, 873-874.

Englyst, H.N., Hay, S. and Macfarlane, G.T. (1987b) Polysaccharide breakdown by mixed populations of human faecal bacteria. *FEMS Microbiology Ecology*, **95**, 163-171.

Englyst, H.N., Bingham, S.A., Runswick, S.A., Collinson, E. and Cummings, J.H. (1988) Dietary fibre (non-starch polysaccharides) in fruit, vegetables and nuts. *J. Human Nutr. Diet.*, **1**, 247-86.

Evans, E., and Miller, D.S. (1975) Bulking agents in the treatment of obesity. *Nutr. Metab.*, **18**, 199-203.

F.A.O. (1969) *The state of Food and Agriculture.* Rome, Food and Agriculture Organisation.

Fadden, K., Owen, R.W., Hill, M.J., Latymer, E., Dow, G. and Mason, A.N. (1985) The use of multiple cannulated pigs to examine the effect of dietary fibre supplements on bile acid metabolism in the porcine hindgut. In *Digestive Physiology in the Pig.* (eds A. Just, H. Jorgensen and J. Fernandez). National Institute of Animal Science, Copenhagen, pp 192-194.

Fairweather-Tait, S.J., Johnson, A., Eagles, J., Ganatra, S., Kennedy, H., Gurr, M.I. (1989) Studies on calcium absorption from milk using a double-label stable isotope technique. *Br. J. Nutr.*, **62**, 379-388.

Faivre, J., Boutron, M., Hillon, P., Bedenne, L., Klepping, C. (1985) Epidemiology of colorectal cancer. In *Diet and Human Carcinogenesis.* (eds J. Joossens, M. Hill and J. Geboers) Excerpta Medica, Amsterdam, pp123-136.

Farah, D.A., Calder, I., Benson, L. and Mackenzie, J.F. (1985) Specific food intolerance: its place as a cause of gastrointestinal symptoms. *Gut*, **26**, 164-168.

Federation of American Societies for Experimental Biology. (1987) *Physiological Effects and Health Consequences of dietary fiber.* Life Sciences Research Office, Bethesda.

Fernandez, R., Kennedy, H., Hill, M. and Truelove, S. (1985) The effect of diet on the bacterial flora of ileostomy fluid. *Microbiol. Aliments. Nutr.*; **3**, 47-52.

Figdor, S.K. and Bianchine, J.R. (1983) Caloric utilization and disposition of 14C-polydextrose in man. *J. Agric. Food. Chem.*, **31**, 389-393.

Findlay, J.M., Smith, A.M., Mitchell, W.D., *et al.* (1974) Effects of unprocessed bran on colon function in normal subjects and in diverticular disease. *Lancet*, **2**, 146-149.

Finotti, P. and Piccoli, A. (1990) Long-term blood glucose control and diabetic retinopathy. *Lancet*, **1**, 107-108.

Firestone, A.R., Schmid, R. and Muhlemann, H.R. (1982) Cariogenic effects of cooked wheat starch alone or with sucrose and frequency controlled feeding in rats. *Arch. Oral Biol.*, **27**, 759-763.

Fischer, H. (1913) *Z. exp. Path. U. Therap.*, **14**, 179.

Fisher, F.J. (1968) A field study of dental caries, periodontal disease and enamel defects in Tristan da Cunha. *Br. Dent. J.*, **125**, 398-401, 447-453.

Fisher, N., Berry, C.S., Fern, J, *et al.* (1985) Cereal dietary fiber consumption and diverticular disease: a lifespan study in rats. *Am. J. Clin. Nutr.*, **42**, 788-804.

Food and Agriculture Organisation. (1947) *Energy-yielding components of food and computation of caloric values.* Washington DC.

Food and Agriculture Organisation (1980) *Carbohydrates in human nutrition.* FAO Papers in Food and Nutrition No. 15. FAO Rome.

Food and Agriculture Organisation (1983) *A comparative study of food consumption data from food balance sheets and household surveys.* FAO, Rome.

Food and Agriculture Organisation (1985) *Guidelines on nutrition labelling.* ALINORM 85/22A. FAO. Rome.

Food and Agriculture Organisation (1988) *FAO production yearbook 1987*, **41**. FAO, Rome.

Foster, D.W. (1989) Insulin resistance - a secret killer? *N. Eng. J. Med.*, **320**, 733-734.

Freeland-Graves, J. (1988) Mineral adequacy of vegetarian diets. *Am. J. Clin. Nutr.*, **48**, 589-862.

French, D. (1972) Fine structure of starch and its relationship to the organisation of starch granules. *J. Jap. Soc. Starch Sci.*, **19**, 6-26.

Friend, B., Page, L. and Marston, R. (1979) Food consumption patterns in the United States: 1909-1913 to 1976. In *Nutrition, lipids and coronary heart disease.* (eds R.I. Levy, B.M. Rifkind, B. Dennis and N. Ernst), Raven Press, New York, pp488-522.

Fuessl, H.S., Williams, G., Adrian, T.E. and Bloom, S.R. (1987) Guar sprinkled in food: effect on glycaemic control, plasma lipids and gut hormones in non-insulin dependent diabetic patients. *Diabetic Med.*, **4**, 463-468.

Furda, I. (1983) *Unconventional Sources of Dietary Fibre.* American Chemical Society, Washington.

Galea, H., Aganovic, I. and Aganovic, M. (1986) The dental caries and periodontal disease experience of patients with early onset insulin dependent diabetes. *Int. Dent. J.*, **36**, 219-24.

Gallaher, D. and Schneeman, B.O. (1986) Intestinal interaction of bile acids, phospholipid, dietary fibres and cholestryamine. *Am. J. Physiol.*, **250**, G420-26.

Garcia-Palmieri, M.R., Sorlie, P., Tillotson, J., Costas, R., Cordero, E. and Rodriguez, M. (1980) Relationships of dietary intake to subsequent coronary heart disease incidence: the Puerto Rico Heart Health Program. *Am. J. Clin. Nutr.*, **33**, 1818-1827.

Gatti, E., Catenazzo, G., Camisasca, E., Torri, A., Denegri, E. and Sirtori C.R. (1984) Effects of guar-enriched pasta in the treatment of diabetes and hyperlipidaemia. *Ann. Nutr. Metab.*, **59**, 1-10.

Gear, J.S.S., Ware, A., Fursden, P. *et al.* (1979) Symptomless diverticular disease and intakes of dietary fibre. *Lancet*, **1**, 511-4.

Gee, J.M. and Johnson, J.T. (1985) Rates of starch hydrolysis and changes in a range of common foods subjected to simulated digestion 'in vitro'. *J. Sci. Food Agric.*, **36**, 614-620.

Gerrard, J.W. (1979) The diagnosis of the food-allergic patient. In *The Mast Cell: its Role in Health and Disease*, (eds J. Pepys and A.M.Edwards) Pitman Medical, Bath, pp416-421.

Gidley, M.J. (1987) Factors affecting the crystalline type (A-C) of native starches and model compounds: a rationalisation of observed effects in terms of polymorphic structures. *Carbohydrate Res.*, **161**, 301-304.

Gillooly, M., Bothwell, T.H., Torrance, J.D., MacPhail, A.P., Derman, D.P., Bezwoda, W.R., Mills, W., Charlton, R.W. and Mayet, F. (1983) The effects of organic acids, phytates and polyphenols on the absorption of iron from vegetables. *Br. J. Nutr.*, **49**, 331-342.

Glicksman, M. (1969) *Gum Technology in the food industry.* Academic Press, New York.

Goldin, B.R., Swenson, L., Dwyer, J., Sexion, M. and Gorback, S.L. (1980) Effect of diet and Lactobacillus acidophilus supplements on human fecal bacterial enzymes. *J. Nat. Cancer Inst.*, **64**, 255-61.

Goldsmith, G.A., Gibbens, J., Unglaub, W.G., Miller, O.N. (1956) Studies of niacin requirement in man. III Comparative effects of diets containing lime treated and untreated corn in the production of experimental pellagra. *Am. J. Clin. Nutr.*, **4**, 151-60.

Goodlad, E.A., Leaton, W., Chatel, M.A., Adrian, T.E., Bloom, S.R., Wright, N.A. (1987) Proliferative effects of 'fibre' on the intestinal epithelium; relationship to gastrin, enteroglucagon and PYY. *Gut*, **28**, 221-226.

Goranzon, H. and Forsum, E. (1987) Metabolizable energy in humans in two diets. Calculation and analysis. *J. Nutr.*, **117**, 267-273.

Goranzon, H., Forsum, E. and Thilen, M. (1983) Calculation and determination of metabolizable energy in mixed diets to humans. *Am. J. Clin. Nutr.*, **38**, 954-963.

Green, R.M. and Hartles, R.L. (1967) The effect of uncooked and roll-dried maize starch, alone and mixed in equal quantity with sucrose on dental caries in the albino rat. *Br. J. Nutr.*, **21**, 225-230.

Gregor, O., Toman, R. and Prusova, F. (1969) Gastrointestinal cancer and nutrition. *Gut*, **10**, 1031-1034.

Gregory, J., Foster, K., Tyler, H. and Wiseman, M.J. (1990) *The dietary and nutritional survey of British adults*. HMSO, London.

Grenby, T.H. (1965) The influence of cooked and raw wheat starch on dental caries in the rat. *Arch. Oral Biol.* **10**, 433-438.

Griffiths, D.W. (1979) The inhibition of digestive enzymes by extracts of field beans. *J. Sci. Food Agric.*, **30**, 458-62.

Grove, E.W., Olmsted, W.H. and Koenig, K. (1929) The effect of diet and catharsis on the lower volatile fatty acids in the stools of normal men. *J. Biol. Chem.*, **85**, 127-136.

Gustaffson, B.E., Quensel, C.E., Lanke, L.S., Lundquist, C., Grahnen, H., Bonow, B.E. and Krasse, B. (1954) The Vipeholm Dental Caries Study - The effect of different levels of carbohydrate intake on caries activity in 436 individuals observed for five years. *Actu. Odont. Scand.*, **2**, 232-364.

Haber, G.B., Heaton, K.W., Murphy, D. and Burroughs, L.F. (1977) Depletion and disruption of dietary fibre: effect on satiety, plasma, glucose, and serum insulin. *Lancet*, **2**, 679-682.

Hallberg, L. (1987) Wheat fibre, phytates and iron absorption. *Scand. J. Gastroenterol.*, **22** (129),73-79.

Hardwick, J.L. (1960) The incidence and distribution of caries throughout the ages in relation to the English man's diet. *Br. Dent. J.*, **108**, 9-17.

Harley, C.J., Davies, I.R. and Livesey, G. (1989) Digestible energy value of gums in the rat - data on gum arabic. *Food Add. Cont.*, **6**, 13-20.

Harvey, R.F., Pomare, E.W. and Heaton, K.W. (1973) Effects of increase dietary fibre on intestinal transit. *Lancet*, **1**, 1278-1280.

Health and Welfare Canada. (1987) *Report of the Expert Advisory Committee on Dietary Fibre*.

Health and Welfare Canada. (1988) Health Protection Branch, *Information Letter Feb 5*.

Heaton, K.W. (1973) Food fibre as an obstacle to energy intake. *Lancet*, **2**, 1418-21.

Heaton, K.W. (1985) Role of dietary fibre in the treatment of irritable bowel syndrome. In *Irritable Bowel Syndrome*. (ed. N.W. Read), Grune and Stratton, Orlando, Fl, pp203-222.

Heaton, K.W. (1987) Effect of dietary fiber on biliary lipids. In *Nutrition in gastrointestinal disease*, (eds L. Barbara, G. Bianchi Porro, R. Cheli and M. Lipkin) Raven Press, New York, pp213-22.

Heaton, K.W. (1988) Gallstone prevention: clues from epidemiology. In *Bile acids in health and disease*, (eds T. Northfield, R. Jazrawi and P. Zentler-Munro) M.T.P. Press, Lancaster, pp157-69.

Heaton, K.W., Manning, A.P. and Hartog, M. (1976) Lack of effect on blood lipids and calcium concentrations of young men on changing from white to wholemeal bread. *Br. J. Nutr.*, **35**, 55-60.

Heaton, K.W., Marcus, S.N., Emmett, P.M. and Bolton, D.H. (1988) Particle size of wheat maize, oat test meals; effects on plasma glucose and insulin responses and rate of starch digestion in vitro. *Am.J. Clin. Nutr.*, **47**, 675-82.

Hecht, A.F. (1910) *Münch. Med. Woch.*, **57**, 63.

Heller, S.N., Mackler, L.R., Rivers, J.M., Van Soets, P.J., Roe, D.A., Lewis, B.V.A. and Robertson, J. (1980) Dietary fibre: the effect of particle size of wheat bran on colonic function in young adult men. *Am. J. Clin. Nutr.*, **33**, 1734-1744.

Helman, A.D. and Darnton-Hill, I. (1987) Vitamin and iron status in new vegetarians. *Am. J. Clin. Nutr.*, **45**, 785-789.

Henry, R.W., Stout, R.W. and Love, A.H.G. (1978) Lack of effect of bran enriched bread on plasma lipids, calcium, glucose and body weight. *Ir. J. Med. Sci.*, **147**, 249-51.

Hikasa, Y., Matsuda, S., Nagase, M. *et al.* (1969) Initiating factors of gallstones, especially cholesterol stones (III). *Arch. Jap. Chir.*, **38**, 107-24.

Hill, M.J. (1980) The aetiology of colorectal cancer. In *Recent Advances in Gastrointestinal Pathology*. (ed. R. Wright), pp297-310. Saunders, London.

Hill, M.J. (1987) *Microbes and human carcinogenesis*, Edward Arnold. London.

Hill, M.J. and Fernandez, F. (1990) Mechanism of action of dietary fibre in colon carcinogenesis. In *Dietary Fiber* (ed. D. Kritchevsky), Plenum, New York (In press).

Hill, M.J., Morson, B.C. and Bussey, H.J.R. (1978) Etiology of adenoma-carcinoma sequence in large bowel. *Lancet*, **1**, 245-247.

Hill, M.J., Maclennan, R. and Newcombe, J. (1979) Gut and large bowel cancer in three socioeconomic groups in Hong Kong. *Lancet*, **1**, 436.

Hill, M.Y. (1982) Colonic bacterial activity: effect of fiber on substrate concentration and on enzyme action. In *Dietary Fiber in Health and Disease*. (eds G. Vahouny and D. Kritchevsky), Plenum, New York, pp35-44.

Himsworth, H.P. (1935) *Clin. Sci.*, **2**, 67-94.

Hirayama, T. (1985) In *Diet and Human Carcinogenesis* (eds J. Joossens, M. Hill and J. Geboers). Excerpta Medica, Amsterdam.

Hizukuri, S. (1985) Relationship between the distribution of the chain length of amylopectin and the crystalline structure of starch granules. *Carbohydrate Res.*, **141**, 295-306.

Hoff, G., Moen, I., Trygg, K., Frolich, W., Souer, J., Vatn, M., Gjone, E., Larsen, S. (1986) Epidemiology of polyps in the rectum and sigmoid colon. Evaluation of nutritional factors. *Scand. J. Gastroenterology*, **21**, 199-204.

Holland, B., Unwin, I.D. and Buss, D.H. (1988) *Cereals and cereal products*. Royal Society of Chemistry, Letchworth.

Holland, B., Unwin, I.D. and Buss, D.H. (1989) *Milk products and eggs*. Royal Society of Chemistry, Letchworth.

Holloway, W.D., Tasman-Jones, C. and Bell, E. (1980) The hemicellulose component of dietary fiber. *Am. J. Clin. Nutr.*, **37**, 253-255.

Holm, J., Lunquist, I., Björck, I. *et al.* (1988) Degree of starch gelatinisation, digestion rate of starch in vitro, and metabolic response in rats. *Am. J. Clin. Nutr.*, **47**, 1010-1016.

Holt, S., Heading, R.C., Carter, D.C., Prescott, L.F. and Tothill, P. (1979) Effect of gel-forming fibre on gastric emptying and absorption of glucose and paracetamol. *Lancet*, **1**, 636-9.

Hood, K., Gleeson, D., Ruppin, D. and Dowling, H. (1988) Can gallstone recurrence be prevented? The British/Belgian post-dissolution trial. *Gastroenterology*, **94**, A548.

Hopman, W.P.M., Honben, P.G.M.P., Speth, J.A.J. and Lamers, C.B.H.W. (1988) Glucomannan prevents post prandial hypoglycaemia in patients with previous gastric surgery. *Gut*, **29**, 930-934.

Hoskins, L.C. (1968) Bacterial degradation of gastrointestinal mucins. *Gastroenterology*, **54**, 218-224.

Huang, C.T., Little, M.F. and Johnson, R. (1981) Influence of carbohydrates on 'in vivo' lesion production. *Caries Res.*, **15**, 54-59.

Hudson, M.J., Borriello, S.P. and Hill, M.J. (1981) Elemental diets and the bacterial flora of the gastrointestinal tract. In *Elemental Diets* (ed. R. Russell), C.R.C Press, Boca Raton, pp105-26.

Hummel, F.C., Shepherd, M.L. and Macy, I.G., (1943) Disappearance of cellulose and hemicellulose from the digestive tracts of children. *J. Nutrition*, **25**, 59-70.

Hungate, R.E. (1985) In vivo metabolism in the rumen fermentation. In *Models of Anaerobic Infection* (ed. M.J. Hill), editor in chief, Martinus Nijlof, Amsterdam, pp139-150.

Hunter, J.O. (1990) Food intolerance and the irritable bowel syndrome. (ed. N.W. Read), In *Neurotic and demented bowels*. Blackwell Scientific Publications, Oxford (In press).

Hunter, J.O., Workman, E., Alun Jones, V. (1985) The role of diet in the management of irritable bowel syndrome. *Topics in Gastroenterology*, **12**, 305-313.

Hyams, J.S. (1983) Sorbitol intolerance: An unappreciated cause of functional gastrointestinal complaints. *Gastroenterology*, **84**, 30-33.

IARC Working Party (1982) Diet, bowel function, faecal characteristics and large bowel cancer in Denmark and Finland. *Nutr. Cancer*, **4**, 5-19.

Ikegamu, S., Tsuchihashi, N., Nagayama, S. and Innami, S. (1982) Effect of viscous indigestible polysaccharides on pancreatic exocrine and bilary secretion in rats. *Nutr. Rep. Int.*, **26**, 263-9.

Imaizumi, K. and Sugaro, M. (1986) Dietary fibre and intestinal lipoprotein secretion. In: Dietary fibre, basic and clinical aspects. (eds G.V. Vahouney and D. Kritchevsky) pp287-308, Plenum Press, NY.

International Life Sciences Institute. (1987) Diet and health: Scientific concepts and principles. Simopoulos, A.P. (ed.) *Am. J. Clin. Nutr.*, **45**, (supp) 1015-1414.

Isaakson, G., Asp, N.-G. and Ihse, I. (1983) Effect of dietary fibre on pancreatic enzyme activities of ileostomy evacuates and on excretion of fat and nitrogen in the rat. *Scand. J. Gastroenterol.*, **18**, 417-23.

James, D.E., Strube, M. and Mueckler, M. (1989) Molecular cloning and characterisation of an insulin - regulatable glucose transporter. *Nature*, **338**, 83-87.

James, W.P.T. (1980) Dietary fibre and mineral absorption. In *Medical Aspects of Dietary Fibre*, (eds G.A. Spiller and R.M. Kay) Plenum Press, New York, p239.

Jenkins, D.J.A., Leeds, A.R., Newton, C., Gassull and M.A. (1975) Effect of pectin, guar gum and wheat fibre on serum-cholesterol. *Lancet*, **1**, 1116-1117.

Jenkins, D.J.A., Goff, D.V., Leeds, A.R., Alberti, R.G., Wolever, T.M.S., Gassuld, M.A. and Hockaday, T.D.R. (1976) Unabsorbable carbohydrates and diabetes: decreased post-prandial hyperglycaemia. *Lancet*, **2**, 170-174.

Jenkins, D.J.A., Wolever, T.M.S., Leeds, A.R. *et al.* (1978a) Dietary fibres, fibre analogues and glucose tolerance: importance of viscosity. *Br. Med. J.*, **1**, 1392-1394.

Jenkins, D.J.A., Wolever, T.M.S., Nineham, R., Taylor, R., Metz, G.H., Baccon, S. and Hockaday, T.D.R. (1978b) Guar crispbread in the diabetic diet. *Br. Med. J.*, **2**, 1744-1746.

Jenkins, D.J.A., Leeds, A.R., Slavin, B., Mann, J. and Jepson, E.M. (1979) Dietary fiber and blood lipids: reduction of serum cholesterol in type III hyperlipidaemia by guar gum. *Am. J. Clin. Nutr.*, **32**, 16-18.

Jenkins, D.J.A., Reynolds, D., Slavin, B., Leeds, A.R., Jenkins, A.L. and Jepson, E.M. (1980) Dietary fiber and lipids: treatment of hypercholesterolemia with guar crispbread. *Am. J. Clin. Nutr.*, **33**, 575-581.

Jenkins, D.J.A., Wolever, T.M.S. and Taylor, R.H. (1981) Dietary fibre, fibre analogues and glucose transport: importance of viscosity. *Am. J. Clin. Nutr.*, **34**, 362-66.

Jenkins, D.J.A., Wolever, T.M.J., Taylor, R.H., Griffiths, C., Krzeminska, K., Lawrie, J.A., Bennett, C.M., Goff, D.V., Sarson, D.L. and Bloom, S.R. (1982) Slow release dietary carbohydrate improves second meal tolerance. *Am. J. Clin. Nutr.*, **35**, 1339-1346.

Jenkins, D.J.A., Wolever, T.M.S., Jenkins, A.L. *et al.* (1983) Glycemic response to wheat products: reduced response to pasta but no effect of fiber. *Diabetes Care*, **6**, 155-9.

Jenkins, D.J.A., Wolever, T.M.S., Jenkins, A.L. *et al.* (1984) In *Dietary Fibre: Basic and Clinical Aspects* (eds G.V. Vahouny and D. Kritchevsky), Plenum Press, New York, pp167-179.

Jenkins, D.J.A., Wolever, T.M.S. and Jenkins, A.L. *et al.* (1986) Low glycaemic response to traditionally processed wheat and rye products: bulgur and pumpernickel bread. *Am. J. Clin. Nutr.*, **43**, 516-520.

Jenkins, D.J.A., Thorne, J.J. and Wolever, T.M. (1987a) The effect of starch protein interaction in wheat on the glycaemic response and rate of in vitro digestion. *Am.J. Clin. Nutr.*, **45**, 946-951.

Jenkins, D.J.A., Wolever, T.M.S., Collier, G.R. *et al.* (1987b) Metabolic effects of a low glycemic index diet. *Am. J. Clin. Nutr.*, **46**, 968-75.

Jensen, M.E. and Schachtele, C.F. (1983) The acidogenic potential of reference foods and snacks at inter-proximal sites in the human dentition. *J. Dent. Res.*, **62**, 889-892.

Johnson, C.K., Kolasa, K., Chenoweth, W. and Benwick, M. (1980) Health, laxation and food habit influences on fiber intake of older women. *J. Am. Diet. Assoc.*, **77**, 551-557.

Johnson, I.T. and Gee, J.M. (1981) Effect of gel forming food gums on the intestinal unstirred layer and sugar transport in vitro. *Gut*, **22**, 398-403.

Johnson, I.T. and Gee, J.M. (1986) Gastrointestinal adaptation in response to soluble non-available polysaccharides in the rat. *Br. J. Nutr.*, **55**, 497-505.

Jorgensen, T. (1987) Prevalence of gallstones in a Danish population. *Am. J. Epidemiol.*, **126**, 912-21.

Judd, P.A. (1982) The effects of high intakes of barley on gastrointestinal function and apparent digestibilities of dry matter, nitrogen and fat in human volunteers. *J. Plant Foods*, **4**, 79-88.

Judd, P.A. and Truswell, A.S. (1981) The effect of rolled oats on blood lipids and fecal steroid excretion in man. *Am. J. Clin. Nutr.*, **34**, 2061-2067.

Kahaner, N., Fuchs, H.M. and Floch, M.H. (1976) The effect of dietary fiber supplementation in man. I. Modification of eating habits. *Am. J. Clin. Nutr.*, **29**, 1437-42.

Karlstrom, B., Vessby, B., Asp, N.G. and Ytterfors, A. (1988) Effects of four meals with different kinds of dietary fibre on glucose metabolism in healthy subjects and non-insulin-dependent diabetic patients. *Eur. J. Clin. Nutr.*, **42**, 519-526.

Karlstrom, B., Vessby, B., Asp, N-G., Boberg, M., Gustafsson, I-B., Lithell, H. and Werner, I. (1984) Effects of an increased content of cereal fibre in the diet of Type 2 (NIDDM) diabetic patients. *Diabetologia*, **26**, 272-277.

Karlstrom, B., Vessby, B., Asp, N-G., Boberg, M., Lithell, H. and Berne, C. (1987) Effects of leguminous seeds in NIDDM patients. *Diab. Res.*, **5**, 199-205.

Kasper, H. (1986) Effects of dietary fiber on vitamin metabolism. In *Handbook of Dietary Fiber in Human Nutrition*, (ed. G.A. Spiller), CRC Press, Florida, USA. pp201-208.

Katz, J.R. (1934) X-ray investigation of gelatinisation and retrogradation of starch and its importance for bread research. *Bakers Weekly*, **81**, 34-37.

Kay, R.M., Truswell, A.S. (1977) The effect of wheat fibre on plasma lipids and faecal steroid excretion in man. *Br. J. Nutr.*, **37**, 227-235.

Kay, R.M., Sabry, Z.I. and Csima, A. (1980) Multivariate analysis of diet and serum lipids in normal men. *Am. J. Clin. Nutr.*, **33**, 2566-72.

Keagy, P.M., Shane, B., Oaoe S. (1988) Folate bioavailability in humans: effects of wheat bran and beans. *Am. J. Clin. Nutr.*, **47**, 80-88.

Kearsley, N.W. and Sicard, P.J. (1989) The chemistry of starches and sugars present in foods. In: Dietary starches and sugars in man: a comparison. (ed. J. Dobbing) pp1-33, Springer-Verlag, London.

Kelsay, J.L. (1982) Effects of fibre on mineral and vitamin bioavailability. In *Dietary fibre in Health and Disease*. (eds G.V. Vahouney and D. Kritchevsky), Plenum Press, New York, pp91-104.

Kelsay, J.L. (1986) Update on fibre and mineral availability. In *Dietary fibre, basic and clinical aspects*. (eds G.V. Vahouney and D. Kritchevsky) Plenum Press, New York, pp361-372.

Kelsay, J.L. (1987) Effects of fibre, phytic acid and oxalic acid in the diet on mineral bioavailability *Am. J. Gastroenterol.*, **82**, 983-6.

Kelsay, J.L., Behall. K.M. and Prather, E.A. (1978) Effects of fiber from fruit and vegetables on the metabolic responses of human subjects. I Bowel transit time, number of defecations, fecal weight, urinary excretions of energy and nitrogen and apparent digestiblilities of energy, nitrogen and fat. *Am. J. Clin. Nutr.*, **31**, 1149-1153.

Kelsay, J.L., Behall, K.M. and Prather, E.S. (1979) Effect of fiber from fruits and vegetables on metabolic responses of human subjects. II. Calcium magnesium, iron and silicon balances. *Am. J. Clin. Nutr.*, **32**, 1876-1880.

Khan, A.R., Khan, G.Y., Mitchel, A. and Quadeer, M.A. (1981) Effect of guar gum on blood lipids. *Am. J. Clin. Nutr.*, **34**, 2446-2449.

Kiehm, T.G., Anderson, J.W. and Ward, K. (1976) Beneficial effects of a high carbohydrate, high fiber diet on hyperglycaemic diabetic men. *Am. J. Clin. Nutr.*, **29**, 895-899.

Kinmonth, A-L., Angus, R.M., Jenkins, P.A., Smith, M.A. and Baum, J.D. (1982) Whole foods and increased dietary fibre improve blood glucose control in diabetic children. *Arch. Dis. Child.*, **57**, 187-194.

Kirby, R.W., Anderson, J.W., Sieling, B., Rees, E.D., Chen, W.J.L., Miller, R.E. and Kay, R.M. (1981) Oat-bran intake selectively lower serum low-density lipoprotein cholesterol concentrations of hyper-cholesterolaemic men. *Am. J. Clin. Nutr.*, **34**, 824-829.

Kirwan, W., Smith, A.N., McConnell, A.A., *et al.* (1974) Action of different bran preparations on colonic function. *Br. Med. J.*, **1**, 187-189.

Konig, K.G. (1967) Caries induced in laboratory rats. *Br. Dent. J.*, **123**, 585-589.

Kritchevsky, D. (1974) Dietary fibre. *Ann. Rev. Nutr.*, **8**, 301-328.

Kritchevsky, D. (1986) Fiber and cancer. In *Dietary Fiber: Basic and Clinical Aspects*. (eds G. Vahouny and D. Kritchevsky), Plenum, New York, pp427-32.

Kromhout, D., Bosschieter, E.B. and Coulander, C.L. (1982) Dietary fibre and 10-year mortality from coronary heart disease, cancer and all causes. The Zutphen study. *Lancet*, **2**, 518-522.

Krotkiewski, M. (1984) Effects of guar gum on body weight, hunger ratings and metabolism in obese subjects. *Br. J. Nutr.*, **52**, 97-105.

Krotkiewski, M., and Smith, U. (1985) Dietary fibre in obesity. In *Dietary Fibre Perspectives: Reviews and Bibliography 1*. (ed. A.R. Leeds), Libbey, London, pp61-67.

Kumar, A., Kumar, N., Vij, J.C. *et al.* (1987) Optimum dosage of isphagula husk in patients with irritable bowel syndrome - Correlation of symptom relief with whole gut transit time and stool weight. *Gut*, **28**, 150-155.

Kushi, L.H., Lew, R.A., Stare, F.J., Ellison, C.R., Lozy, M., Bourke, G., Daly, L., Graham, I., Hickey, N., Mulcahy, R. and Kevaney, J. (1985) Diet and 20-year mortality from coronary heart disease. The Ireland-Boston Diet-Heart study. *N. Eng. J. Med.*, **312**, 811-818.

Lairon, D., Latort, H., Vigne, J.L. Nalbone, G., Leonardi, J. and Hauton, J.C. (1985) Effects of dietary fibres and cholestyramine on the activity of pancreatic lipase in vitro. *Am. J. Clin. Nutr.*, **42**, 629-38.

Leeds, A.R. (1982) Modification of intestinal absorption by dietary fibre and fibre components. In *Dietary fiber in health and disease.* (eds G.V. Vahouny and D. Kritchevsky), Plenum Press, New York, pp53-69.

Lessof, M.H., Wraight, D.G., Merrett, T.G., Merrett, J. and Buisteret, P.D. (1980) Food allergy and intolerance in 100 patients. *Quart. J. Med.*, **195**, 259-271.

Levitt, M.D. (1976) Studies of a flatulent patient. *N. Eng. J. Med.*, **295**, 260-262.

Levitt, M.D., Hirsh, P., Fetzer, C.A., Sheahan, M., Levine, A.S. (1986) H_2 Excretion after ingestion of complex carbohydrates. *Gastroenterology*, **92**, 383-389.

Lewis, J. and Buss, D.H. (1988) Trace nutrients 5. Minerals and vitamins in the British household food supply. *Brit. J. Nutr.*, **60**, 413-24.

Lewis, J. and Buss, D.H. (1990) Intake of individual sugars in Britain. *Proc. Nutr. Soc.*, In press.

Liebman, M., Smith, M.C., Iverson, J., Thye, F.W., Hinkle, D.E., Herbert, W.G., Ritchie, S.J., Driskell, J.A. (1983) Effect of coarse wheat bran fiber and exercise on plasma lipids and lipoproteins in moderately overweight men. *Am. J. Clin. Nutr.*, **37**, 71-81.

Life Sciences Research Office. (1983) *A perspective on the application of the Atwater system of food energy assessment.* (eds R.G. Alison and F.R. Senti). Federation of American Societies for Experimental Biology. Bethesda, M.D.

Lindberg, A.S., Leklem, J.E. and Miller, L.T. (1983) The effect of wheat bran on the bioavailability of vitamin B6 in young men. *J. Nutr.*, **113**, 2578-86.

Livesey, G. (1984) Energy equivalents of ATP and the energy values of food proteins and fats. *Br. J. Nutr.*, **51**, 15-28.

Livesey, G. (1990) The energy values of unavailable carbohydrates and diets: an enquiry and analysis. *Am. J. Clin. Nutr.*, **51**, 617-37.

Livesey, G. and Elia, M. (1985) The potential variation in (A) energy costs of substrate utilization and (B) the energy yield and RQ for lipogenesis. In *Substrate and energy metabolism in man*, (eds J.S. Garrow and D. Halliday), John Libbey, London.

Livesey, G., Davies, I.R., Brown, J.C., Faulks, R.M. and Southon, S. (1990) Energy balance and energy values of α-amylase resistant maize and pea starches in the rat. *Br. J. Nutr.*, **64**, In Press.

Longland, A.C. and Low, A.G. (1988) The digestion of three sources of dietary fibre by growing pigs. *Proc. Nut. Soc.*, **47**, 104A.

Longstreth, G.F., Fox, D.D., Youkeles, L. *et al.* (1981) Psyllium therapy in the irritable bowel syndrome: a double blind trial. *Ann. Int. Med.*, **95**, 53-56.

Low-Beer, T.S. (1979) Colonic bacteria, dexycholate and biliary lipid. In *Biological effects of Bile Acids.* (eds G. Paumgartner, A. Stiehl and W. Gerok). M.T.P. Press, Lancaster, pp71-76.

Lucey, M.R., Clark, M.L., Lowndes, J.O. and Dawson, A.M. (1987) Is bran efficacious in irritable bowel syndrome. A double blind cross over study. *Gut*, **28**, 221-225.

Lund, E.K., Farleigh, C.A. and Johnson, I.T. (1990) Do oats lower blood cholesterol? In: *Fibre 90. Chemical and Biological Aspects of Dietary Fibre* (eds G.R. Fenwick, D.A.T. Southgate, I.T. Johnson and K. Waldron) Roy. Soc. Chem., London.

Lutz, W. (1985) Morbus Crohn unter kohlenhydratarmer Diat. *Colo-proctology*, **5**, 278.

Macagno, E.C., Christensen, J. and Lee, C.I. (1982) Modelling the effect of wall movements on absorption in the intestine. *Am. J. Physiol.*, **243**, G541-50.

Macquart-Moulin, G., Riboli, E., Cornee, J., Charnay, B., Berthezine, P., Day, N. (1986) Case control study on colorectal cancer and diet in Marseille. *Int. J. Cancer*, **38**, 183-91.

Malhotra, S.L. (1968) Epidemiological study of cholelithiasis among railroad workers in India with special reference to causation. *Gut*, **9**, 290-5.

Manning, A.P. and Heaton, K.W. (1976) Bran and the irritable bowel syndrome. *Lancet*, **1**, 588.

Manning, A.P., Thompson, W.G., Heaton, K.W. and Morris, A.F. (1978) Towards a positive diagnosis of the irritable bowel. *Br. Med. J.*, **2**, 653-654.

Manning, A.P., Heaton, K.W., Harvey, R.R. and Uglow, P. (1977) Wheat fibre and the irritable bowel syndrome. *Lancet*, **2**, 417-418.

Manousos, O., Day, N.E., Tzonou, A. *et al.* (1985) Diet and other factors in the aetiology of diverticulosis: an epidemiological study in Greece. *Gut*, **26**, 544-9.

Marcus, S.N. and Heaton, K.W. (1986) Intestinal transit, deoxycholic acid and the cholesterol saturation of bile - three inter-related factors. *Gut*, **27**, 550-8.

Marcus, S.N. and Heaton, K.W. (1988) Deoxycholic acid and the pathogenesis of gallstones. *Gut*, **29**, 522-33.

Marsh, P.D., Hunter, J.R., Bowden, G.H., Hamilton, I.R., McKee, A.S., Hardie, J.M. and Ellwood, D.C. (1983) The influence of growth rate and nutrient limitation on the microbial composition and biochemical properties of a mixed culture of oral bacteria grown in a chemostat. *J. Gen. Microbiol.*, **129**, 755-770.

Marzio, L., Lanfranchi, G.A., Bazzochi, G. and Cuccurullo, F. (1985) Anorectal motility and rectal sensitivity in chronic idiopathic constipation: effect of a high fibre diet. *J. Clin. Gastroenterol.*, **7**, 391-399.

Maxton, D.G., Cynk, E.U. and Thompson, R.P.B. (1987) Small intestinal response to elemental and complete liquid feeds in the rat: effect of dietary bulk. *Gut*, **28**, 688-93.

McBurney, M.I., Horvath, P.J., Jeraci, F. *et al.* (1985) Effect of in vitro fermentation using faecal inoculum on the water holding capacity of dietary fibre. *Br. J. Nutr.*, **53**, 17-24.

McCance, D.R., Hadden, D.R., Atkinson, A.B., Archer, D.B. and Kennedy, L. (1989) Long-term glycaemic control and diabetic retinopathy. *Lancet*, **2**, 824-828.

McCance, R.A. and Lawrence, R.D. (1929) *The carbohydrate content of foods.* Medical Research Council, London.

McCance, R.A., Prior, K.M. and Widdowson, E.M. (1953) A radiological study of the rate of passage of brown and white bread through the digestive tract of man. *Br. J. Nutr.*, **7**, 98-104.

McCance, R.A. and Widdowson, E.M. (1939) *Chemical composition of foods.* HMSO, London.

McCance, R.A. and Widdowson, E.M. (1942) Mineral metabolism of healthy adults on white and brown bread dietaries. *J. Physiol.*, **101**, 44-85.

McConnell, A.A., Eastwood, M.A. and Mitchell, W.D. (1974) Physical characteristics of vegetable foodstuffs that could influence bowel function. *J. Sci. Food Agric.*, **25**, 1457-1464.

McLean Ross, A.H., Eastwood, M.A., Anderson, J.R. and Anderson, D.M.W. (1983) A study of the effects of dietary gum arabic in humans. *Am. J. Clin. Nutr.*, **37**, 368-375.

McNeil, N.I. (1984) The contribution of the large intestine to energy supplies in man. *Am. J. Clin. Nutr.*, **39**, 338-342.

Medalie, J.H., Papier, C.M., Goldbourt, U. and Herman, J.B. (1975) Major factors in the development of diabetes mellitus in 10000 men, *Arch. Intern. Med.*, **135**, 811-818.

Merrill, A.L. and Watt, B.K. (1973) Energy value of foods: basis and derivation. *USDA Handbook 74.*

Metchnikoff, E. (1907) *The prolongation of life.* Heinemann, London.

Meyer, F. and Le Quintrec, Y. (1981) Rapport entre fibres alimentaires et constipation. *La Nouvelle Presse Medicale*, **10**, 2479-81.

Meyer, J.H., Gu, Y., Elashoff, J., Reedy, T., Dressman, J. and Amidon, G. (1986) Effects of viscosity and fluid outflow on postcibal gastric emptying of solids. *Am. J. Physiol.*, **250**, G161-G164.

Meyer, J.H. (1987) Motility of stomach and gastroduodenal junction. In: *Physiology of the Gastrointestinal Tract* (ed. L.-R. Johnson) pp613-629. Raven Press, New York.

Mickelsen, O., Makdani, D.D., Cotton, R.H., Titcomb, S.T., Colmey, J.C. and Gatty, R. (1979) Effects of a high fiber bread on weight loss in college-age males. *Am. J. Clin. Nutr.*, **32**, 1703-9.

Miles, C.W., Kelsay, J.L. and Wong, N.F. (1988) Effect of dietary fiber on metabolizable energy of human diets. *J. Nutr.*, **118**, 1075-1081.

Ministry of Agriculture, Fisheries and Food (1951-1990) *Household food consumption and expenditure: Annual Reports of the National Food Survey Committee.* HMSO, London.

Ministry of Agriculture, Fisheries and Food (1987) *Guidelines on Nutrition Labelling.* MAFF, London.

Ministry of Agriculture, Fisheries and Food (1989) *Food Advisory Committee report on nutrition claims in food labelling and advertising.* MAFF, London.

Mistunaga, T. (1974) Some properties of protease inhibitors in wheatgrain. *J. Nutr. Sci. Vitaminol.*, **20**, 153-9.

Monnier, L.H., Biotman, M.J., Colette, C., Stonnier, M.P. and Mirouze, J. (1981) Effects of dietary fibre supplementation in stable and labile insulin dependent diabetes. *Diabetologia*, **20**, 12-17.

Moore-Gillon, V. (1984) Constipation: what does the patient mean? *J. Roy. Soc. Med.*, **77**, 108-10.

Morgan, L.M., Flatt, P.R. and Marks, V. (1988) Nutrient regulation of the entero-insular axis and insulin secretion. *Nut. Res. Rev.*, **1**, 79-97.

Mormann, J.E. and Muhlemann, H.R. (1981) Oral starch degradation and its influence on acid production in human dental plaque. *Caries Res.*, **15**, 166-175.

Morris, E.R. (1986) Molecular origin of hydrocolloid functionally. In *Gums and Stabilisers for the Food Industry, Vol. 3* (eds G.O. Phillips, D.J. Wedlock and P.A. Williams) Elsevier Applied Science Publishers, London, pp3-16.

Morris, E.R. and Ellis, R. R. (1982) Phytate, wheat bran, and bioavailability of dietary iron. In *Nutritional Bioavailability of Iron.* (ed. C. Kies), American Chemical Society, Washington, DC, pp121-141.

Morris, J.N., Marr, J.W. and Clayton, D.G. (1977) Diet and Heart: a postscript. *Br. Med. J.*, **2**, 1307-1314.

Morrison, W.R. and Laignelet, B. (1983) Apparent and total amylose contents of some starches. *J. Cereal Sc.*, **1**, 9-20.

Morson, D.C. and Dawson, I.M.P. (1972) *Gastrointestinal Pathology.* Blackwell Scientific Publications. Oxford.

Muller-Lissner, S.A., (1988) Effect of wheat bran on weight of stool and gastrointestinal transit time: a meta analysis. *Br. Med. J.*, **296**, 615-7.

NACNE. (1983) *A discussion paper on proposals for nutritional guidelines for health education in Britain.* Health Education Council, London.

Nagahashi, H., Yamazaki, N., Ohi, G. *et al.* (1985) Dietary fiber intake and diverticular disease of the colon. A case control study. *Nippon Eiseigaku Zasshi.*, **40**, 781-8.

Nanda, R., James, R., Smith, H., Dudley, C.R. and Jewell, D.P. (1989) Food intolerance and the irritable bowel syndrome. *Gut*, **30**, 1099-1104.

National Research Council. (1989) *Diet and Health: Implications for reducing chronic disease risk.* National Academy Press, Washington DC, Ch 7 pp159-258.

Neprokoeff, C.M., Lakshmanan, M.R., Ness, G.C., Dugan, R.E., Porter, J.W. (1974) Regulation of the diurnal rhythm of rat liver -hydroxy- -methylglutaryl coenzyme A reductase activity by insulin, glucagon, cyclic AMP, and hydrocortisone. *Arch. Biochem. Biophys.*, **160**, 387-93.

Newbrun, E., Hoover, C., Mettraux, G. and Graf, H. (1980) Comparison of dietary habits and dental health of subjects with hereditary fructose intolerance and control subject. *J. Am. Dent. Ass.*, **101**, 619-626.

Nigro, N.D. (1985) Animal models for colorectal cancer. In *Carcinoma of the Large Bowel and its Precursers.* (eds J.R. Ingall, and A.J. Mastromarino), Alan Liss, New York, pp161-73.

Nordic Nutrition Recommendations, 2nd edition (1989) Nordisk Ministerrad Standing Nordic Committee on Food. *Report 1989*: **2**.

Nugyen, L.B., Gregory, J.F. and Damron, B.L. (1981) Effects of selected polysaccharides on the bioavailability of pyridoxine in rats and chicks. *J. Nutr.*, **111**, 1403-10.

Nyman, M. and Asp N-G (1985) Bulk laxatives: their dietary fibre composition and faecal bulking capacity in the rat. *Scan. J. Gastroenterol.*, **20**, 887-889.

Nyman, M., Asp, N-G., Cummings, J.H. and Wiggins, H. (1986) Fermentation of dietary fibre in the intestinal tract: Comparison between man and rat. *Br. J. Nutr.* **55**, 487-496.

Oberleas, D. and Harland, B.F. (1977) Nutritional agents which affect metabolic zinc status. In *Zinc metabolism current aspects in health and disease.* A.R. Liss, New York, pp11-27.

Oberleas, D. (1975) Factors influencing availability of minerals. In *Proceedings of the Western Hemisphere Nutrition Congress IV.* Publishing Sciences Group, (ed. M.A. Acton), pp156-161.

O'Dea, K., Nestel, P.J. and Anatoff, L. (1980) Physical factors influencing postprandial glucose and insulin responses to starch. *Am. J. Clin. Nutr.,* **33**, 760-765.

O'Dea, K., Snow, P. and Nestel, P. (1981) Rate of starch hydrolysis in vitro as a predictor of metabolic responses to complex carbohydrate in vivo. *Am. J. Clin. Nutr.,* **34**, 1991-1993.

O'Donnell, L.J.D., Emmett, P.M. and Heaton, K.W. (1989) Size of flour particles and its relation to glycaemia, insulinaemia, and colonic disease. *Br. Med. J.,* **298**, 1616-1617.

Ohi, G., Minowa, K., Oyama, T. *et al.* (1983) Changes in dietary fiber intake among Japanese in the 20th century: a relationship to the prevalence of diverticular disease. *Am. J. Clin. Nutr.,* **38**, 115-21.

Ohta, M., Ishiguro, S., Iwane, S. *et al.* (1985) An epidemiological study on relationship between intake of dietary fiber and colonic diseases. *Jap. J. Gastroenterol.,* **82**, 51-7.

Organisation for Economic Co-operation and Development (1988) *Food consumption statistics, 1976-1985.* OECD, Paris.

Osborne, T.W.B. and Noriskin, J.N. (1937) The relation between diet and caries in the South African Banta. *J. Dent. Res.,* **16**, 431-441.

Osuga, T. and Portman, O.W. (1971) Experimental formation of gallstones in the squirrel monkey. *Proc. Soc. exp. biol. Med.,* **136**, 722-6.

Painter, N. (1985) Diverticular disease of the colon. In *Dietary fibre, fibre-depleted foods and disease.* (eds J. Trowell, D. Burkitt and K. Heaton), Academic Press, London.

Painter, N.S. (1975) *Diverticular disease of the colon: a deficiency disease of Western civilisation.* Heinemann, London.

Painter, N.S. and Burkitt, D.P. (1971) Diverticular disease of the colon: a deficiency disease of Western civilisation. *Br. Med. J.,* **2**, 450-4.

Painter, N.S., Almeida, A.Z. and Colebourne, K.W. (1972) Unprocessed bran in treatment of diverticular disease of the colon. *Br. Med. J.,* **2**, 137-40.

Painter, N.S., Truelove, S.C., Ardran, G.M., Tuckey, M. (1965) Segmentation and the localisation of intraluminal pressures in the human colon, with special reference to the pathogenesis of colonic diverticular. *Gastroenterology,* **49**, 169-77.

Paul, A.A. and Southgate, D.A.T. (1978) McCance and Widdowson's *The composition of foods,* 4th edition. HMSO, London.

Paylor, D.K., Pomare, E.W., Heaton, K.W. and Harvey, R.F. (1975) The effect of wheat bran on intestinal transit. *Gut,* **16** 209-213.

Penagini, R., Velio, P., Vigorelli, R., Bozzani, A., Castagnone, D., Ranzi, T. and Bianchi P.A. (1986) The effect of dietary guar on serum cholesterol, intestinal transit, and fecal output in man. *Am. J. Gastroenterol.,* **81**, 123-125.

Percival, S.S. and Schneeman, B.O. (1979) Long term pancreatic responses to feeding heat damaged casein in rats. *J. Nutr.,* **129**, 1609-14.

Phillips, D.R. (1986) The effect of guar gum in solution of diffusion of cholesterol mixed micelles. *J. Sci. Food Agric.,* **37**, 548-52.

Pilch, S.M., (ed) (1987) Physiological Effects and Health Consequences of Dietary Fibre. *A Report Prepared for Center for Food Safety and Applied Nutrition, Food and Drug Administration,* Dept. of Health and Human Services, Washington DC. Bethesda: Life Sciences Research Office, FASEB.

Pixley, F. and Mann, J. (1988) Dietary factors in the aetiology of gallstones: a case control study. *Gut,* **29**, 1511-5.

Pixley, F., Wilson, D., McPherson, K., Mann, J. (1985) Effect of vegetarianism on development of gallstones in women. *Br. Med. J.,* **291**, 11-2.

Preston, D.M. and Lennard Jones, J.E. (1986) Severe chronic constipation of young women: 'idiopathic slow transit constipation'. *Gut,* **27**, 41-48.

Prior, A. and Whorwell, P.J. (1987) Double blind study of ispaghula in the irritable bowel syndrome. *Gut,* **28**, 1510-3.

Prosky, L., Asp, N-G., Furda, I., De Vries, J.W., Schweizer, T.F. and Harland, B. (1984) The determination of total dietary fiber in foods, food products and total diets: interlaboratory study. *JAOAC,* **67**, 1044-52.

Prynne, C.J. and Southgate, D.A.T. (1979) The effects of a supplement of dietary fibre on faecal excretions of humans. *Br. J. Nutr.,* **41**, 494-503.

Pye, G., Crompton, J., Evans, D., Clark, A. and Hardcastle, J. (1987) The effect of dietary fibre supplementation on colonic pH in healthy volunteers. *Gut,* **28**, A1266.

Pyorala, K. (1979) Relationship of glucose tolerance and plasma insulin to the incidence of coronary heart disease. Results from two population studies in Finland. *Diabetes Care,* **2**, 131-141.

Pyorala, K., Savolainen, E., Kaukola, S. and Haapakoski, J. (1985) Plasma insulin as coronary heart disease risk factor. Relationship to other risk factors and predictive value during 9½ year follow up of Helsinki Policemen study population. *Acta. Med. Scand. Supp.,* **701**, 38-52.

Rao, S.S.C., Holdsworth, C.D. and Read, N.W. (1988) Symptoms and stool patterns in patients with ulcerative colitis. *Gut,* **29**, 342-345.

Ravich, W.J., Bayless, T.M. and Thomas, M. (1983) Fructose: incomplete intestinal absorption in humans. *Gastroenterology,* **84**, 26-29.

Read, N.W., MacFarlane, A., Kinsman, R., Bates, T., Blackhall, N.W., Farrar, G.B.G., Hall, J.C., Moss, G., Morris, A.P., O'Neill, B. and Welch, I. (1984) Effect of infusion of nutrient solutions into the ileum on gastrointestinal transit and plasma levels of neurotensin and enteroglucagon in man. *Gastroenterol.,* **86**, 274-80.

Read, N.W., Welch, I.McL., Austen, C.J. *et al.* (1986) Swallowing food without chewing; a simple way to reduce postprandial glycaemia. *Br. J. Nutr.*, **55**, 43-47.

Reaven, G.M. (1980) How high the carbohydrate? *Diabetologia*, **19**, 409-413.

Reaven, G.M. (1988) Role of insulin resistance in human disease. Diabetes, **37**, 1595-1607.

Reinhold, J.G., Faradji, B., Abadi, P. Ismail-Beigi, F. (1976) Decreased absorption of calcium magnesium, zinc and phosphorous by humans due to increased fibre and phosphorus intake as wheat bread. *J. Nutr.*, **106**, 493-503.

Reddy, B.S., Ekelund, G., Bohe, M., Engle, A. and Domellof, L. (1983) Metabolic epidemiology of colon cancer: dietary patterns and faecal sterol concentrations of 3 populations. *Nut. and Cancer*, **5**, 34-40.

Reinhold, J.G., Nasr, K., Lahimgarzadeh, A. and Hedayati, H. (1973) Effects of purified phytate and phytate rich bread upon metabolism of zinc, calcium, phosphorus and nitrogen in man. *Lancet*, **1**, 283-8.

Riboli, E. (1987) Epidemiology of colorectal cancer and diet. In *Causation and Prevention of Colorectal Cancer*, (eds J. Faivre and M.J. Hill), Excerpta Medica, Amsterdam, pp49-60.

Riccardi, G., Rivellese, A., Pacioni, D., Genovese, J., Mastranzo, P. and Mancini, M. (1984) Separate influence of dietary carbohydrate and fibre on the metabolic control in diabetes. *Diabetologia*, **26**, 116-121.

Rice, E.E., Warner, W.D., Mone, P.E. and Poling, C.E. (1957) Comparison of the metabolic energy contributions of foods by growth under conditions of energy restriction. *J. Nutr.*, **61**, 253-266.

Rigaud, D., Ryttig, K.R., Leeds, A.R., Bard, D. and Apfelbaum, M. (1987) Effects of a moderate dietary fibre supplement in hunger rating, energy input and faecal energy output in young, healthy volunteers. A randomized double-blind cross-over trial. *Int. J. Obesity*, **11**, supp 1, 73-78.

Ristow, K.A., Gregory, J.F. and Damron, B.L. (1982) Effects of dietary fibre on the bioavailability of folic acid monoglutamate. *J. Nutr.*, **112**, 750-8.

Ritchie, J.A. and Truelove, S.C. (1979) Treatment of irritable bowel syndrome with lorazepam, hyoscine butylbromide and ispaghula husk. *Br. Med. J.*, **1**, 376-378.

Rivellese, A., Riccardi, G., Giacco, A., Pacioni, D., Genoves, S., Mattioli, P.L. and Mancini, M. (1980) Effect of dietary fibre on glucose control and serum lipoproteins in diabetic patients. *Lancet*, **2**, 447-450.

Roediger, W, (1982) The effect of bacterial metabolism on the nutrition and function of the colon mucosa: a symbiosis between man and bacteria. In *Colon and nutrition*, (eds H. Goebbel and H. Kaspar) M.T.P. Press, Lancaster, pp11-26.

Ross, S.W., Brand, J.C., Thorburn, A.W. and Truswell, A.S. (1987) Glycemic index of processed wheat products. *Am. J. Clin. Nutr.*, **46**, 361-5.

Rossner, S., Andersson, I-L and Ryttig, K. (1988) Effect of a dietary fibre supplement to a weight reduction programme on blood pressure. A randomised, double-blind, placebo-controlled study. *Acta. Med. Scand.*, **223**, 353-7.

Rossner, S., von Zweigbergk, D., Ohlin, A. and Ryttig, K. (1987) Weight reduction with dietary fibre supplements. Results of two double-blind randomised studies. *Acta. Med. Scand.*, **222**, 83-8.

Rotstein, O.D., Kay, R.M., Wayman, M., Strasberg, S.M. (1981) Prevention of cholesterol gallstones by lignin and lactulose in the hamster. *Gastroenterology*, **81**, 1098-103.

Roux, J.C. and Goiffon, R. (1921) *Arch. mal. app. digestif.*, **11**, 25.

Rowe, A.H. (1928) Food allergy. Its manifestations, diagnosis and treatment. *J.A.M.A.*, **91**, 1623-1631.

Rowland, I.R., Mallett, A.K. and Wise, A. (1985) The effect of diet on the mammalian gut flora and its metabolic activities. *Crit. Rev. Toxicol.*, **16**, 31-103.

Royal College of Physicians (1980) *Medical aspects of dietary fibre*. Pitman Medical, London.

Rugg-Grunn, A.J. (1986) *Starchy foods and fresh fruits: their relative importance as a source of dental caries in Britain*. London, Health Education Council, (Occasional paper, no 3).

Rugg-Grunn, A.J., Hackett, A.F., Appleton, D.R., Jenkins, G.N. and Eastoc, J.E. (1984) Relationship between dietary habits and caries increment assessed over two years in 405 English adolescent school-children. *Arch. Oral. Biol.*, **29**, 983-992.

Rugg-Grunn, A.J., Carmichael, C.L. and Ferrell, R.S. (1988) Effect of fluoridation and secular trend in caries in 5-year old children living in Newcastle and Northumberland. *Br. Dent. J.* **165**, 359-364.

Rugg-Grunn, A.J., Edgar, W.M. and Jenkins, G.N. (1978) The effect of eating some British snacks upon the pH of human dental plaque. *Br. Dent. J.*, **145**, 95-100.

Russ, C.S. and Atkinson, R.L. (1985) Use of high fiber diets for the outpatient treatment of obesity. *Nutr. Rep. Int.*, **32**, 193-198.

Russ, C.S. and Atkinson, R.L. (1986) No effect of dietary fiber on weight loss in obesity. *Am. J. Clin. Nutr.*, **43**, abst no 136.

Ryttig, K.R., Larsen, S., Haegh, L. (1984) Treatment of slightly to moderate overweight persons: a double-blind, placebo-controlled investigation with diet and fibre tablets (Dumovital). *Tidssk Nor Laegeforen*, **104**, 898-91.

Ryttig, K.R., Tellnes, G., Haegh, L. *et al.* (1989) A dietary fibre supplement and weight maintenance after weight reduction: a randomised, double-blind, placebo-controlled long-term trial. *Int. J. Obesity*, **13**, 165-71.

Salyers, A.A., Vercelotti, J.R., West, S.E. and Wilkins, T.D. (1977) Fermentation of mucin and plant polysaccharides by strains of *Bacteroide* from the human colon. *Appl. Env. Microbiol.*, **33**, 319-322.

Sandberg, A-S., Carlsson, N-G. and Svanberg, U. (1989) In vitro studies of inositol tri-, tetra-, penta- and hexaphosphates as potential iron absorption inhibitors. In *Nutrient Availability*, (eds D.A.T. Southgate, I. Johnson, and G.R. Fenwick), Royal Society of Chemistry, Cambridge, pp158-160.

Sandstead M.H., Munoz, J.M., Jacob, R.A., Klevay, L.M., Reck, S.J., Logan, G.M., Dintzis, P.R., Inglett G.E., Shuey, W.C. (1978) Influence of dietary fibre on trace element balance. *Am. J. Clin. Nutr.*, **31**, S180-4.

Sandstrom, B. and Lonnerdal, B. (1989) Promotors and antagonists of zinc absorption. In *Zinc in Human Biology*, (ed. C.R. Mills), Springer-Verlag, London, pp57-78.

Saunders, R.M. and Betschart, A.A. (1980) The significance of protein as a component of dietary fiber. *Am. J. Clin. Nutri.*, **33**, 960-61.

Schamschula, R.G., Adkins, B.L., Barmes, D.E., Charlton, G. and Davey, B.G. (1978) *WHO study of dental caries aetiology in Papua New Guinea.* Publ. No. 40. Geneva, WHO.

Scheinin, A. and Makinen, K.K. (1975) Turku sugar studies I-XXI. *Acta. Odont. Scand.*, **33**, supp. 70, 1-350.

Scheppach, W., Fabian, C., Ahrens, F., Spengler, M. and Kasper, H. (1988) Effect of starch malabsorption on colonic function and metabolism in humans. *Gastroenterology*, **95**, 1549-55.

Schlierf, G. and Dorow, E. (1973) Diurnal patterns of triglycerides, free fatty acids, blood sugar, and insulin during carbohydrate induction in man and their modification by nocturnal suppression of lipolysis. *J. Clin. Invest.*, **42**, 732-746.

Scragg, R.K.R., McMichael, A.J. and Baghurst, P.A. (1984a) Diet, alcohol, and relative weight in gallstone disease: a case-control study. *Br. Med. J.*, **288**, 1113-9.

Scragg, R.K.R., Calvert, G.D., Oliver, J.R. (1984b) Plasma lipids and insulin in gallstone disease: a case-control study. *Br. Med. J.*, **289**, 521-5.

Screebny, L.M. (1983) Cereal availability and dental caries. *Community Dent. Oral Epidemiol.*, **11**, 148-155.

Scultati, O., Giampiccoli, L.P., Morandi, D. and Vecciati, A. (1987) Dietary fibre and anorectic patients: war or peace. *Scand. J. Gastroenterol.*, **22**, supp 29, 278-283.

Segi, M. and Kurihara, T. (1972) Cancer mortality for selected sites in 24 countries No 6 (1966-1967), *Jap. Cancer Soc.*, Tokyo, pp1-137.

Selvendran, R.R. (1984) The plant cell wall as a source of dietary fiber: chemistry and structure. *Amer. J. Clin. Nutr.*, **39**, 320-327.

Selvendran, R.R. (1985) Developments in the chemistry and biochemistry of pectin and hemicullulosic polymers. *J. Cell Sci., Suppl.* **2**, 51-88.

Sharma, C.B., Goel, U., Irshad, M. (1978) Myoinositol hexaphosphate as potential inhibitor of alpha amylase. *Phytochemistry*, **17**, 201-3.

Sharma, M., Dhillon, A.S. and Newbrun, E. (1974) Cell-bound glucosyltransferase activity of Streptococcus sanguis strain 804. *Arch. Oral Biol.*, **19**, 1063-72.

Shaheen, S.M. and Fleming, S.E. (1987) High fiber foods at breakfast: influence on plasma glucose and insulin responses to lunch. *Am. J. Clin. Nutr.*, **46**, 804-11.

Shaw, J.H., Krumins, I. and Gibbons, R.J. (1967) Comparison of sucrose, lactose, maltose and glucose in the causation of experimental oral diseases. *Arch. Oral Biol.*, **12**, 755-768.

Simons, L.A., Gayst, S., Balasubramaniam, S,. and Ruys, J. (1982) Long-term treatment of hyper-cholesterolaemia with a new palatable formulation of guar gum. *Atherosclerosis.*, **45**, 101-108.

Simpson, H.C.R., Lousley, J., Geekie, M., Simpson, R.W., Carter, R.D., Hockaday, T.D.R. and Mann, J.I. (1981b) A high carbohydrate leguminous fibre diet improves all aspects of diabetic control, *Lancet*, **1**, 1-5.

Simpson, K.M., Morris, E.R. and Cook, J.D. (1981a) The inhibitory effect of bran on iron absorption. *Am. J. Clin. Nutr.*, **34**, 1469-1478.

Slavin, J.L. and Marlett, J.A. (1980) Effects of refined cellulose on apparent energy, fat and nitrogen digestibilities. *J. Nutr.*, **110**, 2020-2026.

Smith, A.N., Drummond, E. and Eastwood, M. (1981) The effect of coarse and fine Canadian red spring wheat and French soft wheat bran on colonic motility in patients with diverticular disease. *Am. J. Clin. Nutr.*, **34**, 2460-2463.

Smith, M.A., Youngs, G.R. and Finn, R. (1985) Food intolerance, atopy and irritable bowel syndrome. *Lancet*, **2**, 1064.

Smith, U. and Holm G. (1982) Effect of a modified guar gum preparation on glucose and lipid levels in diabetics and healthy volunteers. *Atherosclerosis*, **45**, 1-10.

Soltoft, J., Gudman-Hoyer, E., Krag, B., Kristensen, E., Wulfe, M.R. (1976) A double blind trial of the effect of wheat bran on symptoms of the irritable bowel syndrome. *Lancet*, **2**, 270-272.

Solum, T.T. (1983) Fibre tablets, Dumovital, as a means to achieve weight reduction. *Tidsskr. Nor. Laegeforen*, **103**, 1707-8.

Solum, T.T., Ryttig, K.R., Solum, E., Larsen, S. (1987) The influence of a high-fibre diet on body weight, serum lipids and blood pressure in slightly overweight persons: a randomised, double-blind placebo-controlled investigation with diet and fibre tablets (DumoVital^R) *Int. J. Obesity*, **11**, Suppl 1, 67-71.

Southgate, D.A.T. (1969) Determination of carbohydrates in foods II Unavailable carbohydrates. *J. Sci. Food Agric.*, **20**, 331-335.

Southgate, D.A.T. (1976) *Determination of food carbohydrates.* Applied Science, London.

Southgate, D.A.T. (1986) The relation between composition and properties of dietary fibre and physiological effects. In *Dietary fibre Basic and Clinical Aspects*, (eds G.V. Vahouny and D. Kritchevsky), Plenum Press, New York, pp35-48.

Southgate, D.A.T. (1987) Minerals, trace elements and potential hazards. *Am. J. Clin. Nutr.*, **45**, 1256-1266.

Southgate, D.A.T. and Englyst, H.N. (1985) Dietary fibre; chemistry, physical properties and analysis. In *Dietary fibre, fibre-depleted foods and disease* (eds H. Trowell, D. Burkitt, and K. Heaton), Academic Press, London, pp 31-35.

Southgate, D.A.T. (1988) Dietary fibre and the diseases of affluence. In *A balanced diet?* (ed. J. Dobbing), Springer Verlag, London, pp 117-139.

Southgate, D.A.T. and Durnin J.V.G.A. (1970) Calorie conversion factors: an experimental reassessment of the factors used in the calculation of the energy value of human diets. *Br. J. Nutr.*, **24**, 517-535.

Southgate, D.A.T., Bingham, S. and Robertson, J. (1978) Dietary fibre in the British diet. *Nature*, **274**, 51-52.

Stephen, A.M. (1985) Effect of Food on the Intestinal Microflora. In *Food and the Gut* (eds J.O. Hunter and V. Alun Jones), Bailliere Tindall. Eastbourne, pp57-77.

Stephen, A.M. and Cummings, J. (1980) Mechanism of action of dietary fibre in the human colon. *Nature*, **284**, 283-284.

Stephen, A.M., Wiggins, H.S., Englyst, H.N., Cole, T.J., Wayman, B.J. and Cummings, J.H., (1986) The effect of age sex, and level of intake of dietary fibre from wheat on large-bowel function in thirty healthy subjects. *Br. J. Nutr.*, **56**, 349-61.

Stephen, A.M. and Cummings, J.H. (1979) Water holding by dietary fibre in vitro and its relationship to faecal output in man. *Gut*, **20**, 722-729.

Stevens, J., Burgess, N.B., Kaiser, D.L. and Sheppa, C.M. (1985) Outpatient management of diabetes mellitus with patient education to increase dietary carbohydrate and fiber. *Diab. Care*, **8**, 359-366.

Stevens, J., Levitsky, D.A., van Soest, P.J., Robertson, J.B., Kalkwarf, H.J. and Roe, D.A. (1988) Effect of psyllium gum and wheat bran on spontaneous energy intake. *Am. J. Clin. Nutr.*, **46**, 812-7.

Stock-Damage, C., Bouchet, P., Dentinger, A., Aprahamian, M. and Grenier, J.F. (1983) Effect of dietary fibre supplementation on the secretory function of the exocrine pancreas in the dog. *Am J. Clin. Nutr.*, **38**, 843-8.

Sun, W.M., Read, N.W., Donnelly, T.C., Bannister, J.J. and Shorthouse A.J. (1989) A common pathophysiology for full thickness rectal prolapse, anterior mucosal prolapse and solitary rectal ulcer. *Br. J. Surg.*, **76**, 290-295.

Swain, J.T., Rouse, I.L., Curley, C.B. and Sacks, F.M. (1990) Comparison of the effects of oat bran and low-fibre wheat on serum lipoprotein levels and blood pressure. *N. Eng. J. Med.*, **322**, 147-152.

Tepperman, J., Caldwell, R.T. and Tepperman, H.M. (1967) Induction of gallstones in mice by feeding a cholesterol-cholic acid containing diet. *Am. J. Physiol.*, **206**, 628-34.

Theander, D. (1987) Chemistry of dietary fibre components. *Scand. J. Gastroent.*, **22** (Suppl. 129),21-28.

Thomas, B.J. (1981) How successful are we at persuading diabetics to follow their diet - and why do we sometimes fail? In *Nutrition and Diabetes* (eds M. Turner and B.J. Thomas) Libbey, London, pp57-66.

Thompson, W.G. (1984) Gastrointestinal symptoms in the irritable bowel compared with peptic ulcer and inflammatory bowel disorder. *Gut*, **25**, 1089-1092.

Thomson, H.J., Busuttil, A., Eastwood, M.A., *et al.* (1987) Submucosal collagen changes in the normal colon and in diverticular disease. *Int. J. Colorec. Dis.*, **2**, 208-213.

Thornton, J.R., Emmett, P.M., Heaton, K.W. (1983) Diet and gallstones: effects of refined and unrefined carbohydrate diets on bile cholesterol saturation and bile acid metabolism. *Gut*, **24**, 2-6.

Todd, J.E., Walker, A.M. and Dodd, T. (1982) *Adult dental health*. Vol 2. United Kingdom 1978. HMSO, London.

Tomlin, J. and Read, N.W. (1988a) The relation between bacterial degradation of viscous polysaccharides and stool output in human beings. *Br. J. Nutr.*, **60**, 467-475.

Tomlin, J. and Read, N.W. (1988b) Laxative effects of undigestible plastic particles. *Br. Med. J.*, **297**, 1175-1176.

Trowell, H. (1972) Ischemic heart disease and dietary fibre. *Am. J. Clin. Nutr.*, **25**, 926-932.

Trowell, H. (1972) *Rev. Eur. Etud. Clin. Biol.*, **17**, 345-349.

Trowell, H.C. (1974) Diabetes mellitus death rates in England and Wales 1920-70 and food supplies. *Lancet*, **2**, 998-1004.

Trowell, H.C. (1985) In *Dietary fibre, fibre-depleted foods and disease*, (eds H. Trowell, D. Burkitt and K. Heaton), Academic Press, London, pp1-20.

Tucker, D.M., Sandstead, H.H., Logan, G.M. *et al.* (1981) Dietary fiber and personality factors as determinants of stool output. *Gastroenterology*, **81**, 879-83.

Tuomilehto, J., Voutilainen, E., Huttunen, J., Vinni, S. and Homan, K. (1980) Effect of guar gum on body weight and serum lipids in hypercholesterolemic females. *Acta. Med. Scand.*, **208**, 45-8.

Tuomilehto, J., Karttunen, P., Vinni, S., Kostainen, E. and Uusitupa, M. (1983) A double-blind evaluation of guar gum in patients with dyslipidaemia. *Hum. Nutr.: Clin. Nutr.*, **37C**, 109-119.

Turnbull, W.H. and Leeds, A.R. (1987) Reduction of total and LDL-cholesterol in plasma by rolled oats. *J. Clin. Nutr. Gastroenterol.*, **2**, 177-181.

Turner, P.R., Tuomilehto, J., Happonen, P., Lavilla, A.E., Shaikh, M., Lewis, B. (1990) *Metabolic studies on the hypolipidaemic effect of guar gum atherosclerosis*; (in press).

US Department of Health and Human Services. (1988) The Surgeon General's Report on Nutrition and Health. Public Health Service. *DHHS (PHS) Publication No. 88-50210*, Washington.

US Senate Select Committee on Nutrition and Human Needs. (1977) *Dietary goals for the United States*. US Government Printing Office, Washington.

Vague, J. (1956) The degree of masculine differentiation of obesities: a factor determining predisposition to diabetes, atherosclerosis, gout and uric calculous disease. *Am. J. Clin. Nutr.*, **4**, 20.

Vahouny, G.V. (1986) Dietary fibre and intestinal adaptation. In *Dietary Fibre, Basic and Clinical Aspects*. (eds G.V.Vahouney, and D. Kritchevsky), Plenum Press, New York, pp181-209.

Vahouny, J.V. (1985) Dietary fibres. Aspect of nutrition, pharmacology and pathology. In *Nutritional Pathology, Pathobiochemistry of Dietary Imbalances*. (ed. H. Sidransky), Marcell Dekker Inc., New York, pp207-267.

Valle-Jones, J.C. (1980) The evaluation of a new appetite-reducing agent (Prefil) in the management of obesity. *Br. J. Clin. Pract.*, **34**, 72-4.

Van Der Waaij, D. (1983) *Antibiotic choice: the importance of colonisation resistance*. Research Studies Press, Chichester.

Van Horn, L.V., Lin, K., Parker, D., *et al* (1986) Serum lipid response to oat product intake with a fat-modified diet, *J. Am. Diet. Assoc.*, **86**, 759-764.

Van Itallie, T.B. (1978) Dietary fiber and obesity. *Am. J. Clin. Nutr.*, **31**, S43-S52.

Van Zeben, W. and Hendricks, T.P. (1948) The absorption of carotene from cooked carrots. *Ins. Z. Vitamin-forsch*, **19**, 265-6.

Walsh, D.F., Yaghoubian, V. and Behforooz, A., (1984) Effect of glucomannan on obese patients: a clinical study. *Int. J. Obesity*, **8**, 289-93.

Watters, D.A.K., Smith, A.N., Eastwood, M.A., et al. (1985) Mechanical properties of the colon - comparison of the features of the African, European colon in vitro. Gut., **26**, 384-392.

Weast, R.C., Astle, M.J. and Beyer, W.H. (1984) CRC Handbook of chemistry and physics. CRC Press Inc., Boca Raton, Florida.

Weinreich, J., Andersen, D. (1976) Intraluminal pressure in sigmoid colon. II. Patients with sigmoid diverticula and related conditions. Scand. J. Gastroenterol., **11**, 581-586.

Weinreich, J., Moller, S.H. and Andersen, D. (1977) Colonic haustral pattern in relation to pressure activity and presence of diverticula. Scand. J. Gastroenterol., **12**, 857-864.

Welborn, T.A. and Wearne, K. (1979) Coronary heart disease - incidence and mortality in Busselton with reference to glucose and insulin levels. Diab. Care, **2**, 154-160.

Wenlock, R.W., Buss, D.H. and Agater, I.B. (1984) New estimates of fibre in the diet in Britain. Brit. Med. J., **288**, 1873.

West, K.M. (1972) Acta Diabetol. Lat., **9**, supp 1, 405-428.

Westlund, K. and Nicolaysen, R. (1972) Ten-year mortality and morbidity related to serum cholesterol. A follow-up of 3751 men aged 40-49. Scand. J. Lab. Clin. Invest., **30**, supp 127, 3-24.

Whistler, R.L. and BeMiller, J.N. (eds) (1974) Industrial Gums. Academic Press, New York.

Whorwell, P.J., McCallum, M., Creed, F.H. and Roberts, C.T. (1986) Non-colonic features of irritable bowel syndrome. Gut, **27**, 37-40.

Whyteway, J. and Morson, D.C., (1985) Gastrointestinal disorders in the elderly. In Clinics in Gastroenterology (ed. O.F.W. James), W.B. Saunders, London, pp829-846.

Widdowson, E.M. (1955) Assessment of the energy value of human foods. Proc. Nutr. Soc., **14**, 142-154.

Widdowson, E.M. (1960) Notes on the calculation of the calorific value of foods and of diets. In McCance R.A. and Widdowson, E.M.'s The composition of foods, MRC Spec. Rep. Ser. No. 297, HMSO, London.

Willett, W. (1989) The search for the causes of breast and colon cancer. Nature, **338**, 389-94.

Williams, R.D. and Ormstedt, W.H. (1936) The effect of cellulose, hemicellulose and lignin on the weight of stool: a contribution to the study of laxation in man. J. Nutr., **11**, 433-449.

Williams, R.D. and Olmstead, W.H. (1936) The effect of cellulose, hemicellulose and lignin on the weight of the stool: a contribution to the study of laxation in man. Ann. Int. Med., **10**, 717-727.

Williamson, R.C.N. (1978) Intestinal adaptation. N. Eng. J. Med., **298**, 1393-1401.

Williamson, R.C.N. Buchholtz, J.W., Malt, R.A. (1978) Humoral stimulation of cell proliferation in small bowel after transection and resection in rats. Gastroenterology, **75**, 249-254.

Willis, T. (1684) Practice of Physick: Pharmaceutice Rationales. Ch 3, p76, London.

Winitz, M., Adams, R.F., Seedman, D.A., Davis, P.N. and Jayko, L.G., Hamilton, J.A. (1970) Studies in metabolic nutrition employing chemically defined diets. II Effect on gut microflora populations. Am. J. Clin. Nutr., **23**, 546-559.

Wirth, A., Middelhoff, G., Braeuning, C., Schlierf, G. (1982) Treatment of familial hypercholesterolaemia with a combination of bezafirate and guar. Atherosclerosis, **45**, 291-297.

Wisker, E., Maltz, A. and Feldheim, W. (1988) Metabolizable energy of diets low or high in dietary fibre from cereals when eaten by humans. J. Nutr., **118**, 945-952.

Wolever, T.M.S. and Jenkins, D.J.A. (1986) The use of the glycemic index in predicting the blood glucose response to mixed meals. Am. J. Clin. Nutr., **43**, 167-172.

Wolf, M.J., Khoo, U. and Inglett, G.E. (1977) Partial digestibility of cooked amylomaize starch in humans and mice. Die. Starke., **29**, 401-405.

Wood, F.C. and Bierman, R.L. (1972) Nutr. Today, **7**, 4.

Wu, H.C. and Sarko, A. (1978a) The double-helical molecular structure of crystalline β-amylose. Carbohydrate Res., **61**, 7-25.

Wu, H.C. and Sarko, A. (1978b) The double-helical molecular structure of crystalline α-amylose. Carbohydrate Res., **61**, 22-40.

Wursch, P. (1990) Starch in human nutrition. World Rev. Nutr. Diet, (in press).

Wursch, P., Vedova, S.V. and Koellreutter, B. (1986) Cell structure and starch nature as key determinants of the digestion rate of starch in legume. Am. J. Clin. Nutr., **43**, 25-29.

Wyman, J.B., Heaton, K.W., Manning, A.P. and Wicks, A.C.B. (1976) The effect on intestinal transit and the faeces of raw and cooked bran in different doses. Am. J. Clin. Nutr., **29**, 1474-9.

Yano, K., Rhoads, G.G., Kagan, A., and Tillotson, J. (1978) Dietary intake and the risk of coronary heart disease in Japanese men living in Hawaii. Am. J. Clin. Nutr., **31**, 1270-1279.

Zavoral, J.H., Hannan, P., Fields, D.J., et al. (1983) The hypolipaemic effect of locust bean gum food products in familial hypocholesterolaemic adults and children. Am. J. Clin. Nutr., **38**, 285-294.

Zebrowsky, T. and Low, A.G. (1987) The influence of diets based on whole wheat, wheat flour and wheat bran on exocrine pancreatic secretion in pigs. J. Nutr., **117**, 1212-16.

INDEX

Available from the British Nutrition Foundation

Calcium
The Report of the British Nutrition Foundation's Task Force
Paperback (0 9076 6706 6), 122 pages

Sugars and Syrups
The Report of the British Nutrition Foundation's Task Force
Paperback (0 9076 6704 x), 45 pages

Trans Fatty Acids
The Report of the British Nutrition Foundation's Task Force
Paperback (0 9076 6705 8), 18 pages

BNF Briefing Paper on Dietary Fibre

BNF Briefing Paper on Starches